AF335078

Invisible Sovereign

Invisible Sovereign

Imagining Public Opinion from the
Revolution to Reconstruction

Mark G. Schmeller

Johns Hopkins University Press
Baltimore

Johns Hopkins University Press
2715 North Charles Street
Baltimore, Maryland 21218-4363
www.press.jhu.edu

Library of Congress Cataloging-in-Publication data is available.

A catalog record for this book is available from the British Library.

ISBN 978-1-4214-1870-4 (hardcover)
ISBN 1-4214-1870-3 (hardcover)
ISBN 978-1-4214-1871-1 (electronic)
ISBN 1-4214-1871-1 (electronic)

*Special discounts are available for bulk purchases of this book. For more information,
please contact Special Sales at 410-516-6936 or specialsales@press.jhu.edu.*

Johns Hopkins University Press uses environmentally friendly book materials,
including recycled text paper that is composed of at least 30 percent post-consumer
waste, whenever possible.

For my parents, Wilma and Helmut Schmeller

Contents

Acknowledgments

This book began years ago as a University of Chicago dissertation that proposed to study the changes wrought on the concept of public opinion by the emergence of academic social science, public relations professionals, propaganda, market research, and opinion polling between 1870 and 1940. But one chapter into that project, I ran into a frustrating yet intriguing problem: I had no idea what "public opinion" meant before 1870. As I read back into the nineteenth and eighteenth centuries for answers, a new and better dissertation emerged. Neil Harris generously endured this change of direction and supplied incalculable quantities of aid, insight, and support. Bill Novak's exemplary scholarship and limitless enthusiasm persuaded me that the change was worth the trouble. Barry Karl helped see the project through its early stages, and Amy Dru Stanley stepped in toward the end with helpful criticisms and guidance. Along the way, Ted Cook, Jan Goldstein, Peter Novick, Linda Kerber, David Galenson, Kathleen Conzen, and Bill Brown did me good turns. A fellowship from the Mellon Foundation gave me the freedom to retool myself as a historian of early America. Inestimable aid, intellectual and otherwise, came from the friendship of fellow graduate students—Douglas Bradburn, Andrew Cohen, Michael Willrich, David Tannenhaus, Alexis Dudden, Geoff Klingsporn, Susan Barsy, Jon Aronoff, Elizabeth Dale, and Kate Chavigny, to name but a few.

Turning that dissertation into a book required even more rethinking and revision than I had anticipated. Once again, I was the fortunate recipient of a great amount of personal and institutional support. Colleagues at DePaul, Rice, Binghamton, Northeastern Illinois, and Syracuse Universities provided much encouragement. Allison Sneider, Carl Caldwell, Kerry Ward, Eva Haverkamp, Joel Wolfe, Alex Byrd, Susan Rosa, Patrick Miller, Zachary Schiffman, Michael Tuck, Francesca Morgan, Carol Faulkner, Susan Branson, and James Roger Sharp offered helpful suggestions. And the many students I had the privilege of teaching at these universities prompted me to present my arguments with more precision and clarity.

Fellowships from the National Endowment for the Humanities and the Library Company of Philadelphia allowed me to extend the scope of my research. A year's residence at the Charles Warren Center for Studies in American History at Harvard University really helped me to turn the corner. David Hall and James Kloppenberg were wonderful hosts and mentors, and my compatriots for that year—Carol Anderson, Carrie Tirado Bramen, Charles Capper, Amy Kittelstrom, Jeffrey Sklansky, and Craig Yirush—made the whole experience even better than it had any right to be.

I have also benefited from the opportunity to present portions of my work at the McNeil Center for Early American Studies, the Upstate New York Workshop on Early American History, Princeton University, the Newberry Library, and the University of Paris-Diderot. Conversations with Richard John, Andrew Robertson, David Parker, Leslie Butler, Michael Morrison, John Larson, and Christopher Tomlins helped me to better understand my project. But none of the people named above should be held accountable for its shortcomings.

This book is dedicated to my parents, Helmut and Wilma Schmeller, who inspired me with a love for history and teaching, even if that was not necessarily their intention. I have always been able to count on my brother and fellow historian, Erik Schmeller, for perspective and his unfailingly good sense of humor. Junko Takeda—a wonderful historian, artist, wife, and mother to our son, Takeshi— improved this book and its author in ways too numerous to list here. I am grateful for all the love and happiness she has given me.

Invisible Sovereign

Public Opinion and the American Political Imagination

Of public opinion,
Of a calm and cool flat sooner or later, (how impassive! how
    certain and final!)
Of the President with pale face asking secretly to himself,
    What will the people say at last?
Of the frivolous Judge—of the corrupt Congressman, Governor,
    Mayor—of such as these standing helpless and exposed,
Of the mumbling and screaming priest, (soon, soon deserted,)
Of the lessening year by year of venerableness, and of the
    dicta of officers, statutes, pulpits, schools,
Of the rising forever taller and stronger and broader of the intuitions of
    men and women, and of Self-esteem and Personality
Of the true New World—of the Democracies resplendent en-masse,
Of the conformity of politics, armies, navies, to them,
Of the shining sun by them—of the inherent light, greater than the rest,
Of the envelopment of all by them, and the effusion of all from them.

—Walt Whitman, "Thoughts" (1860)

When Walt Whitman sings of public opinion, politics vanish. One by one, public institutions, authorities, and officials yield before a rising tide of popular intuitions and soon disappear into a calm and cool sea of conformity. This prospect must have held some appeal in 1860, when politics seemed to "enter into everything," pushing the nation to the brink of civil war. For Whitman, who (as one biographer writes) "had come to view American society as an ocean covered with the 'scum' of politicians, below which lay the pure, deep waters of common humanity," poetic legislation will succeed where legislative compromise has failed. The "inherent light" of men and women will trump the tricks and demolish the dicta of party politicos, domineering judges, corrupt legislatures, mercenary journalists, arrogant educators, meddling reformers, and sundry fanatics and fire-eaters.[1]

One could also argue that when Walt Whitman sings of public opinion, public opinion itself vanishes—public opinion, that is, as we understand it today. By the song's end, it effuses from everywhere, envelops everything, and can no longer be distinguished from anything else. Public opinion is not the distribution of opinions across a spectrum of randomly sampled persons that appears in polls today. It has no constructive relationship to the "public sphere," or to any conceivable network of institutions, groups, and forums in which citizens deliberate on matters of shared concern. It cannot be broken down into sociological components and psychological dynamics. Whitman's public opinion is sublime: dreadful, terrifying, and beyond explanation or representation. In his "Thoughts," public opinion ceases to be a distinct and discrete concept and becomes a pervasive and invisible sovereign, a popular will forged not in legislatures, newspapers, public meetings, and polling places but deep "down in the abysms of New World humanity."[2]

Today, Americans have more modest expectations of public opinion, if they have any expectations at all. Public opinion is a largely taken-for-granted fact of everyday politics, something to be surveyed and analyzed, tracked over time and across demographic groups, and incessantly bombarded with constantly evolving techniques and technologies of persuasion, marketing, and social networking. But for all the attention we devote to public opinion, most of us do not speak of it as a sublime, inexorable force of permanent democratic revolution, much less as a reflection of our expanding intuitive powers and mounting self-esteem. Only in the context of contemporary international humanitarian movements are such utopian sentiments still entertained. Social scientists of public opinion are primarily concerned with how individuals struggle to perceive complex issues through a thickening fog of distraction, apathy, and misinformation. More skeptical voices caution that it would be better not to speak of public opinion at all: that the concept is a misleading fiction, an outmoded relic of classical democratic theory, or little more than the "silhouette of a phantom, the haunting fear of democratic consciousness."[3]

Yet it seems highly unlikely that "public opinion" will disappear from our vocabulary any time soon. Despite its vexing ambiguity and imprecision, it is indispensible. The concept of public opinion evokes, as one scholar has put it, "an intuitive, phenomenological sense of civil society." To talk about public opinion is to "indicate, to invoke, and to represent the pure and impure ideas, feelings, and evaluations that members of society hold about one another."[4] Put more simply, we need to think about what other people think, and the concept of "public opinion" helps us to do that. What the most discerning critics of the concept mourn is not the passing of some ideal past public sphere or golden age of deliberative democracy but a loss of meaning. While allowing that it may now be "impossible to recover a useful and usable conception of public opinion," they bemoan the enervation of a "conception, illusion, or idea that once had the capacity to engage the imagination, motivate action, and serve an ideological purpose"—or even inspire Whitmanesque effusions.[5]

So how did the concept of public opinion once engage the imagination? What actions did it motivate, and what ideological purposes did it serve? These are questions worth asking, and they are historical questions. If we go back to the eighteenth century, when the concept first began to take shape, and move forward from there, an eventful, varied, and contested history of claims to represent, measure, and mold public opinion emerges. That history may not be as inspiring, or even edifying, as we might have hoped, but it is an interesting history nonetheless.

The history of any concept should begin with questions about its significance: when and why did it appear, and how and why did it become part of the common vocabulary? "Opinion" played a peripheral role in eighteenth-century Anglo-American political theory. When political philosophers deigned to notice opinion, they saw it as a relatively harmless and apolitical amalgam of popular wisdom and folly. But from the founding era of the 1780s to the crisis of the 1850s, a growing number of Americans invoked "public opinion" to claim political legitimacy in a proliferating array of contexts and circumstances. Federalists introduced the concept to qualify the extent of popular participation in a constitutional republic, and Democratic-Republicans used it to vilify Federalist "aristocracy." Political economists employed it to explain the beneficial operations—or baneful power—of money and credit in an expanding commercial economy. Political party organizers praised its sovereign wisdom to assuage stubborn prejudices against political parties. Men claimed that its irresistible power compelled them to violence or restrained them from abusing their slaves. Women used it both to assert the scope and to protest the limits of their influence. Clergy and other moralists railed against the secular religion of public opinion while identifying its burgeoning power with the inexorable progress of technology and middle-class civilization. Northerners lamented the repressive backwardness of Southern opinion; Southerners mocked the licentious follies of Northern opinion.

A history of a concept should also examine how its meaning—or meanings—

changed. As the concept of public opinion moved from the periphery to the center of American political discourse, the question of what public opinion was became even more vexing, and its relation to political legitimacy more uncertain. Early "political-constitutional" concepts gave way to more modern, "social-psychological" concepts of public opinion. In the former, public opinion was primarily understood in terms of its relation to political institutions and commonly described with the languages of popular constitutionalism and political economy. Public opinion was a guardian of liberty, the voice of a sovereign people, or a political resource that strengthened government, lent authority to the laws, and promoted consensus and comity. While political-constitutional concepts might seem facile and simplistic to the twenty-first-century mind, they helped citizens of the early republic to make sense of the "rise of American democracy" and negotiate the terms on which it would be conducted. They issued from a "different mental universe" that, as Sean Wilentz argues, "regarded political institutions as the foundation of social and economic relations, and not the other way around."[6]

Political-constitutional discourses on public opinion tended to vacillate between confidence and paranoia: a Whitmanesque faith in the wisdom and power of public opinion mingled uncomfortably with a republican fear that power could easily manipulate, if not manufacture, public opinion. As the public sphere grew more expansive and inclusive, these fears intensified, and the constitutional fiction of a sovereign public opinion became difficult to sustain amid a proliferation of expressed opinions and seemingly intractable differences of opinion. In various ways, politicians, jurists, journalists, reformers, clergy, and academics responded by redefining public opinion as an aggregate of private opinions, leaving its political meaning and significance increasingly open to doubt. Public opinion came to be seen less as something expressed through political institutions by a sovereign people and more as something emanating from outside the political sphere. This shift was part of a larger reorientation in nineteenth-century American political and social thought, in which a romantically inflected liberalism and individualism pushed aside republican and Calvinist preoccupations with virtue and corruption and "regrounded political power in the psychosocial stream of 'public opinion' instead of the contractual model of majority rule."[7]

To be sure, the movement from political-constitutional to social-psychological conceptions of public opinion was gradual and incomplete and did not necessarily result in clearer or less ambiguous ways of thinking and talking about public opinion. Indeed, we might say that nineteenth-century Americans slowly replaced one problematic and ambiguous conception of public opinion with another. In the revolutionary and early national eras, appeals to and from the authority of public opinion derived much of their normative force from the ideal of popular sovereignty. The inherent difficulties of fixing a sovereign "people" in space and time, much less divining its will, prompted frequent arguments that often resembled, and frequently intersected with, disputes over public opinion. But the elusiveness of the sovereign people and its voice was both a problem of political legitimacy and a source of potential reform and reinvention.[8]

Concepts of public opinion were never entirely derived from or dependent on abstract notions of popular sovereignty. "Opinion" is (and was) often used to identify a judgment or belief, but it might also denote a sentiment or feeling, and a flourishing culture of sentimentalism supplied antebellum Americans with new ways to imagine and appeal to public opinion. Where historians and literary scholars once consigned sentimental literature and other forms of sympathetic identification of the private and feminine spheres, recent scholarship has convincingly emphasized their public and political dimensions. Antebellum Americans often spoke of public opinion as something that individuals and communities *felt*, be it the humanitarian sympathy of an abolitionist for a whipped slave, patriotic feeling for the union, or a public man's zealous regard for his honorable reputation.[9]

Political and sentimental conceptions of public opinion were not necessarily at odds; they did not reflect some deep conflict between "head" and "heart" in American culture. They did, however, contribute to mounting sectional tensions. In the Northern states, a more active culture of sensibility and benevolence, eager to promote a sense of national "feeling" and supported by more developed networks of communication, worked to create a more expansive and inclusive public sphere. Southerners increasingly viewed such projects as pieces of a larger design for consolidated national government and, following the emergence of radical abolitionism in the 1830s, an existential threat to their peculiar institutions. In defense, they held firm to a more limited, political-constitutional concept of public opinion and called on "traditional" sentiments of honor to defend it. With the realignment of national parties into sectional parties in the 1850s, these divergent conceptions of public opinion became especially manifest. Northern and Southern public opinion appeared to issue from two different mental and moral universes. These apparent differences would pave the path to civil war.[10]

Popular sovereignty, sentimentalism, and sectionalism shaped and complicated American conceptions of public opinion, but not quite as much as that assortment of political practices, ideas, dispositions, aspirations, and feelings that we call "democracy." If democracy means self-governance, public opinion means being governed by our thoughts. For some historians, the increasing power and deference accorded to public opinion in the nineteenth century signal a widespread commitment to the principles and practices of "deliberative democracy." Public opinion calls on people to lay their differences out in the open, argue, persuade, and accept the most persuasive argument. "Public opinion" unveils the secrets of states and the mysteries of professions; it puts the ploughman and the professor on equal moral footing.

There is some truth to this notion. But there is another, largely unacknowledged, side of the story. The concept of public opinion also made it possible to imaginarily escape political conflict and engagement, or to posit grounds for unity and agreement that did not require messy public debates. When antebellum Americans invoked, explained, and imagined public opinion, they drew on seemingly contradictory impulses, desires, and expectations. Like modern democratic liberals, they professed faith in the soundness of popular judgment, the salutary effects of candid public debate, and the right to have and express opinions. At other times (and, occasionally, at the same time), they envisioned a public opinion that transcended unruly controversies, superseded stubborn particularities, sustained civic tranquility, and held individuals tightly within the orbit of Christian morality and republican principle. In the American political imagination, the concept of public opinion could promise a politics of reason and persuasion. But it could just as easily promise a Whitmanesque politics without politics.

CHAPTER 1

The Moral Economy of Opinion

Sooner or later, public opinion, an instrument merely moral in the beginning, will find occasion physically to inflict its sentences on the unjust.

—Thomas Jefferson to James Madison (1804)

Writing from Paris in January 1787, Thomas Jefferson sought news from western Massachusetts, where militias had been dispatched to put down a popular uprising against local courts. Regardless of the outcome of what would become known as Shays' Rebellion, Jefferson urged his American correspondents to compare such "irregular interpositions of the people" and their violent suppression to the gentle rule of "public opinion." But when Jefferson explained the meaning of this relatively new phrase, he did not look to the French salon, the English coffeehouse, or the Virginia Assembly. Rather, he pointed to "those societies (as the Indians) which live without government," for they enjoyed "in their general mass an infinitely greater degree of happiness than those who live under the European governments. Among the former, public opinion is in the place of law, and restrains morals as powerfully as laws ever did anywhere." In his *Notes on Virginia*, written several years earlier, he described a people who had never "submitted to any laws, any coercive power, any shadow of government" but that of their "manners, and that moral sense of right and wrong, which, like the sense of tasting and feeling in every man, makes a part of his nature." Ostracism and exclusion were their only "species of coercion," yet crimes were "very rare among them."[1]

Jefferson's depiction of public opinion among the Indians was not a product of close empirical observation. Believing that Indian societies most closely resembled the original state of nature, he blithely ignored the great variety of native practices of governance and legality. He did, however, acknowledge that the gentle rule of public opinion did not extend to all. Indian women "submitted to unjust drudgery"; force was the "law" of their lives. And if it was "civilization alone which replaces women in the enjoyment of their natural equality," Virginia civilization filled the void of unjust drudgery with African slaves, whose labor gave Jefferson the leisure to cultivate the moral taste of the freeholder.[2] Nor were Jefferson's remarks especially novel: to illustrate opinion's rule, many of his contemporaries resorted to talk of noble savages and primitive states. Benjamin Franklin wrote of Indian government "by the counsel or advice of the sages," in which "there is no force, there are no prisons, no officers to compel obedience, or inflict punishment." New England minister Jedediah Morse believed that "what civilized nations enforce upon their subjects by compulsory measures, they effect by their eloquence."[3] In these ways, the eloquent Indian exemplified eighteenth-century classical republican ideals. In his *History of the Five Indian Nations* (1727), Cadwallader Colden saw the Iroquois propensity for speechifying as "the natural Consequence of a perfect Republican Government: Where no single Person has a Power to compel, the Arts of Persuasion must prevail."[4]

Indian eloquence illustrated the "ancient" and oft-repeated maxim that a people could either be governed by opinion or be ruled by force. Yet Jefferson, Franklin, and other admirers of Indian politics placed government by opinion in the past, or in some ostensibly rudimentary or "savage" form of social organization. For Jefferson, it was a "problem, not clear in my mind," that a society in which "public opinion is in the place of law" was "not the best." But such a "state" was also "inconsistent with any degree of population" and different in essence from those "governments, wherein the will of every one has a just influence." If such governments offered a "precious degree of liberty & happiness" to the "mass of mankind," they were also subject to the sort of "turbulence" then erupting in western Massachusetts. Thinking through this dilemma with James Madison, Jefferson held "that a little rebellion now and then is a good thing, & as necessary in the political world as storms in the physical." To Edward Carrington, he recommended that

> [t]he way to prevent these irregular interpositions of the people is to give them full information of their affairs through the channel of the public papers, & to contrive that those papers should penetrate the whole mass of the people. The basis of our government being the opinion of the people, the very first object should be to keep that right; and were it left for me to decide whether we should have a government without newspapers or newspapers without government, I

should not hesitate a moment to prefer the latter. But I should mean that every man should receive those papers and be capable of reading them.[5]

Jefferson's preference for a "little rebellion now and then" and "newspapers without government" are two of his most frequently quoted aphorisms, but they point in quite different directions: the former suggests an ongoing politics of popular revolutionary violence, the latter a more orderly and routine politics of persuasion and consent.

This was the "problem, not clear" in Jefferson's mind: if "the opinion of the people" was the "basis of our government," what did that mean in practice, much less in theory? Jefferson was not alone in his confusion. For revolutionary-era Americans, anthropological theories of Indian eloquence and philosophical maxims on the gentle rule of opinion did not sit comfortably with the violent realities of revolutionary politics; nor did they translate easily into clear and uncontested ideas about the role of public opinion in the emerging American political order. A faith in the veracity of the commonly held opinions and judgments of ordinary people was one of the more remarkable intellectual inventions of the eighteenth-century Atlantic world. But that faith had few self-evident political implications; it could serve radical arguments for revolutionary change just as readily as it could conservative defenses of tradition and stability. Even the most fair-minded and disinterested political philosophers struggled to square the ostensibly natural, untutored common sense of the people with the complicated contrivances of constitutional law and the elusive fictions of sovereignty.[6]

All of this may explain why American revolutionaries were reticent to invoke "public opinion" in their rhetoric. As Hannah Arendt once observed, they "never referred to public opinion in their own arguments, as Robespierre and the men of the French Revolution did to add force to their own opinions."[7] While American patriots (and loyalists as well) addressed their arguments to a public, and occasionally claimed to speak on its behalf, they did not invoke public opinion as a sovereign force of critical reason. And while ordinary Americans certainly had opinions, and made them known in myriad ways, those opinions were rarely recognized and represented as "public opinion." Arendt attributed this reticence to the classical republicanism of political leaders, who *unanimously* viewed public opinion as "the potential unanimity of all" and thus understood that "the rule of public opinion was a form of tyranny." This erroneously assumes that revolutionaries worried over a possible tyranny of a public opinion that they did not necessarily presume to exist. A more persuasive explanation has been offered by Gordon Wood, who argues that most revolutionary leaders "vaguely held to a largely unspoken assumption that the only public opinion worth worrying about was that of their cultivated peers," an assumption that the democratizing social and political processes unleashed by the Revolution would eventually undermine. While there is much truth in this view, it makes public opinion into little more than a synonym for the leveling impulses of democracy.[8]

Both arguments tend to interpret revolutionary-era conceptions of public opinion through the lens of subsequent eras (twentieth-century totalitarianism for Arendt, Jacksonian democracy for Wood). If we reverse directions and look at things in the context of received early modern ideas about the nature of opinion and its role in public life, the reticence to invoke public opinion and the sources of that "problem, not clear" in Thomas Jefferson's mind become more comprehensible. Eighteenth-century Americans and Britons readily acknowledged that their governments were based on opinion and saw that opinion as a source of civic tranquility, a friend to order, and a security against revolution and civil war. Deeply encoded in the political rhetoric, rituals, and ideas of the British Atlantic world, this "moral philosophy" of opinion cautioned against frequent appeals to popular opinion and demonized dissenters and other "opinionated" persons. It allowed for "irregular interpositions" of the people and their opinions in extraordinary moments of crisis, when they had reasons to fear for their liberty and safety. But those fears could also be dismissed as imaginary and illegitimate.

The Revolution worked profound changes in the way Americans understood and used an array of political concepts: sovereignty, representation, citizenship, law, liberty, and equality to name a few. But it did little to dethrone the traditional moral philosophy of opinion. Indeed, that philosophy was in many respects written into the federal constitution of 1787.

A World Governed by Opinion

Totus mundus regitur opinione. All the world is governed by opinion. Walking the streets near the London marketplace one day in 1638, Henry Peacham saw these words stamped in elaborate letters of gold atop the "great gates" of "a Gentleman or Merchants house." Intrigued, he stopped to take a closer look at the emblem set beneath, which depicted "an old woman who having gathered up into her apron many dead skulls, which shee found scattered upon the ground, with an intent to lay them up in a charnell house, but her apron slipping upon a hill where she stood, some ran one way, and some another; which the old woman seeing, Nay (qouth shee), goe your own waies, for thus ye differed in your opinion when ye had life, every one taking his severall way as he fancied." Reflecting on this tribute to worldly folly, Peacham asked why "the ancient Pagans," who deified so many things, "passed by opinion, bearing a far greater sway than dogs, onions and leeks in Ægypt." The emblem hinted at the answer: "since deifying was wont to bee done with a generall consent, Opinion was never to expect it, every man where she reignes being of severall minde."[9]

Unlike the "public opinion" of modern political theory, "opinion" does not rule the world by forging consensus or inducing conformity. Opinion generates dissent, diversity, and singularity. The empire of opinion is a confusing and enervating Babel of ever-changing and incommensurable standards, principles, and beliefs that will never converge at the bar of reason or congeal into a cake of custom. For Peacham, a moderately successful poet and essayist best known for such conduct books as *The Compleat Gentleman* and *The Worth of a Penny*, opinion is the general cause of the general crisis of the seventeenth century. In a rapidly expanding market economy, opinion is the "compasse" by which men sail a "vast Ocean of Ignorance" and "make shipwracke of their credits, estates, and lives." In an increasingly fluid social order, "vulgar opinion" breeds a confusion of standards that allows men of ill breeding to claim the status of "gentleman."[10]

Worse still, opinion multiplied the controversies that, by the late 1630s, had pushed England to the brink of civil war. The Anglican and Royalist Peacham entered the fray with a series of pamphlets that decried the publication of pamphlets and sought to persuade the public of the futility of persuading opinion. His 1641 *The World is Ruled and Governed by Opinion* (fig. 1.1) featured a striking illustration by Wenceslas Hollar. Lady Opinion, the world resting in her lap and the tower of Babel on her blindfolded head, sits in a tree fruited with the "idle books and libells" found "in everie streete on everie stall."[11] Her only nourishment is the folly poured at her roots, but it is sufficient, for "one opinion many doth devise, and propagate till infinite they bee." Opinion (like Fortune) is a woman—a fecund and fickle creature who, as Machiavelli infamously said, must be taken by force. The equation between opinion and fortune appeared just a year later in Peacham's *Square-Caps Turned into Round-Heads*, a dialogue between "Time," which desires "no *Innovation* either in *Church* or *Common-wealth*," and "Opinion," a weak-willed woman captivated by Puritan fanaticism. As the wheel of fortune turns between them, "Time" eventually persuades "Opinion" of her own folly, but it is to little avail. She can "doe no other than I doe," for she is always carried "with violence in the throng." "Time" ends by declaring that "nothing violent lasts long" and admonishes lady opinion to "keep a good tongue" in the interim.[12]

There was nothing especially novel in Peacham's poems and essays on the perils of opinion. Early modern English folklorists found a variety of such "an-

Figure 1.1. Wenceslas Hollar, illustration for Henry Peacham, *The World Is Ruled and Governed by Opinion;* London, 1642. © Trustees of The British Museum.

cient" adages in wide circulation: "Things are not as they seeme, Not what they be themselves; all is opinion; All that exists, Takes valuation from opinion, A Giddy minion now. Opinion is the Queen of the World; Opinion is the greatest Lady that swayeth the world."[13] Moreover, such proverbial wisdom closely mirrored the discussions of opinion offered in learned texts. Entering Northern European languages in the thirteenth century from the Latin *opinari*, opinion came freighted with largely depreciatory meanings, many of them handed down from Stoic philosophers. In Plato and Aristotle, opinion might refer to a judgment on matters of uncertainty or a proposition that could be neither proved nor disproved. Stoics accepted these definitions but emphasized the passive nature of opinion, often treating it as an impression formed on a weak and plastic mind or a product of unchecked imagination and unbridled passion. Proper care of the self required an ascetic rejection of opinion both personal and popular. In rejecting opinion, the Stoic sought to attain a state of *apatheia* in which the laws of nature could be comprehended. "Nature's wants are small," Seneca advised, "while those of opinion are limitless." If "someone irritates you," Epictetus taught his students, "realize that it is your own opinion that has irritated you."[14]

The appeal of Stoic teachings to seventeenth-century philosophers and men of letters is not difficult to understand. Wearied by the confessional conflicts and religious wars set into motion by the Protestant Reformation and the Catholic Counter-Reformation, fearful of the flourishing fanaticism that they saw as antithetical to civil society, and appalled by the seeming Babel of opinions flying from printing presses across Europe and Britain, neo-Stoics hoped for citizens and subjects who could resist the influence of popular opinion and set aside their particular passions and opinions in the interest of self-preservation, civil peace, and the public good. They desired, as Richard Tuck has put it, a "skeptical and disengaged" people who would subordinate "their own wills, desires and beliefs to those of their sovereign, not because the sovereign knows better, but because the disciplining of an individual psychology is necessary for one's well being."[15]

As it happened, the English were neither as disengaged nor as skeptical as Henry Peacham and other neo-Stoics had hoped. A protracted civil war, a regicide, and a tumultuous Commonwealth ensued. For Thomas Hobbes, writing in exile from Paris in 1651, the proposition that opinion governs the world was no longer a lamentation of worldly folly. It was instead the cornerstone of his political science: "the power of the mighty hath not foundation but in the opinion and belief of the people." But those opinions and beliefs required both a "common power to keep them in awe" and a "mutual and common fear." To be sure, the question of whether it was better to rule through opinion or fear was at least as old as Augustine, if not Aristotle. Machiavelli, Erasmus, and Luther counseled the latter: the people loved the prince when they cared to, but they feared at his will. Hobbes saw this as a false choice. Fear alone had not been sufficient to keep religious and political fanatics in due submission, and a sovereign could not govern by opinion if opinion was divided. But fear—of violence and civil disorder, of foreign invasion and subversion, of poverty and disease—could be used to unify opinion. The people had to be taught to fear the heresies that incited civil discord and war. Because peace required the "well governing of Opinions," a "private opinion, obstinately maintained" and "contrary to the opinion which the public person (that is to say, the representant of the Commonwealth) hath commanded to be taught" was by definition "heresy." A shared fear, deliberately cultivated by the state, would have to substitute for the uniformity of opinion and belief that no longer existed (if it ever had).[16]

Hobbes was probably the first serious theorist of public opinion in English political thought. Rejecting humanist and neo-Stoic indifference to popular folly, he saw clearly the connections between opinion and the exercise of power, as well as the role of religious, educational, social, and political institutions in shaping that opinion. But his theories were not particularly influential. His materialism made him a frequent and favorite target of theologians, and his draconian prescriptions for the "well governing of opinions" made Leviathan into a synonym for absolutism. More cautious political writers reiterated the maxim that opinion governed the world but only to explain how the well-born few could govern the many. "Power, arising from Strength, is always in those that are governed," while the "Authority arising from Opinion" was, according to Sir William Temple, "in those that Govern, who are few." For Temple, opinion was identical to "custom and use": it was a river in "which the Humours and Manners of the People run with the strongest current."[17]

The Glorious Revolution of 1688, and the political order and culture that would slowly and fitfully emerge from it, appeared to promise a different relation between opinion and power. The ostensibly bloodless and orderly nature of that revolution diminished the fear of civil war that bound Leviathan's subjects together. A constitution premised on limited monarchy and the supremacy of Parliament promised additional securities against future civil wars and tentatively winked at ideas of popular sovereignty. A bill of rights, an act of religious toleration, and the lapsing of the licensing act on printing allowed something resembling a Habermasian "public sphere" to emerge at the political margins of a carefully managed parliamentary oligarchy. The post-1688 English state and the expanding British Empire also instilled national and imperial loyalties with a careful cultivation of fear that Hobbes would have appreciated. In churches, prints, and the public square, Whigs preached up the imminent dangers posed by Catholics, Jacobins, Frenchmen, Spaniards, and any other available villains.[18]

If John Locke can be taken as a spokesman for this new political order, it is possible to see some lineaments of a modern concept of public opinion in his political writings. In sharp contrast to Hobbes, he did not regard private opinions as potentially heretical. When entering "politic societies," individuals resigned "up to the public the disposing of all their force" but retained the "power of Thinking well or ill." The people retained a right to revolt, but only after enduring "a long train of abuses, prevarications, and artifices, all tending the same way" that somehow made their "design visible to the people." Locke's psychological theory also left some doubt as to whether individuals could really have "opinions," much less "selves." While the "nature of the understanding" was such "that it cannot be compelled by outward force," the understanding remained subject to a "law of opinion" more powerful than the civil or divine law. Established by "a secret and tacit consent" in the "several Societies, Tribes, and Clubs of Men in the World," the law of opinion acted as a measure "of what is every where called and esteemed *Virtue* and *Vice*."[19] If force could not control opinion, Locke realized that fear of opinion often controlled individuals. In this way, Locke expunged fear from the social contract and took it out of the hands of the magistrate. He *privatized* fear. In some respects, he internalized it: his sensationalist psychology gave anxiety an instrumental role in human motivation. Volition arose out of "uneasiness," and the "anxiety of freedom" became the fountain of all willed action. With Locke, fear loses its public face and becomes a product of village morals and individual anxieties.[20]

It is possible to see Locke's "Law of Opinion" as an anticipation of nineteenth-century critiques of social conformity and the tyranny of public opinion. But aside from a few barbs directed against "opinionaetry" ("the floating of other men's opinions in our brains," which "makes us not one jot more knowing"), Locke did not appear particularly concerned with the problems of individuality and personal identity. Indeed, many eighteenth-century British philosophers and theologians worried that the sensationalist premises of Lockean psychology failed to adequately account for the continuous and indivisible nature of the self. Finding Locke's discussion of identity "hasty," Bishop Butler warned that it could lead to the dangerous belief that "personality is not a permanent, but a transient thing"—a belief that seemed to diminish the moral agency and responsibility of individuals. Others took exception to Locke's "law of opinion," arguing that it conflated morality with mere convention and subjected virtue to the shifting climate of opinion. The Third Earl of Shaftesbury complained that his former teacher had thrown "all order and virtue out of the world, and made the very idea of these . . . *unnatural*."[21]

To restore order to the moral world and integrity to the self, many eighteenth-century British philosophers turned their attention from the understanding to the emotions, from Lockean sensationalism to "sense," be it common, moral, aesthetic, or otherwise. Rejecting the Hobbesian and Lockean portrayal of humanity as atomistic, antagonistic, and calculating, Shaftesbury, Francis Hutcheson, Thomas Reid, Lord Kames, and Adam Smith depicted human nature as social, imitative, and affective. Individuals and communities alike possessed a common sense that insured the moral integrity and continuity of self and society against fickle changes and fractious conflicts of opinion. Standards of virtue and vice were not set by the law of opinion but by a less mutable law of sentiments arising from an innate "public *sense*," which Hutcheson defined as "our determination to be pleased with the happiness of others, and to be uneasy at their misery." The cultivation of such social affections would make persons less opinionated. As "the pleasures of society thicken upon us," Lord Kames counseled, "we learn to submit our opinions." For Edmund Burke, people acquired their manners and opinions less by dry "precept" than through the social "passion" of "imitation," which constituted "one of the strongest links of society," a "species of mutual compliance which all men yield to each other, without constraint to themselves, and which is extremely flattering to all." Far from being an element of well-being, having opinions was frequently regarded as symptomatic of dogmatism, pedantry, ill breeding, or basic mental befuddlement (as in Laurence Sterne's *Life and Opinions of Tristram Shandy*, where Shandy's surfeit of opinions overtakes the story of his life).[22]

Sensibility and sociability became the defining values of a culture of refinement and gentility that took shape in a proliferating array of coffeehouses, clubs, salons, and drawing rooms and expressed itself in forms of "polite" literature ranging from published novels, essays, biographies, histories, poetry, newspapers, and reviews to private letters and privately circulated manuscripts. Beneath this culture of refinement lay a rapprochement of sorts between agrarian and mercantile interests, as well as a more inclusive ethos that opened the circle of polite society to qualified men and (significantly) women. A growing literature on civility instructed aspirants to refinement on the control of private passions and opinions. A "polite philosopher" understood that all "vehemence in discourse" proceeded from "an impatience at finding others differ from us in Opinion." To "start Questions, or manage Debates, which offend the Public Ear," Shaftesbury admonished, was "to be wanting in that Respect which is due to common Society." Britons had become "so wrought on, and confounded, by different modes of Opinion, different Systems and Schemes imposed by Authority," he feared "that they may wholly lose all Notion or Comprehension of Truth." Particular opinions—a "Rust upon Men's Understandings"—stood in the way of a true and universal opinion. For Adam Ferguson, it was this "common sense and opinion of mankind, which, struggling with the private views of individuals, and the claims of party, may be considered as the great legislator of nations."[23]

The philosophical and literary discourses of sense and sociability seeped into the political culture of post-1688 Britain, settled comfortably into the new Whig order, and produced a "political language" that John Pocock aptly called "polite Whiggism." Invoking invidious distinctions between the passionate and militant "prophetic man" of the seventeenth century and the polite and refined man of the eighteenth, polite Whigs developed an "irenic, established, and oligarchic" rhetoric "capable of being deployed against Puritan, Tory, and republican alike" while "making them all look curiously similar."[24] The ridicule of "enthusiasts" furnishes an instructive example of polite Whiggism in practice. In many respects little more than a new term for "fanatic," "enthusiast" became a common "smear word" thrown back and forth among competing political factions, religious sects, philosophical schools, and literary circles. Although neoclassical poets would slowly rehabilitate the "divine influx" of enthusiasm as a desirable source of inspiration, the social image of the enthusiast remained fixed: narrow-minded, isolated, unsociable, unreasonable, and ill-bred.[25]

In the aesthetic moralism of polite Whiggism, "opinion" became a catch-all explanation for political stability and civic tranquility. "Despite the influence of coffee-houses, daily newspapers, and the volatile population of London," J. A. W. Gunn has argued that "the idea of the public as a constant actor in the political process did not materialize." Indeed, the role of opinion was thought to be infrequent and largely passive. For David Hume, there was nothing

> more surprising to those, who consider human affairs with a philosophical eye, than to see the easiness with which the many are governed by the few; and to observe the implicit submission with which men resign their own sentiments and passions to those of their rulers. When we enquire by what means this wonder is brought about, we shall find, that as Force is always on the side of the governed, the governors have nothing to support them but opinion. 'Tis therefore, on opinion only that government is founded; and this maxim extends to the most despotic and most military governments, as well as the most free and popular.

The "maxim" that all government was founded on opinion was little more than a truism, but it was a truism well suited to the predominantly irenic tenor of British political culture. Opinion was anything and everything but physical force, no matter how contrary: nature and culture, reason and folly, declared consent and silent assent, fleeting fashions and established traditions.[26]

At the same time, Whiggish celebrations of the natural, gentle, and "surprising" rule of opinion made the presence of fear in political society seem unnatural. For polite writers of the mid-eighteenth century, the progress of commerce, the refinement of society and sentiment, the moderation of religion, and the spirit of Enlightenment worked together to remove sordid and superstitious fears from the social, spiritual, and natural worlds and led them to hope for similar changes in the political sphere. Consider, for example, Samuel Johnson's 1770 response to Wilkesite agitators:

> One of the chief advantages derived by the present generation from the improvement and diffusion of philosophy, is deliverance from unnecessary ter-

rours, and exemption from false alarms. The unusual appearances, whether regular or accidental, which once spread consternation over ages of ignorance, are now the recreations of inquisitive security . . . The advancement of political knowledge may be expected to produce in time like effects. Causeless discontent and seditious violence will grow less frequent, and less formidable, as the science of government is better ascertained by diligent study of the theory of man.

Johnson would soon direct his pen against Americans and their allegedly chimerical fears of imperial tyranny, fears stirred up by patriot "incendiaries" who had been "taught, by some master of mischief, how to put in motion the engine of political electricity; to attract, by the sounds of liberty and property; to repel, by those of popery and slavery."[27] To better understand that engine, which we would today call "public opinion," it is necessary to take those fears and their political implications more seriously.

The Opinion of Safety

Mid-eighteenth-century Britons frequently boasted of the stability and seeming harmony of their political order, attributing it to the genius of their constitution, its complementary mixture of monarchical and republican principles, and the balance it struck between king, lords, and Parliament. The colonists of British North America shared in this celebration and imagined that their various provincial governments, while different in structural details, faithfully mirrored the constitution of the mother country. Along with William Blackstone (and possibly even above him), the most influential admirer and interpreter of the English Constitution was a Frenchman: Charles Secondat, Baron de Montesquieu, author of *The Spirit of the Laws* (1748).[28] Montesquieu distilled the role of opinion in the English constitutional order into a succinct formula that American colonists would later deploy to resist intrusive imperial laws and regulations, and ultimately to declare their independence. Linking the liberty of political subjects to the "opinion" they held of their own safety, Montesquieu's formula lent clarity, force, and credibility to the popular discontents and fears that Samuel Johnson disdainfully dismissed.

Like Hobbes and Locke, Montesquieu hypothesized that all "societies" originated in fear, but he went on to argue that they developed different constitutions structured and animated by different measures and varieties of fear. Only "despotism," that "oriental" form of government, remained fundamentally dependent on the fear of its subjects. In monarchies, a passion for honor among the aristocracy (or "persons capable of setting a value upon themselves") lessened the power of fear over subjects; in republics, a more broadly distributed spirit of virtue did the same. Along with honor and virtue among its aristocracy, gentry, and polite middle classes, the great mass of the English people enjoyed an additional security against despotism and tyranny (its somewhat less fearful occidental cousin): a constitution that separated the legislative, executive, and judicial powers. In Montesquieu's estimation, this constitutionally secured freedom from fear was a cornerstone of English liberty: "The political liberty of the subject is a tranquility of mind arising from the opinion each person has of his safety. In order to have this liberty, it is requisite that the government be so constituted as one man need not be afraid of another."[29]

With this, Montesquieu effectively psychologized liberty, making it as much a bundle of rights held by a subject as a freedom from the fear that those rights can or will be taken away. Liberty thus exists not in the past or present tense but in the conditional and future tenses, and for this reason it is as dependent on laws and political institutions as it is on the opinion of individual political subjects. Montesquieu went on to assert that the English possessed a peculiar character trait that enabled them to maintain their liberties: an "impatience of temper" that impelled them to resist the slightest encroachment of tyranny, real or imagined, at its inception. Tyranny, being "always slow and feeble in its commencement," stood little chance of success.[30]

Like many eighteenth-century philosophers, Montesquieu believed that the intemperance of the North Atlantic climate instilled this "impatience of temper" in the English. But more immediate causes of this anxiousness can be found in English religion and political culture. Protestant denunciation of Catholic "priestcraft" charged priests with the "invention" of "timid and abject superstition" and the cunning manipulation of "absurd" ceremonial and sacrificial forms designed to ward off "infinite unknown evils." In politics, "Country Party" opponents of Prime Minister Robert Walpole repeatedly warned of corruption and conspiracies against English liberties and urged the people to resist Whig efforts to "awe" them into submission. Both "false religion" and "arbitrary government," Country Party propagandist "Cato" warned, used "dark and dreadful horrors, which banish reason, and contract and embitter the heart."[31]

In both religious and political contexts, the fear to be feared was not a reverent fear of God or a salutary fear of the law but a powerful and potentially debilitating emotion. This intense species of fear attracted much interest and speculation among proponents of philosophical and literary sentimentalism, who saw the capacity to perceive such fears in others as the defining characteristic of human sympathy and sociability. "Fear," according to Adam Smith, was "a passion derived altogether from the imagination, which represents, with an uncertainty and fluctuation that increases our anxiety, not what we really feel, but what we may hereafter possibly suffer." (Smith opined that only "women, and men of weak nerves" were actually overcome with fear in such situations.) Sympathetic fear, as Smith's fellow Scotsman Francis Hutcheson argued, constituted the basis of the human mind's "public *sense*," an "inward pain of compassion" that "solely arises from an opinion of misery felt by another, and not immediately in visible form." Throughout the eighteenth-century Atlantic world, writers and orators frequently resorted to what has been called the "pathetic sublime," a mode of expression designed to produce an irresistible flood of emotion at the sight of fear and suffering.[32]

The fear of fear itself, and the corresponding idea of liberty as freedom from "servile" fear, cast a pall of suspicion over any apparent use of fear as an instrument of political rule. For example, the notion that the king of Britain was God's appointed vice-regent, and should be feared as such, died a quiet death. William III (1689–1702) was commonly addressed as the "dread Sovereign," but by the time of George I (1714–1727) declarations of love for the king prevailed, and divine right became little more than a convenient legal-constitutional fiction. Though a "philosophical mind will consider the royal person merely as one man appointed by mutual consent to preside over many others, and will pay him that reverence and duty which the principles of society demand," William Blackstone worried that

> the mass of mankind will be apt to grow insolent and refractory, if taught to consider their prince as a man of no greater perfection than themselves. The law therefore ascribes to the king, in his high political character, not only large political emoluments which form his prerogative and revenue, but likewise certain attributes of a great and transcendent nature; by which the people are led to consider him in light of a superior being, and to pay him that awful respect, which may enable him with greater ease to carry on the business of government.[33]

There is considerable evidence that the subjects of mid-eighteenth-century British North America loved and revered their king. Following the death of George I, numerous colonial officials, clergy, and publicists breathed new life into the concept of divine right. But proponents of this attempted resanctification of the monarchy, as Brendan McConville has shown, took care to distinguish between the natural bonds of love between Protestant subjects and their monarch and the base, sordid fear that bound Catholic subjects to theirs. Accordingly, provincial Americans developed a political culture of "benevolent royalism" that celebrated the Protestant succession, cheered the expansion of the British Empire, and praised the monarch as protector of their safety, rights, and prosperity. Colonial calendars marked as many as twenty-six holidays—coronation days, royal birthdays, and Pope's Day, to name a few—for colonists to demonstrate their allegiance. But the "large political emoluments" and prerogatives of the crown had relatively slight influence on the actual governance of the colonies. With little power over colonial patronage or land tenure, royal authority was largely symbolic and rhetorical, and thus more dependent on bonds of affection and fears of common enemies than calculations of interest or Blackstone's pragmatic "principles of society." The British Crown, it was often said, governed by "opinion," not force.[34]

But what did that mean in practice? If benevolent royalism gave colonists a sense of connection to the empire, it could not answer some persistent and vexatious questions concerning its constitution and governance. And it could do little to resolve the recurring scrimmages for power between colonial governors and legislatures, much less the shifting factions within those legislatures. Colonial politicians readily accused their opponents of harboring dark designs against public liberty and the common good in a fashion that has often struck historians as markedly, if not pathologically, paranoid. Yet such rhetoric is better understood (as Gordon Wood has argued) as a basic feature of eighteenth-century political mentalities, less a psychological affliction than a product of enlightened, Newtonian conceptions of causality that were at once both rationalistic and personal. "Concatenations of events" were not readily or easily attributed to chance or general social forces—like "public opinion"—but to the "concerted designs of individuals" and, ultimately, "the moral nature of man himself."[35]

When "opinion" appeared in colonial political debates, the discussion usually had less to do with what actual opinion was thought to be than with broad assumptions about its moral nature and tendencies. What colonists thought, either as individuals or in the aggregate, about particular public events or policies could not be easily discerned, much less fashioned into a useful rhetorical weapon. Instead, colonial political writers relied on received maxims about opinion or leaned on the authority of "great" philosophers like Montesquieu. For example, when in 1763 the possibility arose that the Massachusetts lieutenant governor and several judges might be appointed to the upper legislative chamber (the Council), critics charging that this violated traditional prohibitions against multiple office holding turned to *The Spirit of the Laws*. Because political liberty was "a tranquility of mind arising from the opinion each man has of his own safety," a writer in the *Boston Gazette* declared, the "entrusting of the same gentlemen with legislative and judiciary power" could only upset that peace and liberty. An opposing writer in the *Boston Evening Post* agreed in principle with Montesquieu's maxim but contended that it did not apply to this particular case as it did not actually violate the separation of powers. Not persuaded, the *Gazette* writer retorted that the maxim was "an independent proposition" that reached beyond specific constitutional questions: *anything* that "whatsoever has a tendency to destroy the opinion which each man has of his own safety, and the tranquility of mind arising therefrom, is inconsistent with political liberty."[36]

While this 1763 debate over multiple office holding was not especially significant, it illustrates how political scrimmages over the distribution of power easily could turn from seemingly minor points of constitutional law to sweeping assertions about the moral psychology of fear. The mere possibility that a political action might lead men to fear for their safety could be an argument against that action. From here it required no great leap of logic to infer that if men were anxious, their liberties might have already been violated. And from 1763 onward, as the fears of colonists appeared to multiply, this inference became increasingly prominent in the reasoning of American revolutionaries, who repeatedly and insistently traced the cause of those fears back to British policies. The "American mind" was, according to John Adams, "possessed with all that fear, which is essentially the characteristic of monopolized colonies."[37]

If revolutionaries did not make public opinion a part of their arguments, they had much to say about public fear. After all, an American mind possessed by common fears of imperial tyranny was much easier to conceive than one positively defined by shared traditions, interests, or opinions. The variety of political cultures among the thirteen colonies, and the increasing ethnic and religious diversity within each of them, made it difficult to posit any notion of an American people, much less an American nation. Networks of political, social, and commercial communication and association between the colonies—if they existed at all—tended to be weaker than those linking each colony to Britain.[38] To forge a sense of cohesion among colonists, revolutionaries frequently resorted to the pathetic sublime, stocking their rhetoric with dreadful scenes of tyranny and oppression. For some, this was the natural and necessary response to an increasingly frightening series of events. With more canny politicians like Samuel Adams, the cultivation of popular fear was a tactic essential to a larger political strategy of resistance; "THE SPIRIT OF APPREHENSION should be kept up" among the people, he declared, especially when there appeared to be "EVIDENCE OF TY-RANNICAL DESIGNS."[39]

In some respects, the French and Indian War had already taught Americans how to fold sentimentalized portrayals of fear into their political arguments. Colonial propagandists wrapped their denunciations of native savagery and Gallic barbarism in what Peter Silver has called "an enraptured discourse of fear." First devised to convey the paralyzing terror felt by the rural victims of Indian raids, this discourse became an indispensable tool in forging postwar political coalitions and articulating the sense of "indignant vulnerability" and "violent self-pity" so characteristic of revolutionary rhetoric. While protests against the Stamp, Townsend, and Coercive Acts and the countless misdeeds of colonial governments and officials drew on a wide and occasionally contradictory array of political and constitutional ideas, they seldom failed to allude to the dreadful apprehensions of the colonists and to assail the heartless indifference of loyalists and the mother country. At their most extravagant, such portraits of colonial suffering could read like a parody of sentimentalism, as with this 1769 petition from aggrieved North Carolinian regulators: "How relentless is the breast without sympathy, the heart that cannot bleed on a View of our calamity; to see tenderness removed, cruelty stepping in; and all our liberties and privileges invaded and abridg'd by (as it were) domesticks who are conscious of their guilt and void of remorse: O how daring! how relentless! whilst impending judgments loudly threaten and gaze upon them, with every emblem of merited destruction."[40]

Clergy had a particular affinity for talking about fear and understood its uses and moral psychology better than most. The task of alerting the people to impending tyranny came naturally to men accustomed to warning them of their imminent damnation. Whether Liberal or Calvinist, New or Old Light, Congregational or Episcopalian, New England clergy were famously strident in their opposition to British policies, secular or religious, real or imagined. The growing fear that Britain aimed to establish an Anglican episcopacy in the colonies rapidly merged with traditional New England anti-papist paranoia, leading many clergy to speculate that the Antichrist had established a second residence in London. In the face of such grave threats, any nice distinctions between spiritual exhortation and political agitation ceased to matter. The Reverend William Gordon of Massachusetts could promise George Washington that he and his brethren would continue to "preach up the dangers we are in," as it would "do no hurt, and may have a good effect of tending to awaken the stupid, for we still abound with lethargic souls."[41]

For clergy, the fearful state of the colonists offered lessons at once religious, moral, and political. The lessons often began with Micah 4:4 ("that they should sit every man under his vine, and under his fig-tree, and none should make them afraid") or Proverbs 29:25 ("The fear of man brings a snare, but whoever trusts the Lord shall be safe"). The former gestured nostalgically to a tranquil and bucolic colonial past untroubled by imperial intrusions, while the latter identified both the source of and the solution to the present troubles. In "The Snare Broken," a sermon delivered shortly after the repeal of the Stamp Act, the Reverend Jonathan Mayhew of Boston described at length the "universal consternation and anxiety among people of all ranks and ages" (even slaves) occasioned by that measure throughout the colonies and the ways it affected different people "according to the diversity of their natural tempers and constitutions, their education, religious principles, or the prudential maxims which they had espoused." Some became melancholy and lethargic; others were incapacitated by a frenzied, all-consuming rage. Timid characters and those "who had no religious scruples of any kind" counseled submission. But the great majority of men, in Mayhew's estimation, cast aside their fears and stood prepared to choose death before "what they esteemed so wretched and inglorious a servitude"—and a good number of women had "so far metamorphosed into men on this sad occasion" that they would have done the same.[42]

While perturbed by this seeming erasure of gender distinctions, Mayhew was more troubled by the disturbance of public tranquility and the "great animosities, mutual censures and reproaches" that the controversy over the Stamp Act produced. The snare of fear may have been broken, but Mayhew worried that "good order," civility, and due respect for government had been irreparably damaged and that there could be no end to popular "fears and jealousies once they are thoroughly alarmed" without them. Despite his sharp criticism of British policies, the lessons Mayhew and many of his brethren drew from the Stamp Act crisis were ultimately conservative: if colonists did not properly fear God, diligently reapply themselves to their respective stations, and reject the "general dissipation" and selfishness that had become prevalent among them, their societies would only become more turbulent, embittered, and anxious. Clergy talked up popular fear to bring the people to moral reformation, not incite them to political revolution.[43]

But images of colonists seized with fear could and would be put to different uses. Americans influenced by the congeries of civic humanism, classical history, and English Commonwealth and Country Party thought that we today somewhat clumsily categorize as "republicanism" were also strongly disposed to see fear as a grave threat to liberty and had at their disposal an extensive repertory of rhetorical strategies to alarm audiences to its inexorable tendency to corrupt governments and enslave men. The republican interpretation of history as a recurring assault on the fragile blessings of liberty by the designs of executive power, political faction, and personal ambition taught its students to view public events with keen suspicion and regard constitutions as the strongest, if not the only, bulwark against tyranny. Republican literature offered a gallery of heroes who rose above popular fears to defend the constitution and the rule of law, as in James Thomson's popular *Liberty* (1734): "'Mid the low murmurs of submissive fear / And mingled rage, my Hampden raised his voice / And to the laws appeal'd."[44]

Thomson sounded a similar theme in his most popular work: the lyrics to "Rule Britannia," which famously boasted that "Britons never will be slaves." In eighteenth-century Anglo-American republican thought, slavery represented the sum of all fears, the annihilation of liberty and independence, whether corporate or individual. For John Dickinson (himself a slaveholder), the logical implications were clear: "Those who are taxed without their consent, expressed by themselves or their representatives, are slaves." While the question of what intellectual connections colonists made between this political-theoretical "slavery" and the real institution of African chattel slavery remains open to speculation, the fear of insurrections and the more general racial anxieties fostered by the institution shaped the political culture of the Southern colonies in profound ways. Slavery, Edmund Burke argued, made Southerners exceptionally jealous of their rights by adding "the haughtiness of dominion" to a traditionally English spirit of liberty.[45]

But the republicanism of the Southern gentry made them averse to popular government. Believing that public virtue rarely resided in the great mass of men, they viewed democratic legislatures as the natural enemy of civic tranquility and the security of property. If they supported independence, they kept their distance from the ideas of its most effective advocate, Thomas Paine. *Common Sense* masterfully melded the rhetorical strategies of sentimentalism, dissenting Protestantism, and republicanism but largely avoided talk of colonists seized by fear. Paine boldly asserted that colonists had little to fear and much to gain by declaring their independence and establishing a republic. Those who refused to assent to these self-evident truths were either terribly confused by the fallacious complexities of political philosophy or as unmanned by fear as the wealthy Londoners who submitted to "courtly power with the trembling duplicity of a spaniel." Any colonist persuaded by arguments for reconciliation had not only "forfeited his claim to rationality" but had "sunk himself beneath the rank of animals" and stood condemned to "crawl through the world like a worm." While confident that common sense would eventually prevail over fear and confusion, Paine was less certain of its chances against "the mind of the multitude," which was always "subject to change" and to the whims of "fancy or opinion."[46]

Paine's ambivalence toward popular opinion was understandable, as the ostensibly commonsense ideas he advocated were not necessarily common throughout the colonies. Many loyalists viewed colonial protest as a product of irrational fears ginned up by "enthusiast" clergy, ambitious lawyer-politicians, and sundry ink-stained wretches who filled the public mind with "imaginary grievances" and "horrid Phantoms." For other loyalists, the problem was a lack of proper, constructive fear. Jonathan Sewall believed that the colonists had become "totally incapable of attending to the dictates of reason, and will remain so until the passion of Fear is awakened." Mere "threats" or the "appearance of force" would not suffice. The British must "strike Terror through the continent." By making common folk immune to fear, patriots like Paine had thrown the social order into chaos:

> Men deprived, who quit their sphere
> Without remorse or shame or fear,
> And boldly rush, they know not where
> Seduced alas! By fond applause,
> Of gaping mobs and loud huzzas.[47]

At times, the most perceptive loyalists saw a deeper and more dangerous principle at work. With their too-literal notions of representation and their unbending insistence on consenting to the laws, patriots threatened an elementary principle of civil society: the submission of the individual to public opinion. In his unpublished history of the "American Rebellion," Peter Oliver theorized that when one left the state of nature and entered society, he necessarily submitted "his private Opinion to the publick Judgment of the many, confiding in their united Sense, as of more Authority than the Sentiments of any individual." Indeed, individuals were required to "consent to the Opinion of the Majority of the Society, be it ever so small a Majority." To do otherwise would be to "introduce a Principle on which may be founded such Dissentions as would be destructive of the very Existence of such a Society."[48] Patriots, Oliver warned, aimed to overturn the gentle authority of common opinion and leave in its place a violent and unruly politics of perpetual conflict.

From Popular Jealousy to Public Opinion

Put another way, Peter Oliver alleged that American revolutionaries opposed, both in principle and practice, the commonly accepted understanding of the relationship between popular opinion and the exercise of authority—the "moral philosophy" of opinion. Such an allegation would, of course, be difficult to substantiate and impossible to prove. But there is little evidence to suggest that patriots harbored any particularly novel or radical ideas about the political role of opinion. Americans did not identify public opinion as a distinguishing feature of the new governments they created. During the brief confederate or "critical period" of the 1780s, revolutionary celebrations of the common sense and virtue of the people gave way to more traditional concerns about popular passions, ignorance, and vice. Political elites worried over the excesses of democracy and the legislative "despotism" prevalent in the states, but they did not complain about the excesses of public opinion. If anything, they were more disposed to lament the absence of a public opinion to which the people would submit. These were the worries of men who continued to subscribe to the moral philosophy of opinion. Like Hume, they saw opinion as something that allowed the few to govern the many without force or coercion. Like Montesquieu, they identified political liberty with a tranquility of opinion that could only prevail when men did not fear for their safety. After the revolution, neither "opinion" appeared to exist.

To be sure, few dared deny that the Revolution was a popular revolution or question the principle of popular sovereignty that animated it. But the role of popular opinion in the Revolution and in the new political order that it created remained open to interpretation and contestation. Two particular concepts informed this discussion, and they did so in ways that tended to diminish the significance of popular revolutionary action. The first was "enthusiasm." Once synonymous with unreasonable, intemperate, and fervent belief, especially of a religious nature, the concept underwent several renovations in the mid-eighteenth century. English Whig writers secularized it and equated it with patriotism and "public spirit," while "New Light" proponents of revivalism defended enthusiasm as a necessary travail of a sinner on the path to redemption. Revolutionaries soon applied this more positive conception to their own cause. John Adams declared that "no great enterprise for the honor or happiness of mankind was ever achieved without a large mixture of that noble infirmity." Mercy Otis Warren praised the "enthusiasm of opinion" that had put "down opposition like a torrent, and enkindled the flame which emancipated the United States." Other patriots invoked enthusiasm while praising the success of boycotts, the faith with which citizens accepted debt certificates and paper money at face value, and the "heroic" actions of antiloyalist mobs, committees of correspondence, and militias. Even clergy who had once decried religious revivalism now championed, as Charles Chauncy did, the "enthusiasm for liberty."[49]

The image of the Revolution as an outpouring of enthusiasm was shared by the genteel and the common, but in potentially different ways. "Enthusiasm" could explain the Revolution as something akin to a holy war and lead an ordinary "Jersey Soldier," armed with bayonet and Bible, to believe that "nothing but a kind of enthusiasm, in the sacred cause of freedom," could have sustained him and his brethren. But "enthusiasm" could also explain why "the people" acted as *a* people: leaders and elites frequently equated revolutionary enthusiasm with uniformity of opinion. Unlike traditional outbreaks of enthusiasm, the enthusiasm for liberty did not produce factions or sects. James Madison believed that this had been due to "an enthusiastic confidence of the people in their patriotic leaders, which stifled the ordinary diversity of opinion on great national questions." But the revolutionary meaning of "enthusiasm" did not necessarily alter the understanding of its general dynamics, its irrationality, and its "passionate" nature. Enthusiasm remained an ephemeral force, useful in circumstances that required popular mobilization but unnecessary in times of peace and, in the final analysis, an argument for the rule of the refined.[50]

The social disorder, political factionalism, and popular rage for speculation and luxury revolutionary leaders observed in the 1780s were often attributed to the dissipation of enthusiasm. The zeal for liberty and leaders had held other passions in check. "Jealousy" was one of these passions, and it provided another way of explaining revolutionary opinion. Unlike today, jealousy was carefully distinguished from envy and more closely related to apprehension. In eighteenth-century English usage, it was equated with the vigilance necessary to safety and a suspicion that was not necessarily distrustful. Nevertheless, jealousy was usually regarded as a popular vice, a passion that if not moderated, destroyed social confidence and consensus. As a passion, it could be either benevolent or selfish, partaking of either love or hate: the Christian God was, after all, a "jealous" God. Jealousy was often used in tandem with metaphors of vision: there was "watchful jealousy," "hawk-eyed jealousy," or the "jealous eye" of the people. As James Hutson has shown, American revolutionaries self-consciously endeavored to arouse this mixture of fear and alertness, anxiety and attentiveness. "The great object of all our public and private institutions," Alexander Hamilton recalled, had been to "nourish this spirit" in "the public mind."[51]

But jealousy remained a passion that tended toward dangerous extremes. Alarm over the political upheavals of the 1780s brought condemnations of the "extreme jealousy of power," which Hamilton thought "attendant on all popular revolutions," a perversion of revolutionary ideals that always "endangered the common cause." Without enthusiasm and public spirit to discipline it, jealousy appeared as an all-consuming and corrupting passion. To Fisher Ames, "the people" had "turned against their teachers the doctrines, which were inculcated in order to effect the late revolution." Connecticut governor John Trumbull chastised his jealous constituents in verse:

> You've but pursued the self-same way
> With Shakespeare's Tinc'lo in the play;
> "You shall be Viceroys here, 'tis true,
> "But we'll be Viceroys over you."
> What wild confusion hence must ensue?
> Tho' common danger yet cements you:
> So some wreck'd vessel, all in shatters,
> Is held up by surrounding waters,
> But stranded, when the pressure ceases,
> Falls by its rottenness to pieces.

A centrifugal force unleashed by the passing of "common danger," jealousy seemed to run riot across the Confederation. Americans, one Pennsylvanian complained, continued to deify this vice at the expense of the "amiable goddess of confidence," doing so under a system of representative government that demanded more of the latter than the former.[52]

As passions that shaped and moved opinions, "enthusiasm" and "jealousy" explained the extraordinary degree of popular political activity during revolution. But both retained their more latent connotations as irrational impulses and passionate vices that endangered public tranquility. In the 1780s, nationalists revived these meanings and reasserted the antithesis between passion and opinion. Dr. Benjamin Rush's diagnosis of the psychosomatic influence of the Revolution vividly phrased this concern:

> The excess of the passion for liberty, inflamed by the successful issue of the war, produced, in many people, opinions and conduct which could not be removed by reason nor restrained by government. For a while, they threatened to render abortive the goodness of heaven to the United States, in delivering them from the evils of slavery and war. The extensive influence which these opinions had upon the understanding, passions and morals of many of the citizens of the United States, constituted a species of insanity, which I shall take the liberty of distinguishing by the name of *Anarchia*.

Passions stirred by the war had produced opinions that, in turn, inflamed passions verging on anarchy.[53]

Proponents of stronger national government depicted local and state governments as hotbeds of anarchy, and cast the actions of "the people out of doors" and rural "regulations" of taxes, prices, rents, and court fees in increasingly sinister hues. Reactions to Shays' Rebellion are, once again, instructive on this point. Critics quickly identified Shays and his followers as wild enthusiasts desiring, as one newspaper warned, "to totally annihilate the evils which have, till this aurora of the Millennium, been tacked to human life!" Superintendent of War Henry Knox reported to George Washington that the rebels were "seeking a common division of property, annihilation of all debts both public and private, and to have agrarian laws and unfounded paper money," even if it meant "spreading anarchy and bloodshed the length and breadth of this land." Rumors circulated that Shays had received gunpowder from Montreal and that the British had moved regiments to their frontier forts, leading the *New York Journal* to conclude that Americans would soon be driven "into the pit of POLITICAL DAMNATION" if they did not make their "FEDERAL HEAD adequate to the *requisite* purposes of government."[54]

In this way, nationalists stoked popular fears of anarchy and British invasion to build support for a new constitutional convention. But once that convention had completed its work, Federalist supporters of the proposed federal constitution asserted that it had been created under circumstances free from fear. "Other nations have been driven together by fear and necessity," Noah Webster observed, but the Philadelphia convention had consulted the "wisdom of all ages . . . as well as the opinions and interests" of millions of Americans. "The foundation of our Empire," George Washington instructed the American people, "was not laid in the gloomy age of Ignorance and Superstition, but at an Epoch when the rights of mankind were better understood and more clearly defined, than at any former period." Should Americans fail to seize this opportunity and become "completely free and happy, the fault will be entirely their own."[55]

In the "great national discussion" of 1787, Federalists stressed their sobriety, their candor, their devotion to facts and established principles—especially in contrast to their opponents. "Publius" promised to expose the "over-scrupulous jealousy" of anti-Federalists as "mere pretense and artifice, the stale bait for popularity at the expense of public good." Anti-Federalist arguments were "the inflammatory ravings of chagrined incendiaries or distempered enthusiasts"; to speak of "tyranny, and the subversion of our liberties," was to speak "the language of enthusiasm."[56] Benjamin Franklin likened anti-Federalists to the "artful men" who had "work'd upon" the jealousy of the ancient Israelites in order to rob them of their "newly-acquired Liberty." But Federalists did not so much reject "enthusiasm" as lament the loss of that revolutionary and "enthusiastic confidence of the people in their patriotic leaders, which had stifled the ordinary diversity of opinion on great national questions."[57]

The "enthusiasm" that remained in 1787 seemed more a passionate zeal for particular opinions than an enthusiasm for union and liberty. "Publius" thus appealed to "the more powerful sentiment of self-preservation," which could "overcome the zeal for . . . opinions and supposed interests." To replace the national enthusiasm of a bygone era, he offered a "public opinion" that would speak through an enlarged scheme of political representation and exercise its influence through a national executive.[58] By "extending the authority of the federal head to the individual citizens of the several States," the new republic would secure the "due obedience to its authority which is enjoyed by the government of each State, in addition to the influence on public opinion which will result from the important consideration of its having power to call to its assistance and support the resources of the whole union." This "public opinion" was a federal resource to be set against the disruptive tendencies of local opinion, a higher tribunal that would referee conflicts between the states. It was also a refined resource. An enlarged scheme of political representation, in Madison's classic formulation, would "refine and enlarge the public views through the medium of a chosen body of citizens." In this system, "the public voice, pronounced by the representatives of the people, will be more consonant to the public good than if pronounced by the people themselves, convened for that purpose."[59]

To explain why this would be the case, "Publius" emphasized contexts in which "opinion" could be protected from "passion" and directed toward reason. As a result, he devoted little attention to those aspects of civil society today deemed essential to the formation of public opinion. The role of the press was rarely mentioned; when newspapers appear in the *Federalist*, they are but one of the means by which common people depend on "the information of intelligent men, in whom they confide." Voluntary associations, if alluded to at all, were viewed with suspicion. "Collective meetings of the people," according to Madison, made popular ignorance "the dupe of cunning, and passion the slave of sophistry and declamation." Numbers worked in favor of passion, for "the more numerous any assembly may be, of whatever characters composed, the greater is known to be the ascendancy of passion over reason." When individuals reasoned "coolly and freely on a variety of distinct questions," they would "inevitably fall into different opinions on some of them." But if they were "governed by a common passion, their opinions, if they are so to be called, will be the same." Large gatherings contained majorities of ill-informed individuals vulnerable to the sway of passionate appeal. Even when republican or democratic feelings called a meeting to order, an oligarchy of demagogues would eventually seize control of the gavel.[60]

"Publius" acknowledged that an individual's passions, reason, and opinions were ultimately inseparable: "as long as the connection subsists between his reason and his self-love, his opinions and passions will have a reciprocal influence on each other; and the former will be objects to which the latter will attach themselves." What mattered most were the "objects" of attachment. When opinions and passions fastened on factions and sects, they disrupted public tranquility and private prosperity. In part, an extended republic helped to protect against this disruption. In the "dispersed situation" of the people, Hamilton found insurance against their being "regulated in their movements by that systematic spirit of cabal and intrigue." A "people spread over an extensive region," Madison believed, would be immune "to the infection of violent passions or to the danger of combining in pursuit of unjust measures." Time as well as space served to protect against such infections: a federal government was also a complex government that would slow the advance of "every sudden breeze of passion, or every transient impulse which the people receive from the arts of men," and stop them before they could be inscribed into policy, legislation, and law. It stood to reason that "under the general government of a UNION, whose members will be farther removed from those fears which spring from popular sources, another kind of eloquence than inflammatory declamation will be necessary for persuasion."[61]

"Publius" considered political deliberation and judgment within very limited, institutional, and "refined" contexts where reason could gain ascendancy over passion. At best, this required a studied ignorance of more informal and extralegal forums of popular deliberation. At worst, it revealed the uncharitable estimate of popular intelligence that historians and political theorists have often found in Federalism. Federalists were only following some established republican maxims of constitutional law, which called for the separation of "elective" (or "constituent") and "deliberative" (or "political") powers—the power to form a government and the power to legislate for it. To retain this separation and realize political stability, Federalists invested considerable hope in a consensus of the elite and their virtuous capacity for compromise. In so doing, they assumed that the "true opinion" of the electorate would continue to honor the best men with offices.[62]

If the "public voice" was to be pronounced by legislators, if this voice was to be utilized as a resource to bind and discipline the union, if in a "large Society the people are broken into so many interests and parties, that a common sentiment is less likely to be felt," what sort of "public opinion" existed outside of government? In many respects, this "public opinion" was equivalent to Montesquieu's "opinion of safety." Madison, for example, observed that "the strength of opinion in each individual, and its practical influence on his conduct, depend much on the number which he supposes to have entertained the same opinion." Individual opinions proceed from a fear of ostracism and wax or wane with the general climate of opinion or, more precisely, what an individual *supposes* that climate to be.[63]

Among a "nation of philosophers," such suppositions would not be necessary, as "reverence for the laws would be sufficiently inculcated by the voice of an enlightened reason." But in reality, the "reason of man, like man himself, is timid and cautious when left alone, and acquires firmness and confidence in proportion to the number with which it is associated," and "when the examples which fortify opinion are *ancient* as well as *numerous*, they are known to have a double effect." Thus, when Madison recited the ancient truism that "all government rests on opinion," it was to illustrate that "frequent appeals" to the people "would, in great measure, deprive the government of that veneration which time bestows on everything" and pose the "danger of disturbing the public tranquility." A public aroused by too many "great national questions" would become a public without an effective public opinion—that is, an opinion safely removed from transient judgments and reinforced by time, a prejudicial opinion. For example, Madison worried that a second constitutional convention, "by opposing influence to influence, would in a manner destroy an effectual confidence in either, and give a loose rein to human opinions; which must be as various and irreconcilable concerning theories of Government, doctrines of Religion."[64]

Only a fixed public opinion could perform its most important function: the restraint of public officials. Hamilton assured Americans that the "two greatest securities they can have for the faithful exercise of any delegated power" were "the restraints of public opinion" and the "opportunity of discovering with facility and clearness the misconduct of persons they trust." Centralized power, he implied, made it easier for the public to observe official conduct while strengthening restraints on it. To make this implication clearer, "Publius" introduced a new word into the English language—"responsibility." Whereas an executive council multiplied authority and acted to "conceal faults and destroy responsibility," a single, national executive made it impossible for "agents" of the public trust to employ "mutual accusations" and shift blame "from one to another with so much dexterity, and under such plausible appearances, that the public opinion is left in suspense."[65] The same fear of ostracism that weakened individual actions and opinions would discipline official actions and opinions. An official's desire for good "opinion" (or even "fame") forged a bond between his interest and the public interest. "What shadow of danger," Hamilton asked, could "there be from men who are daily mingling with the rest of their countrymen and who participate with them in the same feelings, sentiments, habits, and interests?"[66]

This was danger enough in the judgment of some opponents of the proposed constitution. "Opinion," in their estimation, was local opinion and could only be conveyed by local representatives; a national public opinion seemed either impossible to achieve or too susceptible to manipulation. Interests and manners were too diverse to allow for a national representative scheme in which the "sense or opinion" of the people could be the "criterion of every public measure." The "great body of the people" would "never steadily attend to the operations of government, and for want of due information" were "liable to be imposed upon." Richard Henry Lee feared the worst: "*opinion*, founded in the knowledge of those who govern, procures obedience without *force*. But remove *opinion*, which must fall with a knowledge of characters in so widely extended a country, and *force* then becomes necessary to secure the purposes of civil society."[67] An extended republic would not be governed by opinion; a distant government would instead rule opinion. "You must recollect," warned George Clinton, "that opinion and manners are mutable; and may not always be a permanent obstruction against the encroachments of government." Absent an enhanced, localized scheme of representation and more "express political compacts," the inevitable corruption wrought by "the progress of a commercial society" would beget "ambition and voluptuousness," which, "aided by flattery," would "teach magistrates where limits are not explicitly fixed to have separate and distinct interests from the people." This government interest would, in the end, "assimilate the manners and opinions of the community to it."[68]

Anti-Federalists worried that the people feared too little, suspected that they were not sufficiently jealous of their liberties, and sensed that their opinions were too weak and malleable. Federalists, by contrast, took this disengagement as an emblem of popular "confidence" in their leaders. Fear was a local product of passion, narrow self-interest, and factious demagoguery; public opinion was national and disinterested, a refined product of deliberations among polite and literate gentlemen. But the success of the Federalists in the ratification debates of 1787 would do little to quiet anti-Federalist warnings that a powerful national government would mold, if not manufacture outright, public opinion.

CHAPTER 2

Credit and the Political Economy
of Opinion

Wonderful, indeed, is the influence of opinion upon mankind; and
to such a degree does it operate upon the human constitution, that
happiness itself is generally found to consist therein . . . Were opinion
unchangeable, governments, even the most cruel and oppressive, would
forever be the same; fortunately, however, in some degree, for mankind,
the mutability of opinion is the cause of revolutions in the great political
wheel of government; and allows them their intervals of pleasure, as well
as pain. Perhaps in no country is opinion of a more fickle and transient
nature than in the United States, as may more fully appear from the
following Chronological list of Opinions—

> 1789. Public debt *may* be a public blessing.
> 1790. Public debt *is* a public blessing.
> 1791. Public debt *is not* a public evil.
> 1792 (January). Public debt *may* be a public evil.
> 1792 (November). Public debt *is* a public evil.
> 1793. Public debt is the greatest of public evils.
> 1794. It is wonderful that so great a folly of opinion should have
> ever existed in a free and enlightened country.

—Phillip Freneau, "Opinion" (1792)

There are those who believe that the market corrupts politics, and then there are
those who believe that politics corrupts the market. In either case, the belief
hinges on distinctions between the respective roles and proper domains of "the
market" and "the public." But such distinctions can be terribly indistinct. After
all, both terms can denominate a place, a process, or a mode of power. As places,
markets and publics have almost always shared space. The ancient Greeks went
to their agora for commerce and political discussion; moderns have their "mar-

ketplace of ideas." As processes, the market and the public are systems of exchange in which valuations and opinions are made manifest. As such, both require a medium, be it money or language. The Greeks simplified this by using the same word, *seme*, to denote "coin" and "word." Moderns understand that money and language operate on credit, on the confidence that they can be redeemed for something else. But if money "answereth all things" in the marketplace, language serves specific purposes in the public sphere. Markets aggregate individual preferences; publics transform them into consensus. Put another way, publics generate power politically. Conversely, injunctions to "let the market decide" typically express a distaste for politics, a desire to appeal disputes to a power that is ostensibly impersonal, apolitical, or even "natural."[1]

Indistinct distinctions between the market and the public are expressed in the way a culture conceptualizes and represents public opinion. In current usage, "public opinion" is something influenced by the market, but "public opinion" does not influence the market. When opinions do exert economic influence, they are called something else—"consumer confidence," "expectations," or "preferences."[2] The presumption seems reasonable, but it was not one that early national Americans necessarily made. Political opinions mattered in their marketplace because political objectives were often pursued there. They did not perceive their economy as an autonomous system obedient to its own distinctive rhythms and cycles. They spoke of "public opinion" as something that caused inflation and deflation, precipitated panics, incited bank runs, produced prosperity, determined the ease of credit, and eased the burden of debt. This tendency to attribute economic conditions to public opinion was neither a symptom of loose terminology nor a quaint specimen of the analytical imprecision that predated modern economics. Rather, it arose from an understanding of commerce as politics by other means, of "economics" as "*political* economics."

In the previous chapter, I argued that the concept of public opinion played a rather peripheral role in the political discourse of the revolutionary and founding eras. In those rare instances in which "public opinion" appeared, it did not seem to convey any novel political meanings. But in the 1790s, Americans did begin to talk about public opinion, and the meanings were politically charged (fig. 2.1). Performing a simple word count, of course, can only hint at the significance of a concept, telling us little about its meaning and context. But such a count does suggest that in 1790, something provoked politicians and newspaper writers to invoke "public opinion" with new urgency and unprecedented frequency. The controversy over Alexander Hamilton's financial reports and proposals was the source of provocation. In debates over the assumption and funding of public

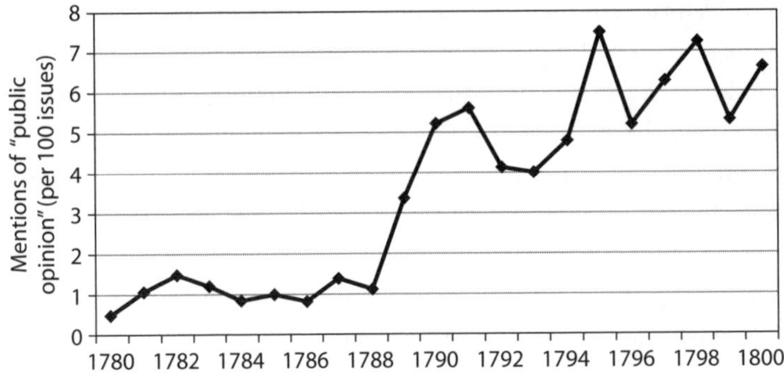

Figure 2.1. Frequency of "public opinion" in U.S. newspapers, 1780–1800 (per 100 issues). *Source: Early American Newspapers, Series 1, Archive of Americana (Chester, VT: Readex).*

debts, and the chartering of the Bank of the United States, previously vague and inarticulate assumptions about the nature and role of public opinion quickly developed into explicit and politicized theories of public opinion. This coincidence of public opinion theory and financial controversy was not simply coincidental. The sciences of public finance and political economy made public opinion "thinkable" in powerful and distinctive ways. Federalist-era controversies over public credit, money, and banking generated "political economies of opinion" that persisted into the "bank wars" and "money questions" of the 1830s. Long before the advent of modernist social science and survey research, Americans frequently employed the languages of finance and economics to define that nebulous entity called "public opinion."

Historians of Europe occasionally have noted the conjoined histories of public finance and public opinion. Indeed, one of the earliest histories of public opinion, William MacKinnon's *On the Rise, Progress, and Present State of Public Opinion in Britain and Other Parts of the World* (1828), did so. Years later, Lord Acton remarked that during the reign of Louis XVI "the sovereignty of public opinion was just then coming in though the rise of national debts and the increasing importance of the public creditor." Patrick Brantlinger has recently offered a somewhat oversimplified formulation: "public credit is to bourgeois economics what public opinion is to bourgeois liberalism." American historians have generally shied away from drawing such analogies, opting to place public opinion in the context of republican ideologies, the influence of Enlightenment thought, "democratization," or the development of "public spheres." While certainly relevant to the history of the concept of public opinion, such interpretations tend toward the macro-historical, or they treat "public opinion" as a rarefied idea constructed outside the sound and fury of ordinary political conflict. But political actors, as Susan Herbst has observed, "tend to define public opinion as part of an argument they make," and the substance of what they argue about also tends to shape the definition of the "public opinion" they invoke. In the early 1790s, controversies over public finance inspired Americans to make "public opinion" an explicit part of their arguments, and the language of political economy shaped the meaning of that novel and nebulous concept. To understand why, it is first necessary to look back into colonial and revolutionary-era financial history.[3]

Public Faith

Stephen Burroughs and his friend Lysander wanted money, but there was little of it to be found in postrevolutionary Connecticut. So they decided to make some, literally. For a small fee, a local alchemist promised to transform their scraps of copper into silver coins. When this proved to be a swindle, Lysander proposed his own counterfeiting scheme:

> Money, of itself, is of no consequence, only as we, by mutual agreement, annex it to a nominal value, as the representation of property . . . We find this verified in fact, by those bills of credit which are in circulation throughout the world. Those bills simply, are good for nothing; but the moment mankind agree to put a value on them, as representing property, they become of as great a consequence as silver and gold . . . Therefore, we find the only thing necessary to make matter valuable, is to induce the world to deem it so; and let that esteem be raised by any means whatever, yet the value is the same, and no one becomes injured by receiving it at the valuation.[4]

Lysander's rationale for counterfeiting parodied an insight crucial to the new science of political economy and the creation of the early modern "fiscal-military" state: that money is credit, and credit is, at bottom, a matter of opinion. From the seventeenth century onward, the proliferation of instruments and institutions of public and private credit—banks, funded public debts, annuities, securities, bonds, stocks, and paper currencies—made states and markets more dependent on such opinions. Although popular maxims and vague proverbs had long deemed "opinion" the "queen of the world," the "financial revolution" made opinion more concrete, quantifiable, and politically consequential. The politics of public finance spawned interest groups and legislative factions, prompted nationalist appeals to public faith, and attracted the jealous gaze of the taxpayer. While subjecting the affairs of states to greater public scrutiny, the financial revolution also tapped into deeper political and cultural anxieties regarding luxury, corruption, and bankruptcy.[5]

On the North American edge of the empire, the British financial revolution of the eighteenth century resulted in frequent shortages of cash. Parliament prohibited the export of British specie, and Crown prerogative prevented colonial governments from minting coins. Trade imbalances and a high demand for liquidity—what Adam Smith called "the enterprising and projecting spirit of the people, their desire of employing all the stock which they can get"—compounded this problem. By the 1730s, every colonial government had resorted to circulating some form of paper currency. Though met with occasional sermonizing on the profligate evils of paper money, such policies usually appeared to promote trade. Bishop Berkeley asked "whether there are not to be seen in America . . . towns, wherein the people are well lodged, fed, and clothed, without a beggar in the streets, although there be not one grain of gold or silver current among them?" Was it not "the opinion or will of the people, exciting them to industry, that truly enricheth a nation?" Advocates contended that a generous sense of common trust and public spirit made colonial paper (almost) as good as gold. Maryland poet Ebeneezer Cooke compared hard-money men to

> The *Scribes* likewise, and *Pharisees*,
> Infected with the same Disease,
> On *Paper Money* look a squint,
> Care not to be made fools in print.
> Thus what is meant for Publick Good,
> I find to be misunderstood,
> And taken in the worser Sense,
> By those, care not for *Paper Pence*.[6]

After 1760, changing imperial policies and mounting trade imbalances gave new force to antipaper sentiments, but the Revolution drove them into temporary exile. Lacking significant reserves of specie or foreign credit, revolutionary leaders had little choice but to finance the war with paper currencies, which ultimately accounted for two-thirds of the war debt. When the Continental Congress issued its "Continental" bills in 1775, its members assumed, as most political economists of the time did, that depreciation could be limited by restricting the amount of money in circulation and balancing it against the volume of foreign and domestic trade—an assumption economists would today call the "quantity theory of money." The remaining depreciation would act as an indirect tax.

Moreover, patriots believed that American "virtue" and "enthusiasm for liberty" would back the value of their currency, that political support for the Revolution would influence economic decisions. Patriots thus portrayed the handling of money as a political act. To make a public debt, Thomas Paine declared in *Common Sense*, was to make a "public bond," and every Continental or state bill that passed at face value testified to the public faith. Revolutionaries condemned those who refused payment in paper as traitors and denounced "wicked and designing men" who questioned the public credit. Those who dared "under-value the credit of the states," wrote "A Tradesman," had joined "with the herd of ungodly men, who are doing all they can to ruin the credit of our money, and overthrow the country." Some read currency values as indices of divine favor for the American cause, warning that "any violation of the public faith on which her public credit rests, would be madness, atheism, and suicide."[7]

The rapid and steep depreciation of Continentals and state paper currencies soon rendered such implications unpalatable. Although wartime inflation resulted from a host of concrete economic causes and political factors—depressed trade, slowed production, and Congress's inability to restrict state currency emissions or limit the money supply through taxation—many saw distressed public credit as a predominantly moral problem. "Speculation, engrossing, forestalling with all their concomitants, evidence the decay of public virtue," complained George Washington, who called in vain for "ways and means to appreciate the currency, on the credit of which everything depends." Believing that "our currency will have that degree of credit we are pleased to give it," state legislatures and local committees of correspondence pledged to assist Congress "in the glorious attempt of appreciating our money." Other patriots sought out scapegoats. Thomas Jefferson deemed counterfeiting and profiteering "the cursed arts of our secret enemies" seeking to "effect by depreciating our money, what the open arms of a powerful enemy could not." Paine accused British officers of counterfeiting Continentals and forging bills of exchange. If the British army could be defeated, he assured Americans that their "currency would rise to millions beyond its present value" and that every "man would be rich, and every man would have it in his power to be happy."[8]

Victory did not, of course, produce such a windfall. Continentals fell out of circulation in 1781, as did many state currencies. As the money supply contracted, debt certificates issued by Congress and the states functioned as makeshift currencies and objects of intense speculation. Taxes levied to redeem war debts drained the money supplies of cash-poor farmers, who in turn bombarded state legislatures with petitions for paper money. Paper emissions, however, drove prices up, forcing more merchants and consumers to borrow. Mounting private debts spurred the popular organization of price-setting committees and sent speculators racing through the countryside. Paine saw an "airy bubble of paper currency . . . continually awakening or creating new schemes of deceit" and turning "the whole country into stock jobbers." This compelled him to reject "the romantic, if not hypocritical, tale that a virtuous people need no gold or silver, and that paper will do as well." The "disease" of speculation had, according to Dr. Benjamin Rush, "unhinged the judgment, deposed the moral faculty, and filled the imagination, in many people, with airy and impracticable schemes of wealth and grandeur." In a similar vein, David Ramsay contrasted the "enthusiasm" for liberty that had brought "such credit and currency to paper emissions, as made the raising of supplies an easy matter" to "the languid years of peace, when selfishness usurped the place of public spirit, and credit no longer assisted, in providing for the exigencies of government."[9]

A more skeptical observer argued that enthusiasm, revolutionary or otherwise, had no place in the sober world of public finance: Americans had errantly "substituted enthusiasm for that opinion which is necessary to national credit." For those more versed in the language of political economy, the problem lay neither in an excess of currency nor in the paucity of postwar enthusiasm and public spirit but in a diminished state of public confidence and opinion. Alexander Hamilton calculated that rates of depreciation stood five times higher than any quantity theory of money could explain. "The excess," he conjectured, "is derived from opinion, a want of confidence," and "we deceive ourselves when we suppose the value will increase in proportion as the quantity is lessened," for the "opinion of objects has more influence than their real nature." James Madison independently arrived at a similar diagnosis: the depreciation of currency and debt certificates had arisen primarily from a growing "distrust of the public ability to fulfill their engagements."[10]

Hamilton and Madison differed however in their understanding of how opinion related to the value of money. For Madison, "opinion" attended to the time between the issue of money and its redemption in specie: longer periods between issue and redemption diminished confidence and accelerated depreciation. Because (as John Locke had argued) "universal opinion" regarded gold and silver as the only genuine standard of value, Madison proposed to infuse specie into the money supply as rapidly as possible, thereby allowing holders to quickly redeem their paper for metal. Delaying specie redemption would, he thought, only benefit profiteers and speculators. For Hamilton and Robert Morris, the restoration of confidence and credit required a more complex remedy. Fearing that infusions of specie into the money supply would encourage hoarding, they gravitated toward the idea of a national bank. Chartered by the Commonwealth of Pennsylvania in 1781, the Bank of North America attempted to pile up specie reserves while circulating notes by redeeming those notes on rare and largely symbolic instances. The resulting high reserves would serve "an everlasting emblem of public confidence" that would inhibit depreciation and speculation.[11]

Assuming that public confidence would emanate from wealthy gentlemen throughout the nation, Hamilton and Morris sought to ally them to their nascent system of national finance, and to make that alliance public. Morris encouraged public creditors to form organizations, issue publications, and initiate petition drives for the support of Congress, the Bank of North America, and a national impost. He also helped these groups to ally their efforts with those of army officers seeking pensions. Hamilton moved (unsuccessfully) to open the doors of Congress to a group of public creditors during a debate on the war debt. Irritated by the aggressive lobbying of this "aristocratic junto" of officers, merchants, and financiers, the Pennsylvania legislature revoked the Bank of North America's charter in 1785. Writing in defense of the bank, James Wilson explained that such measures had been necessary "to sooth the timidity of some of their friends. The credit of a bank, as well as all other credit, depends upon opinion. Opinion, whether well or ill founded, produces, in each case, the same effects upon conduct."[12]

Though a truism (if not a tautology), the claim that credit depends on opinion carried a particular political valence in the 1780s. Nationalists like Wilson repeatedly used the truism to argue against the interference of state legislatures in matters of currency and credit. If (private) opinion could not—and should not—be altered by sheer legislative fiat, then the same held true for credit. State tender laws requiring the acceptance of paper money at face value provided an object lesson in this political economy of opinion. Tender laws failed because "the whole value of paper is imaginary, and men do not believe by compulsion. Every attempt to force a man to believe that paper is equal in value to silver implies a consciousness that it is not equal. It injures what it is intended to serve." But "credit," as Pelatiah Webster argued, could not be anything other than "the forcing an opinion upon another, who is possessed of something we want, and which we have no right to take from him without his consent." The "most substantial foundation of this opinion" was "public faith," and some device was needed to create this faith. Americans needed a national system of public finance, and Wilson knew why: "The millennium is not yet come."[13]

Over the last decade, scholars have placed renewed emphasis on public credit as the prime motivation in the Federalists' push for a stronger central government. The constitutional ban on state currency emissions, assumption and funding of war debts, and other Federalist financial policies were not (as progressive historians have often argued) simply means to promote particular economic interests or curb the power of more democratic state governments. For Federalists, the crisis of public credit degraded national honor, imperiled national security, and symbolized a deeper yet more diffuse problem: a diminished state of common trust that impeded the exercise of legitimate authority. Federalists—especially those of the Hamiltonian persuasion—gave this problem a name. They called it "public opinion" and complained not of its power but of its weakness. In their 1790 campaign for the adoption of Hamilton's financial system, Federalist politicians, editors, and pamphleteers presented the first extensive and systematic explanation of the role of public opinion in the new American political order. Their conception of public opinion, though narrow in its scope and often freighted with Anglophilic and elitist pretension, is best understood as a by-product of their preoccupation with public credit.[14]

Public Opinion as Public Resource: Federalism

While serving as General Washington's aide-de-camp during the Revolutionary War, Alexander Hamilton kept up with his reading. As proof of this, we have his pay books. Scrawled between pages of accounts and provisions lists are the study notes of an aspiring political economist and classicist: depreciation tables, foreign exchange rates, outlines from Postlethwayt's *Universal Dictionary of Trade and Commerce*, and remarks on Plutarch's *Lives*. Though he made no specific mention of it, one of Plutarch's biographies must have deeply impressed Hamilton, the story of Eumenes, a Cardian of obscure origin who rose to power in the Macedonian army as principal secretary to Alexander the Great. When Alexander died, Eumenes found himself in danger. Though the Macedonians respected his military abilities, they despised his foreign origins. Sensing that they "sought an opportunity to kill him," he "pretended to be in want of money, and borrowed many talents, of those especially who most hated him, to make them at once confide in him and forbear all violence to him for fear of losing their own money. Thus his enemies' estates were the guard of his person, and by receiving money he purchased safety, for which it is more common to give it." Hamilton, a newcomer to America who rose to power through the patronage of its greatest general, arrived at a comparable insight: that political security could be created through debt, and enemies could become allies by making them creditors.[15]

Debt is a political instrument because it creates a manageable form of trust. Trust can be a passion or a policy: "as a passion, a sentiment, it can be evanescent or durable," but "as a modality of action it is essentially concerned with coping with uncertainty over time." Credit—certainty of payment over time—is one such modality. The debtor is beholden to the creditor, but the creditor is interested in the debtor's financial prospects. When the debtor is the government and the creditor is a citizen, a layer of complexity is added. After all, not all citizens hold equal shares of public debt. If those shares can be traded, public credit comes to depend not only on individual expectations regarding the capacity of the government to redeem its debts but also on what individuals imagine the expectations of others to be. In other words, people become "speculators," engaging in what John Maynard Keynes called "third-degree thinking," wherein "we devote our intelligences to anticipating what average opinion expects average opinion to be." The forces cementing the interests of creditor and debtor become generalized, and public opinion—what average opinion expects average opinion to be—becomes a financial and political x factor.[16]

For these reasons, Alexander Hamilton and his allies could not talk about public credit without talking about public opinion, and vice versa. In his reports to Congress as secretary of the Treasury, he declared that "in whatever regards Credit . . . Opinion is the soul of it, and this is effected by appearances, as well as realities." When proposing a national mint, he wrote of a "depreciation of the public opinion" regarding the currency, worrying that "the effect of the debasement in the public opinion is not easy to be calculated. It is always to be remembered however that the effects of the imagination and prejudice are not to be disregarded in anything that concerns money." Opinion represented an incalculable intangible that made the "geometrically true" but "abstract calculations" of financial science "false as they relate to the concerns of beings governed more by passions and prejudice than by an enlightened sense of their interests." A well-administered government would encourage such beings to refine their opinions into a "rational calculation of probabilities." Hamilton believed that the "confidence of the people" would not be gained by a "numerous representation" in Congress but by "good administration." Public opinion would become fixed, stable, and influential through the centralization of executive power. Such an administration could enter "into those objects which touch the most sensible chords and put in motion the most active springs of the human heart." Simply put, money was "the vital principle of the body politic."[17]

Hamilton's allies echoed these themes. John Fenno of the *Gazette of the United States* traced the "misfortunes in this country" to "a scattered unproductive publick opinion." Lacking a "common standard, to which the jarring prejudices could be referred, and by which they may be controlled," the government had to "produce a reaction upon public opinion. It should search for it, estimate it, trace its origin, examine its effects, endeavor to remove its errors," and "collect the scattered sentiments of the public and form them into proper shapes; and in some instances create opinions and attachments wholly new." Public credit did this in a manner suited to a republic because it was "the necessary offspring of public faith; and without it, no nation on earth can exist, under the enjoyment of a free constitution and government"—or so another essayist conjectured. In "arbitrary" governments, "public faith to the subjects is of no consequence; force answers the purpose of credit, and the monarch takes what he wants, and compels thanks for leaving the residue." Oliver Wolcott Jr., Hamilton's deputy in the Treasury Department, regarded the financial system as important "in no other respect than as an engine of government." Indeed, republican government came equipped with few other such engines, for "the influence of a clergy, nobility and armies, are and ought to be out of the question in this country." Unless "some active principle of the human mind can be interested in the support of the government, no civil establishments can be formed, which will not appear like useless and expensive pageants, and by their unpopularity weaken the government which they intend to support." With Hamilton's financial system in place, Wolcott looked forward to the transformation of "public sentiment" into "a fund of good sense in this country, upon which those who administer the public affairs may safely rely."[18]

The "engine of government" laid out in Hamilton's proposals for public credit, minting, national banking, and the promotion of manufactures sought to create public opinion by institutionalizing and stabilizing political-economic expectations. By 1790, combined foreign, state, and national war debts stood at around $76 million, and annual interest payments on the debt exceeded federal government revenues. Rejecting the options of either repudiating the debt, discriminating between original and present holders of debt certificates, or fully redeeming all debts through tax increases, Hamilton proposed to assume all state debts and "fund" them by permanently setting aside revenues for interest payments. In so doing, he sought to tie the interests of both federal and state creditors to the new government by treating debt certificates (which contained no specified date for redemption) as annuities. Redemption would not be necessary if good faith were restored, for the value of certificates would rise and eventually stabilize. Hamilton also created a "sinking fund" to purchase enough government securities in the open market to "peg" their value. With public credit restored, government debt would become a large pool of liquid capital. Hamilton hoped that individuals would invest some of this capital through subscriptions to the proposed Bank of the United States—"a political machine of the greatest importance to the State." In turn, the bank would provide short-term loans to the government and private lenders.[19]

Within less than a year, assumption and funding of the debt had created $30 million in capital out of $76 million in debt because, as Forrest McDonald has written, "the public, instilled with illusions and expectations, changed its opinion about the value of those pieces of paper." The success of Hamilton's program inspired something of a cult of the administrator among Federalists, who hailed Hamilton as the "great American Necker." Like Hamilton, the French finance minister Jacques Necker possessed a romantic view of the finance minister as a "rare genius" of "frankness and publicity" who "must at once enlighten, pacify and lead the minds of men" and "by a line of conduct constantly wise, just, and beneficial, moderate the action of separate interests, by imperceptibly bringing them back to the social principles, and to the ideas of public order." He preferred the "secret benedictions of the people which he will not hear, and that public opinion which is slow in forming itself, but whose decisions must be waited for patiently, to all the courtly praise and adulation." Genuine "public opinion" stood above "those rumours of the day, which commonly take their rise in particular societies only." Turning a deaf ear to such transitory talk, the finance minister remained loyal to a "public opinion . . . rendered sacred, by reason, time, and a universal conformity of sentiments."[20]

In a similar fashion, Hamiltonians described public opinion as a rare yet inelastic public resource, frequently denying its existence on any particular issue. Fenno's *Gazette of the United States* spent more ink informing its readers what public opinion was not than what it might be. Though any newspaper "must ultimately depend on publick opinion," Fenno promised to refrain from the common editorial practice of "anticipating that approbation through the medium of *professions*" regarding the state of public opinion. The columns of the *Gazette* repeatedly warned that "there cannot be a more plausible cover for bad intentions, than a pretense that they correspond with the public opinion. Such a pretext is the more convenient as it cannot be easily detected." Rarely seen or heard, "public opinion cannot be distinguished by unequivocal marks" and was "often too indefinite to be admitted as a rule of conduct." Even if one could "gather the public opinion by obtaining that of every individual in the community, it would be not only fluctuating, but contradictory. It would amount to nothing." The true "solemnity and force" of public opinion could "only prevail in situations of a very momentous nature," as "most questions that are discussed are not obvious or interesting enough to affect and touch the great bulk of mankind." Public opinion mattered, but only as the "*ultimate* arbiter of every measure of government," and Hamiltonians often called for a "suspension of the public opinion" on a variety of issues. Fenno asserted that public opinion should only "be exercised upon a measure after it is put into operation, rather than while it is in contemplation. It can try and prove the law better than it can direct its origin or passage."[21]

Arguing that public opinion could provide no clear, substantive direction on complex questions of policy, Hamiltonians set it to the more limited task of keeping watch over the republic by protecting public authority from lawless, arbitrary, and seditious forces. Public creditors exerted an especially salutary influence in this arena. Their vested interests fostered an attentive yet cautious political attitude that would both mitigate occasional outbursts of popular enthusiasm and offset the enervating effects of everyday public apathy. One essay in Fenno's *Gazette of the United States* stated this case in vivid terms. Because "a national debt attaches many citizens to the government who, by their numbers, wealth, and influence, contribute more perhaps to its preservation than a body of soldiers," it could sustain the republic over time.

> It only remains to calculate the influence that this body of men will have, first, upon the public opinion, and next upon the government itself. In this country, they are powerful by their numbers; by their property; by their patriotism; for it was that which made great numbers of them public creditors. They are justly denominated by the Secretary "enlightened men." Their dispersed situation enables them to give a strong impulse to the public mind in different parts of the country at the same instant. Interest will wake when patriotism sleeps. As these persons have a common interest, and that corresponds with the general interest of the society, self love is combined with the love of country. They become watchmen, and continue such, when other citizens, less interested, relax their attention to public affairs for the sake of private concerns. Much has been said in favour of republican jealousy. The creditors can never have an interest against liberty—for tyranny and public credit can never exist together.[22]

The Mirror of Republicanism

When James Madison took the floor of Congress in New York in February 1790 to argue that "public opinion" stood overwhelmingly against Hamilton's proposed assumption of state debts and for the discrimination between original and present holders, Federalists leapt from their seats in protest. Fisher Ames found it "an unusual thing for a gentleman in a public assembly to assert, that four-fifths of the people are of his way of thinking." Though it was "not strange for persons to mistake their own opinion for that of the public," he dismissed such "fond prepossessions" as irrelevant. Ames could just as easily claim "four-fifths of the wise and worthy men, in a very wide extent of the country," agreed with him. Congress agreed by a lesser margin, and Madison's amendments to Hamilton's finance system failed. "Such a decision," Benjamin Rush wrote to Madison, "would not have taken place had the Congress been seated on the Banks of the Delaware or the Potomac. Public Opinion is a species of influence—and this I well know has been exerted too successfully in New York" by the throng of speculators swarming Federal Hall. Madison agreed, lamenting that "nothing is more contagious than opinion, especially on questions, which being susceptible to very different glosses, beget in the mind a distrust of itself," making it difficult "to avoid confounding the local with the public opinion."[23]

The debate over Hamilton's financial system represents the first significant argument over the definition and role of "public opinion" in the history of American political discourse. Hamiltonians, as Rush and Madison acknowledged, won the first round. Opponents attributed Hamiltonians' success to superior organization: acting in concert with speculators and other suspect interests, Hamilton's Treasury had manufactured a powerful "in and out of door influence" over Congress. While outmaneuvered logistically, opponents encountered comparable difficulties on the rhetorical front. To support the claim that "public opinion" opposed assumption and favored discrimination, opponents could offer little more than anecdotal evidence and sermons on the "justice" owed to poor soldiers and other original creditors. Confusion over the arcane language of financial legislation, uncertainty as to who held debt certificates, seeming public indifference, and a lack of clear party distinctions weakened opposition invocations of "public opinion." Speaking in support of Hamilton's proposals, congressman and former anti-Federalist Elbridge Gerry explicitly rejected such talk, "first because we know not the public opinion; secondly because conjecture is endless and useless."[24]

Frustrated by the seemingly unchecked influence of Hamiltonian interests, James Madison dug deeper into his library for a more theoretically robust and rhetorically potent concept of public opinion. The ideas of French physiocrats proved, as Colleen Sheehan has argued, particularly instructive. In the writings of Mirabeau, Turgot, Le Mercier de La Riviére, and Jacques Peuchet, *opinion publique* appeared as a sovereign force of reason wholly distinct from the state, a *puissance invisible* that emerged from the institutions of civil society. Like Adam Smith, they portrayed economies as national systems integrated by networks of circulation. Unlike Smith, they extended this economic vision into the political sphere with less hesitance and nuance, analogizing public opinion to the circulation of money. Unlike Montesquieu and Necker (or, for that matter, Hamilton), physiocrats viewed royal and ministerial influence over public opinion and legislatures with keen suspicion. Moreover, physiocratic valorization of agriculture resonated with Madison's own political-economic predilections and prejudices.[25]

Madison's studies produced a series of short essays that appeared from late 1791 to early 1792 in the recently established *National Gazette*. Throughout the essays, he drew invidious distinctions between authentic public opinion and the "counterfeited" version invoked by Hamiltonians. For Hamilton, opinion was a weak and vacillating compound of sentiments and ill-informed conjectures that became public opinion through the agency of energetic governments and public institutions. Madison regarded opinion as a species of private property: if "property" was "every thing to which a man may attach a value and have a right, and *which leaves every one else the like advantage*," it followed that "a man has property in his opinions and the free communication of them." Through dissemination and discussion, opinion became public opinion, which "sets the bounds to every government, and is the real sovereign in every free one."[26]

Madison's concept of public opinion began with the individual citizen and his opinion. Where Hamilton tended to worry over the weakness of public opinion and its enervating effect on government, Madison worried over the politics of public opinion in an extensive republic: the ease with which public opinion could be counterfeited, the timidity of the opinionated citizen, and the dangers both problems posed to liberty. "The larger a country, the less easy for its real opinion to be ascertained, and the less difficult to be counterfeited; when ascertained or presumed, the more respectable it is in the eyes of individuals. This is favorable to the authority of government. For the same reason, the more extensive a country, the more insignificant is each individual in his own eyes. This may be unfavorable to liberty." For this reason, "whatever facilitates a general intercourse of sentiments" would be "*equivalent* to a contraction of territorial limits" and thus "favorable to liberty." Monarchies confined perception to a single sovereign, and even "the eyes of a good prince cannot see all that he ought to know," a problem that increased "with the extent of dominion." Without a monarch, a small dominion "might become a simple democracy" but would likely fall into the hands of an aristocracy "where a concentration of the public will is required by external danger." For Madison, public opinion would have a predominantly negative role as a check on corruption and unconstitutional encroachments of public power. Each citizen would "be at once a sentinel over the rights of the people; over the authorities of the confederal government; and over both the rights and the authorities of the intermediate governments . . . every citizen shall be an ARGUS to espy, and an AEGON to avenge."[27]

Such an alarm system would, Madison thought, counteract the subtle power of British capital and its networks, a "fund of influence" that threatened to undermine American republican principles. Capital in Anglo-American trade amounted to nearly $40 million, and three-fourths of this amount remained in British hands. "The residue in the hands of Americans," Madison worried, "has more effect in Anglicizing them, than in Americanizing the influence it gives." This "specie of influence" made its way into American ports and followed "a thousand streams to the inland towns, and country stores: which, in aid of the influence inherent in British trade and British credit, not infrequently receive from the political zeal of the importing merchants, a stock of British ideas and sentiments proper to be retailed among the people," thereby "recolonizing the American character, and duping us into the politics of a foreign nation." Madison labeled this "stock of British ideas and sentiments" as "fashion" and distinguished it from the "independent situation and manly sentiments" of American farmers and laborers. As individuals fell under the influence of fashion's capricious whims, so too would nations. The *"mutability of fashion"* led to *"mutability of policy."*[28]

In the movements of money and credit, Madison detected a network of influence that could "counterfeit" public opinion and thereby bend law and government to its own purposes. Suspicions of this nature did not, of course, originate with Madison: in *The Wealth of Nations* (1776), Adam Smith lamented the ease with which merchants and manufacturers deceived the public and its officials into identifying the public interest with their particular interests. But where Smith attributed this problem to general ignorance of the principles of political economy, Madison attributed it to general misconceptions regarding public opinion. To correct these errors, Madison posited a broader political economy of opinion. Rejecting the Hamiltonian definition of public opinion as a subjective relationship between government and its creditors, Madison rooted public opinion in the circulation of real goods and opinions throughout the nation. In some respects, the differences between Madisonian and Hamiltonian conceptions of public opinion mirror differences in their larger visions of social and economic development. Where Hamilton emphasized development of time, Madison envisioned development across space. Where Hamilton analogized public opinion to public credit (or the cultivation of trust over time), Madison envisioned public opinion as a network of information and inquiry extended across space.[29]

Though Madisonian visions of development across space contained a rural and agrarian bias, opposition to Hamiltonian finance encompassed a wider range of economic interests, ideologies, and *mentalité*. In addition to agrarians like John Taylor of Virginia and George Logan of Pennsylvania, writers of more commercial (Albert Gallatin of Pennsylvania), plebian (William Manning of Massachusetts), middling (William Findley of Pennsylvania), and Paineite (Phillip Freneau and Joel Barlow) orientations took up their pens against Hamilton's system. As speculation in debt certificates and Bank of the United States stock grew more fervid, criticism intensified. When the collapse of a speculative syndicate headed by William Duer, Hamilton's former Treasury assistant, set off the new nation's first financial panic in April 1792, criticism became especially profuse. While earlier criticism concentrated on the economic injustice of Hamilton's system or questioned his claim that public debt could function as capital, critics increasingly focused on the political, constitutional, and cultural consequences of public finance and the "paper aristocracy."[30]

Here the debate shifted onto more familiar ground, allowing opponents to invoke traditional British "Country Whig" strictures against funded public debts, stock-jobbing, and national banks as enemies of liberty and republican virtue. The Virginia Assembly discerned "a striking resemblance between [Hamilton's] system and that which was introduced into England, at the revolution." Critics repeatedly linked public debts to excessive taxation, legislative corruption, the aggrandizement of the "court," and the creation of a stock-jobbing aristocracy and standing army. The "grand nostrum" for "changing a limited Republican Government into an unlimited hereditary one" was, Philip Freneau warned, "a PUBLIC DEBT." Even William Manning, an uneducated farmer and tavern keeper from rural Massachusetts, understood how perpetuated public debt functioned as a political instrument of "the few."[31]

Hamilton's system was not an exact replica of the British model, and the criticism directed against it did not simply parrot British "Country" precedent. The nascent Democratic-Republican opposition added different normative, constitutional, and rhetorical inflections to their arguments. They laid particular emphasis on the cloak of secrecy that shrouded the doings of a "finance minister" and the generally incomprehensible nature of his "science." Hamilton's *Report on Public Credit* (over 20,000 words long with 11 appendices) prompted George Logan to complain that the secretary's "long reports on finance, by fatiguing the memory confound the judgment, and force his readers into such a labyrinth of error, that the clue of decision has not length enough to reach the extensive mazes of a wandering imagination." Others saw in the reports the "machinations of an inventive genius, directed to amuse and perplex, not to inform and convince," or they found the whole issue to be an "abstruse, intricate, and perplexing." The "science" of public finance itself was "the real art of hocus-pocus; or, the sorceries of Simon Magus revived." John Taylor took his readers through the "dark channel" of the "paper system" to "ferret out the motives" of a "foe . . . concealed from the view of the senses." Previous "forms of tyranny" could be "seen in the persons of kings, nobles, and priests," and even the corruptions of "executive sinecure and patronage" were "visible, and a visible enemy may be subdued." But a *paper* aristocracy was an "invisible enemy" that "could not even be assailed," and the public would be "kept patient by election itself, from an erroneous opinion, that the government is administered according to their will."[32]

Working in secret concert and armed with esoteric knowledge, finance ministers and speculators counterfeited public opinion by manipulating value, and vice versa. George Logan lamented the plight of "the farmers and soldiers" who "had accepted certificates in lieu of their full pay, although public opinion at the very moment of acceptance, had reduced them to one eighth part of their nominal value." They could not have known that the federal government, prompted by "the influences and artifices of a few men," would alter public opinion and appreciate the value of the certificates, creating an imaginary currency that "exists only in name, in paper, in public faith." John Taylor warned that the "paper aristocracy" would "never fail to pass off the false coin of private opinion, under the forged name of the public." Failing this, "the counterfeiters" would "use armies, superstition, penal laws, and paper corruption, to make the laws pass." Joel Barlow defined public finance as "a modern invention calculated to enslave mankind," using the power of the purse to exercise a "secret and silent control over the conduct of influential individuals." Logan thought that "the officer of finance" had no place in republican government.[33]

As they assailed this opaque system of secret influence and counterfeit consent, opposition writers made publicity and transparency the touchstone of genuine public opinion. Rejecting the Hamiltonian equation of public opinion with public confidence, John Taylor dismissed "confidence" as an unthinking, unrepublican "substitution of the understanding and honesty of others for our own." To illustrate the difference between monarchical-aristocratic confidence and republican jealousy, opposition writers frequently employed optical analogies that distinguished the factious lens of federalism from the mirror of republicanism. Taylor dismissed the mere "professions" of Federalists as "magnifying glasses" made to deceive the "the weak weapon of human reasoning." Deeds, however, were "mirrors reflecting political truth." Too many printers, a letter to the *Philadelphia General Advertiser* complained, "instead of being mirrors of the public sentiment, are the creatures and eulogists of [the] administration." Assuming the identity of a mock Federalist, Philip Freneau worried "that the people are seized with the *phrenzy of thinking for themselves*" and urged other Federalists to take up their pens and "become a lens, thro' which the diverging rays of popular opinion and interests will be brought into *focus*. Without this politico-philosophical mode of aggregating things, the people could never be made to understand their true interests."[34]

Needless to say, contrasts between the "lens" of Federalism and the "mirror" of Democratic-Republicanism were the stuff of partisan rhetorical combat. They may have reflected different sincere attitudes toward "the people" and their opinions. They may have expressed different normative understandings of the "public sphere" that translated into more or less democratic styles and practices of governance. But the haphazardly organized, weakly disciplined, and paradoxically antipartisan tenor of the "first party system" makes it difficult to affix firm partisan and ideological labels to something as plastic as concepts of public opinion. Here I have only emphasized the significance of political-economic thought to the development of these concepts. Debates over public finance compelled participants to translate loose ideas and latent attitudes regarding the role of popular opinion into more manifest and politically pointed definitions of public opinion. Thereafter, the politics of public opinion would encompass efforts both to persuade and to define that nebulous entity.[35]

But it is also important to recognize that several broad areas of consensus modified the political conflicts described above. The first, though rather general and possibly trite, is worth mention: most Federalists and even more Democratic-Republicans affirmed that something called "public opinion" played a unique and indispensable role in American politics. Both agreed that its force, when unified and energized, was irresistible. Both, to varying degrees, viewed the rising power of public opinion as inevitable and irreversible. For both parties, the question was not *whether* public opinion should rule but *how* it should rule. And in the course of arguing over how it should rule, both parties promoted the idea that something called "public opinion" existed and that it ruled despite the efforts of the other party to counterfeit or delude it.

The second broad area of consensus was both constitutional and financial. Opposition to Hamilton's financial system played a significant role in the formation of a Democratic-Republican opposition, but it did not produce any fundamental changes to that system. Jeffersonian policies of "economy" reduced the scale of the system, retired the debt more rapidly, and allowed the charter of the politically unpopular Bank of the United States to lapse in 1811. But American republicanism nonetheless found a place for the officer of finance and a modified version of the Anglo-Dutch fiscal state. Beneath the heated debates over discrimination, assumption, funding, and banking lay a nearly uncontested "liberal" commitment to privatizing the sources of monetary value. Few opponents of the Hamiltonian system proposed a return to the colonial system of paper currency finance. The federal constitution of 1787 had, of course, removed this alternative. Prohibiting states from coining money, and restricting congressional authority over currency by tying its value to specie, the Constitution shifted financial power away from legislators and taxpayers and toward public creditors and private banks.[36]

In many respects, Hamilton's system aroused Democratic-Republican suspicions because it made some tacit features of this new financial and constitutional regime—its limitations on state sovereignty and legislative authority and the increased dependence of public credit on private wealth—politically manifest. By openly equating the opinions of public creditors with public opinion, Hamiltonians invited competing conceptions of public opinion into the political and rhetorical arena. An emergent Democratic-Republican opposition responded by defining public opinion as a mirror of popular sentiment coextensive with networks of communication and set it to the difficult task of detecting the corruption of public law by private wealth, ministerial legerdemain, and the chicanery of bankers and speculators. Democratic-Republicans may have asked too much of public opinion, and Hamiltonian Federalists may have asked too little. But both parties, broadly conceived, phrased their demands and expectations in the language of political economy.

A "Bank-Note World"

The Jeffersonian revolution of 1800 nevertheless hurried the larger Federalist vision of an energetic nation-state along its path to extinction. Political opposition to Hamilton's public finance system and the Bank of the United States had already prevented him from implementing his more ambitious designs. The ratification of the Eleventh Amendment in 1798 affirmed that state governments would set the terms of American citizenship, and popular outrage over the Alien and Sedition Acts, passed later that year, suggested that the federal government lacked the authority to police dissent and instill a sense of national identity, much less mold public opinion. Defeated at the polls, a lame-duck Federalist Congress quickly expanded the federal court system through the Judiciary Act of 1801. But with the repeal of the act the following year and the death of Alexander Hamilton two years later, Federalist design to forge a genuinely national public sentiment through energetic government came to an end. Some Federalists aimed to instill national feelings through an "empire" of benevolent societies and a cult of Washington. Others pursued, with mixed success, projects of internal improvement. Still others took refuge in the dry abstractions of John Marshall's constitutionalism, in which the Supreme Court would speak for "the people."[37]

But if the Jeffersonian vision of a decentralized polity triumphed, the Jeffersonian vision of an agrarian economy stocked with virtuous and contented farmers did not come to pass. As we have seen, Jeffersonians opposed Hamilton's system of funded debts and national banks out of the fear that it gave the federal government and a paper aristocracy of speculators the power to manipulate value, and thereby manipulate, if not counterfeit, public opinion. When Jefferson, Madison, or John Taylor made such assertions, they assumed that "opinion" would naturally accept nothing less than specie, that the "universal opinion of mankind" (as Locke had called it) would forever regard gold and silver as the basis of monetary value. When it came to credit, they assumed that the gentry and other "men of credit" would continue to serve as the primary lenders in most communities and would regulate the ease of credit as the laws of honor dictated. But this insistence on honor and metal would prove impractical and moralistic. Specie was scarce in the early republic, and banks multiplied to meet a booming economy's demand for credit and currency. Between 1801 and 1811, sixty-three banks were chartered. By 1820, close to four hundred were in operation. In 1840, there were over nine hundred. America had become, in the melancholy lament of poet Fitz-Greene Halleck, a "bank-note world." Beyond thinking it evidence that Americans were, as John Adams put it, "the most thievish people that ever existed," the majority of the founders never comprehended the popular "Mania for Banks," the force and fury with which state legislatures were bombarded with requests for charters, the wild rush for stock subscriptions that turned every bank opening into something of a civic festival.[38]

In certain respects, the banknote world was the financial correlate of the Jeffersonian polity, in which local politics took precedence and a spirit of voluntarism kept the heavy hand of government at a distance. Public opinion mattered in the banknote world, but it was a local opinion based on personal knowledge and reputation. Most antebellum banks, as Naomi Lameroux has aptly put it, operated like "investment clubs." The greatest share of a bank's initial capital came from stock subscriptions, not deposits. One bought "scrip" because one knew the directors of the bank and hoped to share in their future profits. That bank directors usually loaned much of this capital to family members, friends, and political allies did not raise eyebrows. Indeed, this was expected. Scrip-holders knew they were investing in the families and friends of the bank directors. Chartering a bank or purchasing scrip was just another way of doing politics, and banks in larger towns and cities often aligned themselves with competing parties and factions. In this way, the politicization of banking provided investors with useful guideposts in an information-scarce economy.[39]

Relatives, friends, and political cronies did not always make the most responsible creditors and debtors. For this and other reasons, antebellum banks were subject to an alarming number of runs, suspensions, and failures. Because such events usually preceded economic panics and recessions—especially in 1819 and 1837—banks were often fingered as the culprits. During the panic of 1819, Hezekiah Niles placed the blame squarely on the shoulders of the nation's 8,000 (by his estimate) bankers and board members. "Like harlots," they had "stood in the highway with naked bosoms, to tempt the people to sin."

> Here is a powerful class—a separated people—a sort of nobility, whose interests are more or less at variance with the interests of the community at large; invested with exclusive, or peculiar privileges, and very naturally using them to their own special and individual advantage. It may be estimated that they controul a real or fictitious amount of money and its representative credit in paper . . . to the extent of four hundred millions, with which to build up or put down tens of thousands at their own good will and discretion. Now, who can calculate the influence of such a body, so powerfully commanding the purse-strings of a people? And what is the effect of their example? Who that is made a president, cashier or director of one of our truly modern banks, that does not dash into some extravagance in dress or living? His family follows his lead, for "father can get plenty of money," and the whole economy of his household is changed. Emulation is thus excited—each one a little apes the style that he cannot attain—plainness of dress and manners are cast into the shade, and things are valued rather by their cost than by their utility. We know that a superabundance of real money destroyed the Roman virtue, and laid the foundation on which was erected the despotism under which that people groaned . . . It is this luxurious living—originating in the example of the rag barons and other speculators, that causes the balance of trade to be against us, and it must remain.[40]

The panic of 1819 fanned dormant suspicions toward banks into a political furor that would consume state politics throughout the 1820s. Legislatures across the nation passed debtor-relief laws and imposed new restrictions on bank charters and credit. Bullionist beliefs in "natural" money gained new and influential adherents. All the "arts" of the "paper system," Senator Thomas "Old Bullion" Benton declared, were no match for "the instinctive feeling of the masses . . . which told them that the money which would jingle in the pocket was the right money for them." Though the "sophistry of the Bank men" had silenced the voice of the majority, William Gouge maintained that "common-sense notions of money" had "never been obliterated from the minds of the great body of the people."[41]

By the end of the decade, these notions had helped to install Andrew Jackson in the White House. During the ensuing "bank war," incited by Jackson's veto of a bill to recharter the Second Bank of the United States, the rhetoric repeatedly gestured back to the battles over the First Bank. Jackson men never failed to tout their "Jeffersonian" principles. For pro-bank men like Daniel Webster, Alexander Hamilton was the genius who "smote the rock of the national resources, and abundant streams of revenue gushed forth," a necromancer who "touched the dead corpse of public credit, and it sprung upon its feet."[42] Moreover, Jacksonians frequently accused the Second Bank of the United States of attempting to control public opinion. In most instances, they alluded to the favorable loans that bank president Nicholas Biddle dispensed to pro-bank newspaper editors and politicians. But at other moments, Jacksonians offered more comprehensive critiques of the credit system and its relation to public opinion. As William Cullen Bryant explained to readers of the *New York Evening Post*:

> The credit system is erroneous on two accounts. It is erroneous because it interferes with commerce, which is always better and more safely conducted when let alone. It is erroneous again because it interferes with opinion. We reject the regulation of religion by law as tyrannical and mischievous; we find that a church established by law is the parent of false professions and hypocritical observances. Yet we regulate credit, which, equally with religious belief, depends upon opinion; we make laws defining who are worthy of credit; our state governments take upon themselves to instruct us whose promises are to be trusted. The same effect follows as in other cases where public authorities tamper with opinion. We have insolvency in the disguise of licensed credit, and the licensed few wield their powers to the disadvantage of the unlicensed many.

Here at last is a thoroughly laissez-faire and libertarian political economy of opinion, in which the divorce of bank and state is as essential to the sovereignty of public opinion as the separation of church and state. Bryant, a severe critic of the Jeffersonians in his youth, repudiates the Hamiltonian design to manage public opinion by attaching the interests of the creditworthy to the state, and he does so in a newspaper founded by Alexander Hamilton.[43]

With the lapse of the Second Bank's charter in 1837, Bryant got his wish, and the era of "wildcat banking" moved into full swing. Once again, the supposedly instinctive desire for specie did not prevail. Paper money proliferated, and great leaps of imagination were required to discern the presence of an instinctive and "universal opinion of mankind" at work amid the chaotic patchwork of banks and confusing variety of currencies. Over 5,000 different banknote issues were made during the antebellum period, and it has been estimated that as much as 40 percent of the money in circulation at any given time was counterfeit. Even some counterfeit detectors—popular handbooks that described the distinguishing features of different bank currencies—were counterfeited. Indeed, it is today difficult to fully appreciate the amount of uncertainty, guesswork, haggling, and "humbug" that went into the simple act of passing a note, the confusion and frustration of getting three dollars for a five-dollar note in one town and four in the next. In the banknote world, the opinion that determined the value of money, the ease of credit, and the rates of discount was not universal, instinctual, or timeless. It was a predominantly local and often fluctuating opinion subject to the small politics of personal reputation and factional enmity. To get his money's worth, every buyer had to be an informal opinion pollster, every seller an amateur market researcher. The banknote world demanded that its citizens continuously monitor public men, measures, and moods for movements that might modify the value of their paper. Antebellum money "represented the prose of life"; it was, as Ralph Waldo Emerson wrote, "a delicate meter of civil, social, and moral changes," the "finest barometer of social storms."[44]

The year 1837 brought another financial panic, this one even more severe and prolonged. While most critics sharply denounced banks for encouraging excessive speculation, many spread the blame more widely. Democrats reflexively fingered Nicholas Biddle as the culprit. Whigs, while targeting the failed policies of Jackson and Martin "van Ruin," tied the panic to the dissolute state of popular morals. Most political economists also minimized the role of banks. As Janet Riesman has argued, American economists had by then arrived at a more broad and complex understanding of their subject "as not just a matter of considering money and the problems of money, but as the study of all the variables that were part and parcel of the market."[45] Then again, economists had no theories of business cycles on hand to explain why good times suddenly turned hard. Instead of viewing a panic as the periodic self-adjustment of an autonomous economic system, they saw it "as an unhappy interruption of a normal trend of business" brought about by "overtrading." They could not, however, explain overtrading without emphasizing the influence of paper money, banking, and speculation on public opinion, or vice versa.[46]

But by the mid-1840s, the political economy of opinion had lost much of its explanatory power and political potency. The "divorce" of bank and state Jacksonian Democrats desired, and eventually realized with the Sub-Treasury Act of 1846, removed financial controversies from the center of the national political stage. As banking became a more commonplace and accepted institution, old republican fears of paper aristocracies and counterfeited public opinion receded into the background of popular political consciousness. Perhaps more importantly, the financial expectations of the public came to appear increasingly inconsequential as capital concentrated into private, large-scale industrial enterprises.[47] As commercial capitalism gave way to industrial capitalism, it became more difficult to perceive connections between public opinion and economic phenomena— and easier to make distinctions between the market and the public.

CHAPTER 3

Partisan Manufactories of Public Sentiment

There are nations which *have* no public opinion. The having it requires what a pedantic writer might call the *co-ordination of judgments*. Some people must be recognized to be wiser than others are. In every district there must be people generally admitted by the judgment of their neighbors to have more sense, more instructed minds, more cultivated judgments than others have. Such persons will not naturally or inevitably, or in matter of fact, agree in opinion; on the contrary, they will habitually differ: great national questions will divide the nation; great parties will be formed. But the characteristic of a nation capable of public opinion is, that those parties will be *organized*; in each there will be a leader, in each they will be criticized and accepted by the many.

—*Walter Bagehot, "The History of the Unreformed Parliament and Its Lessons" (1858)*

It is difficult to imagine public opinion without political parties. We are daily bombarded with survey results that depict public opinion as a distribution of opinions spread across a partisan spectrum. Our popular historical narratives often treat public opinion as a product of conflicting partisan opinions. Seen in this light, Bagehot's logic seems inescapable: in an "age of discussion" and representative democracy, differences of opinion will invariably result, requiring the organization of parties.[1]

But must a nation have parties in order to have a public opinion? The political history of the early American republic complicates Bagehot's tidy English logic. Before Americans made a nation, they formed parties: in the 1780s, the founders organized themselves under the banner of "federalism," produced a constitution that promised to check the evils of party, and branded their opponents as partisans. From the 1790s to the 1840s, partisan conflict and organization promoted the development of the nation-state and instilled nationalist sentiments. "Great national questions" created parties, and parties created "great national questions."[2] The relation between parties and public opinion presents additional complications. Bagehot saw parties as originating in a moment of deference: wise men are recognized, parties form around them, and their disputes create public opinion. American political historians reverse this sequence: parties emerged as deference to "wise men" declined.[3] For Bagehot, parties are legitimate and "accepted by the many" because they are led by wise men. But in the early American republic, both wise men and a good number of "the many" doubted the legitimacy of parties.

Debates over the legitimacy of party generated concepts of public opinion that would, in turn, legitimate partisan organization.[4] The anti-partyism of the founding generation rested on classical humanist ideas of popular opinion as weak, unstable, and easily counterfeited by designing men. As these ideas fell into disuse, a new generation of politicians, journalists, and other "public men" reconfigured the relation between party and public opinion along party lines. Democrats advanced a "political-constitutional" rationale for party government. They equated public opinion with the will of the people and saw parties as a necessary means for implementing that will. Whigs developed a weaker "social-psychological" defense of party organization. They defined public opinion as a product of civilization and economic improvement, arguing that it would restrain leveling impulses and constrain the violence of partisan conflict.

Public Opinion against Parties

The founding generation of American political leaders rejected, if not reversed, Bagehot's logic. They repeatedly insisted that a nation with parties could not have a *legitimate* public opinion. As republicans, they regarded factions as self-interested conspiracies against the public good. As sentimental moralists, they condemned party spirit as an illiberal and unsociable passion. As constitutionalists, they viewed partisan organizations as mechanisms designed to cheat the people of their sovereignty. Parties and factions, in their estimation, could do little else but deceive, delude, and counterfeit public opinion.[5]

Avowed anti-party principles did not deter politicians from electioneering, attending legislative caucuses and nominating meetings, and subsidizing a rapidly expanding network of partisan newspapers. While it is tempting to dismiss such "antipartisan partisanship" as standard political double-talk, most historians have adopted a more charitable view. The founders, as Richard Hofstadter put it, "stood at a moment of fecund inconsistency" between eighteenth-century factions (fluid alliances among elites that promoted a particular interest or individual leader) and the permanent, mass-based parties that emerged in the mid-nineteenth century.[6] While recognizing that differences of opinion were inevitable by-products of liberty, the founders did not embrace pluralism as a positive good. Because "truth is a thing, not of divisibility into conflicting parts, but of unity," John Taylor surmised that "the situation of the public good, in the hands of two parties nearly poised as to numbers, must be extremely perilous." While allowing that organized opposition could be justified in rare and revolutionary instances, they could not imagine a political culture animated by perpetual party competition. It seemed a logical certainty that "[t]wo factions of nearly equal strength, violently played off against each other by ill designing or mistaken men, would either mutually destroy each other, and suffer a third power to prevail, or the contest would terminate in the utter extinction of one, and the insolent triumph of the other. Either event would introduce a most insupportable tyranny."[7]

In this spirit, the framers of the Constitution proposed to "break and control the violence of faction" by extending the sphere of republican government. Representatives chosen from large districts that comprehended a "greater variety of parties and interests," James Madison believed, would be less likely to serve any particular faction or interest. Stocked with *disinterested* men of "the most diffusive and established characters," Congress would act as firewall against the factionalism that seemed to consume state politics. It would "refine and enlarge the public views" and speak with a public voice "more consonant to the public good than if pronounced by the people themselves, convened for that purpose."[8] Of course, this national public opinion could only be legitimate if it remained uncorrupted by party spirit. "Publius" repeatedly assured his readers that a stronger national government would not, as several anti-Federalists warned, lead to the formation of national parties. In the "dispersed situation" of the people, Alexander Hamilton saw insurance against their being "regulated in their movements by that systematic spirit of cabal and intrigue." A "people spread over an extensive region," Madison believed, were immune "to the infection of violent passions or to the danger of combining in pursuit of unjust measures." An extended republic slowed the advance of "every sudden breeze of passion, or every transient impulse which the people receive from the arts of men."[9]

None of these reassurances were meant to guarantee that factions and cabals would not emerge within the halls of Congress. The framers were far too experienced with legislative assemblies to harbor such naïve expectations. Here they hoped that the president—presumably the most established character in the nation—would stand above the fray, counsel moderation and compromise, and promote popular affection for the Union. But what if such a Washingtonian character failed to materialize? The presidential selection process would likely devolve into a scrimmage between the favored sons of each state, one from which no clear winner could emerge without partisan intrigue. The answer to this vexing problem, cobbled together in the eleventh hour of the convention after much deliberation and delay, was the Electoral College. The convention rejected a direct presidential election as impractical, injurious to the interests of southern states (whose slaves could not be apportioned into a popular vote count), and, in Elbridge Gerry's opinion, "radically vicious":

> The ignorance of the people would put it in the power of some one set of men dispersed through the Union & acting in Concert to delude them into any appointment. [Gerry] observed that such a Society of men existed in the Order of the Cincinnati. They are respectable, united, and influential. They will in fact elect the chief magistrate in every instance, if the election be referred to the people. The prospect of Congress selecting the president proved equally unfeasible: it compromised the independence of the executive and legislative branches, and could only encourage party spirit and intrigue in both.[10]

The eventual solution created a separate and discrete ad hoc congress, excluded congressmen and persons holding an "Office of Trust or Profit under the United States," and labeled it a "college" to evoke an image of disinterested and professional association. To encourage the selection of a truly "national character," the college gave each state elector two votes but required him to cast one vote for a resident of another state. Because "the electors would vote at the same time throughout the U.S. and at so great a distance from each other," Gouvernour Morris explained, "the great evil of cabal was avoided." Moreover, "the aim of this Enlightenment machine," as Bruce Ackerman has pointed out, "was to create the artificial impression that the president was a man of truly national character even if the pickings were pretty slim. A man could become president if he was the second choice of a bare majority of the electors."[11]

Needless to say, the Constitution did not successfully "break and control the violence of faction." While the new federal government may have helped to curb the animosities that agitated state politics under the Confederation, it did so by removing some of the most divisive issues—public debts and currency in particular—from the agendas of state legislatures. When those issues resurfaced at the federal level, partisan rancor soon followed. In the previous chapter, we saw how a nascent Republican opposition denounced Hamilton's financial system as

a factious design to counterfeit public opinion, enrich a clique of paper aristocrats, and steer the republic toward monarchy. Federalists predictably responded
by painting their opponents as a carefully orchestrated cabal of treasonous Jacobins, manipulative mobocrats, and embittered anti-Federalists. By the elections
of 1792, voting patterns within Congress exhibited early signs of partisan align-
ment, and the rudiments of party organization—party newspapers, nominating
meetings, and political clubs—began to materialize out-of-doors. Over the next
eight years, voting patterns solidified, organizations proliferated, and the acrimony of partisan rhetoric grew exponentially.

Polarizing controversies over the French Revolution, the Genet mission, the
Neutrality Act, the Jay treaty, the Whiskey Rebellion, the XYZ Affair, and other
events drove this dynamic, but they did little to legitimate partisanship. If anything, the public controversies of the 1790s promoted a peculiar ideology of antipartisan partisanship that fueled partisan animosities while demonizing partisan
behavior and organization. In this climate, extraconstitutional efforts to organize
or represent public opinion could be readily branded as factious designs against
the republic. Even when politicians grudgingly acknowledged the existence of
parties and identified themselves as Federalists or Democratic-Republicans, they
invariably charged their opponents with the crime of counterfeiting public opinion. In doing so, they necessarily depicted genuine public opinion as an unmed-
iated and unrehearsed expression of popular judgment that stood outside the
realm of everyday politics. If "public opinion did not come forth spontaneously,"
Walter Lippmann sardonically remarked, "nobody in that age believed it would
come forth at all."[12]

The brief and controversial history of the Democratic-Republican societies
illustrates this dilemma. In the summer of 1793, former anti-Federalists, ardent
supporters of the French Revolution, and critics of the Washington administration began to meet in societies modeled after the London Corresponding Society
and the Jacobin Clubs of France. By the following summer, more than thirty-five
Democratic societies existed across the nation, with a membership drawn primarily from the middling ranks. They sponsored dinners and patriotic festivities,
listened to orations and debated public affairs, and circulated petitions and resolutions steeped in the language of Paineite radicalism and popular constitutionalism. Portraying themselves as patriotic associations for the diffusion of political
information, they vowed to guard *the real principles of the constitution, and the
original intention of the revolution*" from the "machinations of men in power."
Disavowing any intention to engage in electioneering or other partisan tricks, the
societies pledged to confine their activities to the arena of public opinion. They

would promote "careful and attentive deliberation," encourage citizens to "hear and impartially weigh the arguments on both sides of all questions," and expose the efforts of their "enemies" to "mould public opinion."[13]

Federalists immediately denounced the Democratic societies as hothouses of faction and sedition. Society members responded by vehemently insisting that they had the right to censure public men and measures. Matthew Lyon, a Vermont politician and newspaper editor, complained that the societies were "ridiculed by men who consider the science of government to belong naturally to only a few families." Stung by repeated insults from anonymous newspaper essays and broadsides, the New York society demanded that their critics "form amongst *themselves* a permanent political society in this city," place the names of their members before the public, and submit to a debate regarding "the characters, the opinions, and the general conduct of each person composing the two societies, from the memorable 19th of April, 1775, to the present moment."[14]

Asserting a right, if not an obligation, to examine public men and measures, the Democratic societies directly challenged a premise central to traditional conceptions of deference: that the "few" were best equipped to debate political questions while the "many" were best suited to listen and judge the results, preferably in silence.[15] On July 4, 1794, members of the Democratic Society of Chittenden County, Connecticut, claimed their right to openly inspect the measures of public officials, citing a passage from Justice Nathaniel Chipman's *Sketches on the Principles of Government* as authority. Chipman, a Federalist, immediately dispatched a letter to the *New York Herald* disavowing any connection with "self created societies" that presumed "to speak the sentiments of the people." By deliberating on public questions *before* public officials, they violated the principles of "representative democracy," which Chipman explained thusly: "Such is the state of things, that knowledge in the complicated affairs of civil society comes not by intuition. The means of information, and frequently, diligent investigation are necessary. *The knowledge of the people will follow, but can rarely precede, a public discussion.* They will generally approve or disapprove with judgment, but in dictating, are exposed to all the rashness of ignorance, passion, and prejudice." The letter prompted replies in the New York press. Were "the people" not "the public"? If Chipman meant to confine the task of investigating public measures to "particular members of the community, on what possible principle" could he "exclude those who meet for this express purpose in societies styled democratic"? Did the judge intend to limit it to members of the bench and bar? And what distinguished a "self created society" from any other form of association?[16]

The last question soon became a subject of congressional and popular debate.

In his November 1794 message to Congress, President Washington (who had privately complained of the "arrogant presumption" of the Democratic societies for months) held "certain self-created societies" responsible for inciting the recent Whiskey insurrections in western Pennsylvania. Opposition newspapers condemned the remark, and at least six new Democratic societies quickly formed in protest. Washington's supporters counterattacked, unleashing a deluge of orations, sermons, pamphlets, and newspaper essays that branded the societies as factious and seditious instruments of French influence. In Congress, they pushed for a motion of censure against the societies.[17]

The Federalist case against self-created societies began with the charge that they usurped the legitimate authority of legislatures. Congressman William Vans Murray of Maryland claimed that the Pennsylvania Democratic societies had "arrogated the management of public opinion and affairs," and Fisher Ames of Massachusetts asked if other Democratic societies would not soon "avail themselves as substitutes for representation"? The recent history of the Jacobin clubs in France indicated that they might. While Federalists recognized that popular committees had played a vital role in the American Revolution, and acknowledged that the people had never surrendered their right to occasionally gather in protest, they contended that permanent extraconstitutional associations were unnecessary under a republican form of government. What possible purpose could avowedly democratic societies serve, Vans Murray asked, when "the whole country is full of well-established organs of the People's will"?[18] Noah Webster could detect only one possible purpose, and it was not at all democratic:

> Each individual member of the state should have an equal voice in elections; but the individuals of a club have more than an equal voice because they have the benefit of another influence; that of extensive private attachments which come in aid of each man's political opinion. And just in proportion as the members of a club have an undue share of influence, in that proportion they abridge the rights of their fellow citizens. Every club therefore formed for political purposes, is an aristocracy established over their brethren.

Clubs exhibited "all the properties of aristocracy" but produced "all the effects of tyranny." A man might join a club to add weight to his opinion, but he checked his "individual independence of mind" at the door. From that moment on, he became "a mere walking machine, a convenient *engine of party leaders*." Worse still, club meetings exposed him to more grievances than he would have otherwise heard or imagined. In this way, political societies artificially promoted popular discontent, poisoned confidence in the government, and encouraged slander, libel, and sedition.[19]

Few Republican politicians openly defended the Democratic societies. Sensing that the Federalist "game was to connect the Democratic societies with the odium of the insurrection" and then "connect the Republicans in Congress with those Societies," James Madison carefully argued against censuring the societies without appearing to defend them. He simply maintained that Congress had no authority to censure the opinions of citizens. The good sense of the people guaranteed that "no lasting evil" would "result from the publications of these societies; they will stand or fall by the public opinion." Madison and his allies steered clear of any questions regarding the legitimacy of extraconstitutional societies, which they may well have doubted.[20] Even members of the Democratic societies exhibited some defensiveness and ambivalence on this point. "We make no apology for thus associating ourselves," proclaimed one Vermont Democratic society. Tunis Wortman would later admit that the conduct of "literary associations" should be closely monitored, for "they were too often rendered subservient to the particular views of sectaries or factions." The "improvement" of society would in time render them less dangerous. As men on both sides of a question came to learn that they had "the same right and the same spirit of association," the "collision produced will be favorable to the eventual reception of truth."[21]

Did the opprobrium cast on self-created societies influence political behavior? Did the dubious legitimacy of extraconstitutional associations deter Americans from associating for political purposes? For the most part, it did not. While Federalist attacks certainly damaged the Democratic societies, most remained active until 1796, when the ratification of the Jay treaty and the election of President John Adams demoralized their rank and file. Still, it could be argued that the vocal animosity and quiet ambivalence toward self-created societies directed popular political energies into forms of association that *seemed* more constitutional and patriotic. If the right of the people to associate for the purpose of criticizing the government remained in doubt, the right to assemble and celebrate the nation seemed above reproach. Public holidays and festivals soon became pretexts for partisan rituals and oratory, with Federalists and Republicans staging separate celebrations of Independence Day, Washington's Birthday, and other national anniversaries and events. Such events, as David Waldstreicher has argued, allowed Americans to practice "a divisive politics and a unifying nationalism at the same time."[22]

Party spirit could also disguise itself as philanthropy and take up residence in a rapidly growing number of benevolent, honorary, literary, and fraternal societies. Federalists found these associations particularly congenial to their ideals of sociability, deference, and antipartisanship. Indeed, the two largest and most extensive associations—the Society of the Cincinnati and the Freemasons—were widely (and justly) perceived as Federalist fronts: George Washington himself was president general of the former and a proud member of the latter until his death in 1797. Even the Bavarian Illuminati panic of 1798, during which Masonic lodges stood accused of harboring a dangerous sect of Jacobin radicals, did not shake the general image of Masonry as a Federalist stronghold. As John Brooke has shown, the panic had less to do with anxieties over French influence than with a fear that the lodges were no longer *exclusively* Federalist.[23]

The Illuminati panic was but one minor terror in the annus horribilis that was 1798. The threat of war with France, the Alien and Sedition Acts, and the direct house tax pushed partisan fervor to a new and alarming peak. While historians often characterize these animosities as a battle between two parties before the court of public opinion, it might be more precise to view them as a contest of public spheres: two distinct yet loosely organized networks of politicians, caucuses, presses, celebrations, benevolent societies, and fraternal organizations that embodied and articulated divergent conceptions of public opinion.

Federalists, as we have come to expect, defined public opinion as a public resource—"the great auxiliary of good government" that faction, Fisher Ames argued, invariably weakened and, if left unchecked, would ultimately destroy. Thomas Day's 1798 *Oration on Party Spirit*, perhaps the most unalloyed expression of high Federalism, explained why. Speaking before the Connecticut Society of the Cincinnati on July Fourth, Day, a recent Yale graduate and student at the Litchfield Law School, began with a Humean proposition:

> All subordination depends upon opinion. There exists not a government on earth, where the physical strength does not reside in the governed. Some obey from reason, and some from self-interest: but it is a reverence, founded in prescription, for the laws and magistrates of their country, which alone prevents a large majority of the subjects, from exercising their natural powers, and trampling those laws, with their authors, under foot. Party spirit always weakens, and not unfrequently destroys, this reverence.

Party spirit encouraged the "lower classes of society" to overestimate their intelligence and discouraged the upper classes from public service. The repeated "false alarms" raised by demagogues put "visionary scenes of danger" into fearful and credulous minds and perplexed otherwise reasonable and discerning persons with doubts and anxieties. The fearful and anxious alike would seek defense in factions, and factions would incite violence: "in the lower ranks of society, club-fighting; in the higher ranks, dueling."[24]

The Sedition Act translated this logic into law: if "the strength of a government, as ours, lies in the opinion of the people," the Federalist jurist Alexander Addison reasoned, "the corruption of public opinion will ruin the government."[25] In opposing the act, Democratic-Republicans defined public opinion in narrowly political-constitutional terms as a popular security against misrule. With the exception of a few radical arguments for liberty of opinion and the "uncontrollable" nature of the human mind (discussed in chapter 4), most Jeffersonians focused their attacks on the constitutionality of the act and its encroachment on the rights of the states. And if the act had intended to effectively outlaw opposition to the government, the Republicans steered clear of any public defenses of party. Writing to John Taylor, Thomas Jefferson speculated that "in every free and deliberating society, there must, from the nature of man, be opposite parties, and violent dissensions and discords; and one of these, for the most part, must prevail over the other for a longer or shorter time. Perhaps this party division is necessary to induce each to watch and relate to the people the proceedings of the other." Jefferson closed by cautioning Taylor to not let these sentiments "get before the public."[26]

Good Feelings: Public Opinion without Politics

The election of 1800 swept the Jeffersonian Republicans into office. Federalists did not go quietly, but they went without bloodshed. But Thomas Jefferson did not view the election of 1800 as a party victory. It was a "revolution" effected by a new and "mighty wave of public opinion" that had rolled over the republic, and "the most pleasing novelty is, it's so quickly subsiding over such an extent of surface to its true level again." Americans had not chosen one legitimate party over another; they had simply recovered from a "delusion" induced by a small faction of Federalist crypto-monarchists. Convinced that the vast majority of Americans were Republicans at heart, Jefferson pursued a policy of conciliation toward moderate Federalists, hoping to absorb them into a great Republican majority. A small band of recalcitrant Tories—"the weakly and the nervous, the rich and the corrupt seeing more safety and accessibility in a strong executive"—would remain, and temporary schisms between "moderate and ardent republicanism" might surface on occasion. But he remained confident that party spirit would abate and make no more mighty waves of public opinion.[27]

President Jefferson and his Virginian successors, James Madison and James Monroe, remained as committed as Washington and Adams to Bolingbrokean conceptions of the chief executive as a disinterested patriot king. A president should, Jefferson explained, "unite in himself the confidence of the whole people" and, when necessary, point the people "in a single direction as if all constituted but one body and one mind." Unlike Washington and Adams, the Virginia presidents placed greater emphasis on the popular nature of the office. In practice, this required them to distance themselves even farther from anything that smacked of party organization. As a result, the nascent national party structures built during the 1790s fell into disuse. If the anti-partyism of the Washington and Adams administrations encouraged both party development and nationalization, the anti-partyism of the Virginia dynasty appears to have had the opposite effect.[28]

While anti-partyism remained the official public creed from the age of Jefferson to the age of Jackson, a series of developments slowly worked to weaken its structural supports and undermine its basic premises. First, constitutional amendments and revisions at the national and state level created a more hospitable environment for party development. With the Twelfth Amendment in 1804, the Constitution formally acknowledged the existence of political parties. By requiring electors to cast separate ballots for president and vice president, the amendment eased the efforts of parties to nominate national tickets and add them to slates of congressional and local candidates. Moreover, states moved to allow voters to pick electors directly. In 1800, legislatures chose electors in ten of fifteen states. By 1828, voters made that choice in twenty-one of the twenty-four states. Most importantly, a growing number of voters made these choices. In 1800, two-thirds of the states imposed some property requirement for suffrage. New York and Massachusetts abolished their property restrictions 1821. By 1828, a majority of states offered near-universal suffrage to white males, including eight of the nine states added to the union since 1800.[29]

Second, this expanding electorate, and the younger generation of politicians who courted their votes, did not necessarily share the founders' disdain for the bare-knuckle factionalism and besotted electioneering of state and local politics. From 1800 to 1816, intense partisan competition in New England and the Mid-Atlantic pushed participation in state and congressional elections to unprecedented levels. In some areas, conflicts among avowed Republicans drove voters to the polls. In others, a resurgent Federalist party produced similar effects. A cohort of young Federalists exchanged the overt elitism and anti-partyism of their tie-wig elders for covert elitism and party organization. Convinced that "opinion" had triumphed over true republicanism in the election of 1800, Fisher Ames advised his allies to study "popular opinion and accommodate measures to what it is." The new-model Federalists subsidized newspapers, fêted voters, sponsored "Washington Benevolent Societies," and organized an extensive network of committees, caucuses, and conventions.[30] As political participation widened, politicians of all persuasions increasingly stressed their "friendship" for the people. Electioneering rituals demanded fewer displays of popular deference to candidates, placing new emphasis on the shared principles and loyalties that united voters and candidates in battle against their partisan foes. Although this new political style directly challenged the aristocratic and deferential premises of traditional anti-partyism, it did not cause politicians to dispense with anti-party rhetoric. The allegation of "faction" could still sting a partisan enemy. But some cliques of politicians, most notably the Republican Bucktails of New York, began to make a case (which I return to below) for the positive benefits of party.[31]

Third, and most important for our purposes, "public opinion" took on new and different meanings. The anti-partyism of the founding generation drew on a classical and humanist (or, to be more precise, "neo-Stoic") psychology and political science of "opinion." As discussed in chapter 1, neo-Stoicism defined opinions as impressions stamped on weak and passive minds by inconstant bodily urges, overheated passions, and runaway imaginations. Politically, opinion was a malleable and potentially dangerous force—especially in a republic. It could be prudently governed and educated by just laws, sound traditions, and virtuous elites, or deluded and counterfeited by demagoguery, priestcraft, and the arts of faction. The oft-repeated maxim that "all governments are founded upon opinion" was not a tribute to popular wisdom but a reminder that even the best governments remained vulnerable to instability of opinion.[32]

By 1816, such dour and pessimistic assessments of public opinion had all but disappeared from public discourse. Phantasms of opinion had not destroyed the republic, and the evils of party spirit gave way to an "era of good feelings." In the absence of distinct party ideologies, politicians climbed over each other to applaud the rise of public opinion. In the "age of good feelings," no oration or essay seemed complete without a tribute to the diffusion of knowledge, the march of civilization, and the apotheosis of "public opinion." The frequency with which the phrase appeared in periodicals (fig. 3.1) is a rough indication of this. As Sampson Reed observed,

> Nothing is a more common subject of remark than the changed condition of the world. There is a more extensive intercourse of thought, and a more pow-

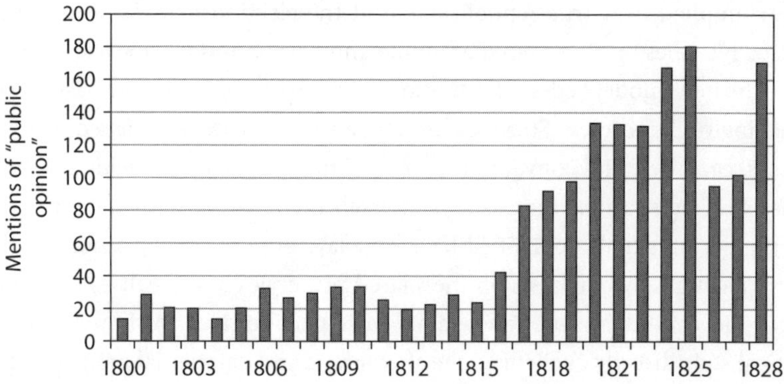

Figure 3.1. Occurrence of "public opinion" in American periodicals, 1800–1828. *Source: American Periodicals Series Online (Ann Arbor, MI: ProQuest).*

erful action of mind upon mind than formerly. The good and the wise of all nations are brought nearer together, and begin to exert a power, which though yet feeble as infancy, is felt throughout the globe. Public opinion, that helm which directs the progress of events by which the world is guided to its ultimate destination, has received a new direction. The mind has attained an upward and onward look, and is shaking off the errors and prejudices of the past.

Edward Everett announced that a "public opinion of a new kind has arisen among men—the opinion of the civilized world." No longer constrained by the infirmities of human nature, the "field in which mind may labor," Francis Wayland conjectured, "has now become as wide as the limits of civilization." The printing press, steam power, and an array of internal improvements had established what Joseph Story called "a new and mighty empire, the empire of public opinion."[33]

What accounts for this outburst of effusive praise for public opinion? To be sure, some of this enthusiasm can be attributed to the antebellum penchant for high-flown rhetoric. Michael Kammen has attributed the "rather mindless (and sometimes insincere) manner" in which Americans celebrated "the emergence of public opinion as a sign of the progress of civilization" to burgeoning notions of American exceptionalism. A more charitable interpretation might view celebrations of public opinion as clumsy attempts to come to terms with (and further promote) some concrete and arguably revolutionary changes in transportation and communication. Roads, bridges, canals, steamboats, and the postal system inspired language every bit as rapturous and sublime as the Bunker Hill Monument, and politicians frequently employed it to stoke a popular clamor for internal improvements. John C. Calhoun famously proposed to "bind the republic together with a perfect system of roads and canals" that would "conquer space." Because "public opinion exerts a controlling influence" in a republic, an 1816 committee report to the Virginia House of Delegates concluded that internal improvements were "an important auxiliary, if not a necessary ingredient of political liberty."[34]

For Calhoun and the Virginians, internal improvements extended republicanism across space by empowering public opinion as a guardian of liberty. Their ideas remained rooted in the revolutionary enlightenment and the Jeffersonian principles of 1798. For Webster and his fellow Bostonians, the relation between republicanism and the "empire of public opinion" was more subtle and complex: internal improvements created a more orderly and governable republic by civilizing public opinion. Their ideas derived from what Henry May once called the "didactic" enlightenment: an amalgam of conservative moral philosophy, moderate political science, and liberal political economy that became the standard fare of college curricula and elite journals of opinion after 1800. The didactic enlightenment was in many respects a Scottish import. American moral philosophers drew heavily on the writings of Adam Smith, Francis Hutcheson, Lord Kames, Thomas Reid, Adam Ferguson, and their students. Libraries and booksellers stocked the histories of William Robertson and the novels of Sir Walter Scott, newspapers and periodicals excerpted the speeches of James Mackintosh, Francis Jeffrey, and Henry Brougham, and frequently republished essays from the *Edinburgh Review*, which had many American subscribers.[35]

If there was anything resembling an accepted academic theory of public opinion in the early American republic, it can be found in Dugald Stewart's *Elements of the Philosophy of the Human Mind*. First published in 1793, the book went through eight American editions in the ensuing thirty years.[36] Stewart, pupil and biographer of Adam Smith and professor of moral philosophy at the University of Edinburgh, began with the premise that "in the present age" the "rapid communication, and the universal diffusion of knowledge, by means of the press" had rendered "the situation of political societies essentially different from what it ever was formerly." Stewart greeted this development with nearly unqualified optimism. The printing press represented a great leap forward in the "natural history of man." It had revealed the "mysteries of courts," widened the "circle of science and civilization," and enlarged the "basis of equitable governments, by increasing the number of those who understand their value." Moreover, print promised to diminish the "influence of popular eloquence; both by curing men of those prejudices upon which it operates, and by subjecting it to the irresistible control of enlightened opinions."[37]

For these reasons, "public opinion" had "acquired an ascendant in human affairs, which it never possessed in those states of antiquity from which most of our political examples are drawn." Modern civilization required a new political philosophy, and Stewart found it in the science of political economy. The "enlightened and humane philosophy" offered a *juste milieu* between the revolutionary spirit of innovation and unthinking, obstinate traditionalism. By eschewing republican preoccupations with virtue, corruption, and constitutions, political economy tempered the "violent and sanguinary" tone of political discourse. By extending "our views to the whole plan of civil society, and showing us the mutual relations and dependencies, of its most distant parts," political economy could not "fail to check that indiscriminate zeal against established institutions, which arises from partial views of the social system; as well as to produce a certain degree of skepticism with respect to every change, the success of which is not insured by the prevailing ideas and manners of the age."[38]

Stewart had little to say about factions and parties, other than to imply that they arose from inherited prejudices and "partial views of the social system" that the progress of civilization and the diffusion of political-economic science would gradually moderate and enlighten. Indeed, it could be argued that in positing public opinion as the driving force of civilized political society, Stewart rendered politics increasingly unnecessary. It is not difficult to imagine why, in an era of good feelings, this sublime vision of pubic opinion without politics appealed to American academics, professionals, and other elites. By defining public opinion as a product of civilization, Stewart's philosophical system placed it under the careful tutelage of the most civilized. Unfailingly moderate and optimistic, it equated material improvement with moral improvement in ways that eased lingering republican and Calvinist anxieties regarding commercial society.[39]

Parties of Public Opinion

The belief that economic development could quiet the voice of faction formed the basic premise of Matthew Carey's *The Olive Branch; or, Faults on Both Sides, Federal and Democratic* (1814), the most extensive, widely circulated, and celebrated work of anti-party literature in its time. In the course of reviewing the recent war with Britain, Carey, a prominent Philadelphia printer and journalist, blasted Federalists for their wartime disloyalty, disregard for the public will, and libelous attacks on the characters of Jefferson and Madison. At the same time, Carey criticized his fellow Republicans for their misguided and unbending opposition to standing armies, central banks, and other necessary instruments of energetic national government. With independence from Britain now fully secured, Carey urged both sides to bury old grudges and outmoded policies and turn their attention to the promotion of economic prosperity. While allowing that partisan differences over the means of economic development would surface, Carey believed that "calm, dispassionate, and moderate" politicians could recognize the underlying harmony of interests that linked the fortunes of farmers, merchants, craftsmen, and manufacturers in all parts of the nation. To ensure the election of moderate men, Carey proposed to dismantle old party mechanisms and replace them with processes more sensitive to public opinion. For example, the nomination of candidates could not, he argued, be left to the workings of secret party caucuses.[40]

As it turned out, Carey's *Olive Branch* became an ironic blueprint for the second party system: the promotion of economic development revived partisan animosities, and the opening of the nomination process led to the construction of more elaborate party organizations. The panic of 1819 fanned smoldering anti-banking sentiment into a political furor that consumed state politics throughout the 1820s and carried over to national politics in the ensuing decade. The practice of nominating candidates for state and national office in legislative caucuses had been criticized intermittently before 1815. Defenders of the caucus system argued, with apparent success, that legislators could best ascertain the preferences of fellow partisans in their districts and select the right candidate for the party as a whole. With the subsequent demise of the Federalist Party at the national level, this argument lost much of its weight. Now, in clear violation of the separation of powers, a caucus of congressional Republicans effectively selected the president. The presidential caucus of 1816, in which James Monroe of Virginia narrowly defeated William Crawford of Georgia, roused public criticism (especially in the North) of "King Caucus" and permanently damaged its credibility. John Taylor nevertheless defended the party caucus, arguing that it actually discouraged faction. But should the caucus "ever attempt to control public opinion instead of expressing it, their doings would have little influence in the nation other than to embitter party animosity and to sharpen the edge of political strife."[41]

President Monroe, an even more ardent advocate of one-party government than Madison or Jefferson, failed to identify a clear successor. The prospect of King Caucus deciding the 1824 election, though remote, was sufficient to provoke a barrage of criticism from opponents of Crawford, the presumptive caucus nominee. Supporters of Andrew Jackson, Henry Clay, and John Adams raced to condemn the caucus as a usurpation of the sovereignty of the people and, in the words of Rufus King of Massachusetts, a "self-created central power . . . regulated by a sort of freemasonry, the sign and password of each at once placing the initiated in full confidence and communion with each other in all parts of the union." Publisher Hezekiah Niles of Maryland, a Clay man, insisted that he "would rather learn that the halls of Congress were converted into common brothels" than see a nominating caucus conducted within them. When the state legislatures of New York and Virginia resolved to abide by the decision of the caucus, Niles complained of "the present broad attempt to bring *public opinion* into contempt and make the voice of people a thing to be laughed at, under the cant of '*preserving the republican party.*'" This party no longer existed: "when what was called the 'era of good feelings' first began, I expressed my fear of it, considering the absence of political excitement as the precursor of less safe divisions among the people, because *local*—instead of being *general,* as our former divisions were."[42]

Here Niles moved past the traditional defense of party as an occasional and necessary evil and inched toward a rationale for party as a positive good. National parties could produce the sort of general excitements that prevented sectional divisions, but only if they were popular parties. They had to abandon any pretense of *directing* public opinion through caucuses and present themselves to the people as mechanisms for *concentrating* public opinion through conventions. The "period has surely arrived," an 1824 convention of "democrat republicans" at Harrisburg, Pennsylvania, declared, "when a president should be elected from the ranks of the people." Andrew Jackson came "pure, untrammeled and unpledged, from the bosom of the people" and walked away with 124 of the 125 votes cast.[43]

In some respects, the shift from caucuses to conventions was more nominal than structural. Elected officials continued to exercise considerable influence over the nomination process. But it is difficult to generalize: in some localities, "caucuses" were as open to popular participation as "conventions"; in others, popular "conventions" contested the verdicts of insular "caucuses." In their haste to "get up meetings," most politicians did not fuss over terminology. Although a pyramid of local, state, and national party meetings would become "the heart and soul of mid-nineteenth-century political structure," the "New York system" often encountered stiff resistance from both anti-party ideologues and loyal partisans who doubted its constitutionality. The chief architects of this system, Martin Van Buren and the "Albany Regency," made their case for party organization with a curious blend of popular constitutionalism and traditional anti-partyism. Parties, they argued, were not mere machines for winning elections, alliances of interest groups, or vehicles for mobilizing public opinion—these were the hallmarks of faction. Parties more closely resembled different constitutional orders or estates. There had always been a "democracy" comprising the great majority of the people, and there had always been an "aristocracy" equipped with all "the appliances generally most effective in partisan warfare," determined to pervert the constitution to its own ends. To level the playing field and preserve the Constitution, the democracy needed to organize. An aristocratic party founded on Hamiltonian principles, Van Buren observed,

> does not often stand in need of caucuses and conventions to preserve harmony in its ranks. Constructed principally of a network of special interests,—almost all of them looking to Government for encouragement of some sort,—the feelings and opinions of its members spontaneously point in the same direction, and when those interests are thought in danger, or new inducements are held out for their advancement, notice of the apprehended assault or promised encouragement is circulated through their ranks with a facility always supplied by the sharpened wit of cupidity.

Party organization was necessary to counter the influence of the "money power." Although this power exerted a "liberal influence" and had "elevated public opinion" in England and throughout much of Europe, its American cousin had always "designed to control the public will by undermining and corrupting its free and virtuous impulse and determination."[44]

For Van Buren and his allies, party organization embodied a democratic public opinion that could not be corrupted by the money power, factions of privileged elites, priestcraft, and other aristocratic "appliances." This public opinion—continually reinforced by party newspapers, pamphlets, orations, meetings, clubs, and festivities—instilled the party regularity needed to defeat the foes of democracy. Moreover, a party organized on purely democratic principles, and organized down to every precinct, would counteract the natural tendency of government toward consolidation and oligarchy. As Gerald Leonard has argued:

> The purpose of the new party was to replace lawmaking (and constitutional interpretation, for that matter) by a Madisonian deliberative Congress with lawmaking by expression of popular will through the party; to replace president-making by popular will through party nomination; and to replace constitutional interpretation by the consolidationist Supreme Court (and Congress, for that matter) with constitutional interpretation by a localist people through their party-disciplined representatives in the regular course of policymaking.

To sell this new mode of party organization, politicians had to persuade voters that government had grown unresponsive to the will of the people and rife with favoritism and corruption. This was not a hard sell. Democrats stoked popular outrage over the presidential election of 1824, in which Andrew Jackson lost the presidency to a "corrupt bargain" struck in the halls of Congress. They assailed unelected judges and elected representatives who ignored popular instructions. They attacked the privileges and powers granted to chartered corporations like the Second Bank of the United States, which, in Old Hickory's estimation, aimed to "control public opinion."[45]

But the core issue around which Jackson, Van Buren, and their allies built the Democratic Party was democratic partyism: popular election, equal rights (for white men), and popular influence over the government through party organization. They devoted their attention to the privileges and inequalities created by government and largely ignored those present in society. Their party platforms and campaign materials were almost devoid of what would today be considered "substantive" policy proposals. The Democratic Party was not designed to agitate or educate public opinion; its primary purpose was to embody and concentrate it in defense of "the democracy" and the Constitution.

The brief history of the Anti-Masonic Party provides an instructive contrast to Democratic partyism. In 1826, William Morgan, a disgruntled former Mason from Batavia, New York, made it known that he intended to publish an exposé of the order's secret rites and "mysteries." His subsequent and highly suspect disappearance aroused public curiosity and indignation. Newspapers demanded answers, and grand juries issued indictments against Morgan's alleged Masonic abductors. Nearly all were acquitted. Masonic judges and jurors kept their allegiances secret, and Masonic witnesses refused to testify. Outraged anti-Masons appealed to the state government, but neither Governor Clinton nor the Albany Regency satisfied their demands. Rebuffed by both parties, anti-Masons formed their own. Local committees and popular conventions issued resolutions declaring Masons unfit for public office and nominated candidates to take their place. By 1828, the Anti-Masonic Party had established a strong political foothold in western New York, and an energetic Anti-Masonic press spread the message into New England, Pennsylvania, and the Ohio valley.[46]

Historians are careful to distinguish political Anti-Masonry from a broader anti-Masonic social movement. Although both were infused with a spirit of evangelical, "middle-class moral populism," a good number of anti-Masons rejected party organization and the political proscription of Masons as unchristian. Political Anti-Masons insisted that they had little choice but to organize themselves as a party. They had learned "from a thorough experience that all other means are and will be wholly ineffectual." As a writer in *The Anti-Masonic Review and Mag-*

azine explained, "Free Masonry is a veteran in discipline; and those who would oppose it, must choose some form of action, which, by a combination of effort, will enable them to meet the phalanx of the enemy. To form a society to oppose it, would be inconsistent. Only two forms of association exist, which can be turned to this purpose: these are religion and politics. If the religious societies enter the field, 'priestcraft!' is heard." Having organized themselves as a political party, Anti-Masons held "themselves subject to the verdict of public opinion" that Masons sought to escape. And organize they did: Anti-Masons established over forty newspapers, conducted regular county meetings and state conventions, and, in 1831, held the first national political convention to nominate former attorney general William Wirt for president.[47]

As the party grew, it attracted voters not especially concerned with the mysterious designs of Freemasonry. As Donald Ratcliffe has put it, "Anti-Masonry was Jackson Democracy, in a sense, for those who could not stand Jackson." No political party made more sweeping claims regarding the wisdom and power of public opinion. "Republican government," John Quincy Adams declared during his brief stint as an Anti-Mason, was "essentially the government of public opinion." Because public opinion controlled the will of the people in a republic, it "must govern everything, which is properly subject to government power. This is the theory of our government. It is clearly the only theory consistent with the rights of man." Only public opinion could defeat Masonry, and Anti-Masons vowed to use it as "our shepherd's sling." The purpose of party organization was to excite and awaken it: "what is the virtue of public opinion, while it reposes in its omnipotence, and will not exert its power upon the subject of its displeasure? It must make itself respected, by making itself felt."[48]

The Anti-Masonic emphasis on public opinion can be attributed in part to the moralistic nature of its adherents' crusade against secrecy, and in part to their position as a third party in a developing two-party system. With faint hope of securing a majority, Anti-Masons had little else to hope for but a moral victory in the court of public opinion. And like most third parties, the two major parties regarded the Anti-Masons as a nuisance. In New York, Albany Regency Democrats saw the party as a cat's paw of their Clintonite and National Republican enemies, and argued that attacks on Masonry lay outside the bounds of acceptable *political* discourse. Governor Enos Throop, a Regency man who had once praised the "blessed spirit" of anti-Masonry, had no use for the Anti-Masonic Party. In explaining why, he set forth a carefully circumscribed case for the benefits of the two-party system:

Those party divisions which are based upon conflicting opinions in regard to the constitution of the government, or the measures of the administration of it, interest every citizen, and tend, inevitably, in the spirit of emulation and proselytism, to reduce many shades of opinion into two opposing parties . . . organized parties watch and scan each other's doings, the public mind is instructed by ample discussions of public measures, and acts of violence are restrained by the convictions of the people, that the prevailing measures are the results of enlightened reason.

Legitimate party competition stayed within these bounds. Parties that dealt in "private" questions roused the passions and disturbed social harmony. The "violent and persecuting spirit" of Anti-Masonry, a petition of Rochester citizens complained, had left "the peace of families broken" and deranged "ordinary business transactions between man and man."[49]

Although short-lived as a political party, Anti-Masonry successfully prosecuted its enemy before the bar of public opinion. Masons abandoned the order in droves: New York had 228 Masonic lodges in 1827; ten years later, only 26 remained active. Those who remained and fought defended the Masonic lodge as a place where society's natural leaders cast aside contentious partisan and sectarian differences and united in a spirit of brotherly affection and benevolence. They depicted Anti-Masons as the credulous dupes of designing men and asserted that Anti-Masonic proscription violated individual freedoms of association and conscience. The "public opinion" that Anti-Masons championed was, for Boston poet and Mason Thomas Power, an affront to personal liberty and dignity:

> Boast we of freedom on these Western shores?
> E'en human minds are here transferred by scores!
> With office, honor, flattery, or gold,
> Men's grave OPINIONS now are bought and sold:
> Common commodities, with market price,
> All packed to order, on the first advice . . .
> Opinion's valued!—Thoughts for open sale!
> Shame on the wretch that warrants such a tale![50]

The Dialogue of Parties

The "organizational revolution" in politics initiated by Jacksonians in the 1820s gained momentum throughout the 1830s and gave birth to the second party system. Unlike the first party system of the 1790s, parties openly organized, invited mass participation, and defended (with some lingering ambivalence) party competition as a natural, if not beneficial, aspect of free government. Historians continue to debate the meaning and implications of this revolution. Did the rise of the two-party system indicate a widespread acceptance of pluralism and liberal, interest-group politics? Does the persistence of anti-party rhetoric suggest that republican ideologies remained entrenched in antebellum political culture? Or did politicians simply accept pluralism in practice while denying it in theory? The concept of public opinion helped Democrats and Whigs to resolve, or at least obscure, these discrepancies between practice and theory in different ways. Democrats gravitated toward a "political-constitutional" concept of public opinion. They equated public opinion with popular liberty and sovereignty and advocated popular party organization as a necessary means of defense against corruption and overreaching state power. Whigs gravitated toward a "social-psychological" concept of public opinion. They equated public opinion with the progress of civilization, and (with some difficulty) they organized a party to protect individual conscience against Democratic and majoritarian manufactories of opinion.[51]

Yet another difference between the first and second party systems can be found in the volume of discourse about public opinion. In the 1790s, politicians and political writers invoked the concept in an infrequent, vague, and offhand manner. By the 1830s, the concept had become a keyword in the American political vocabulary. The notion that the American republic was a "government of public opinion" was a bipartisan commonplace and—especially for Democrats—a point of national honor. When Alexis de Tocqueville, Harriet Martineau, and other European observers asserted that Americans lived under the tyranny of majority opinion, Jacksonians fought back. Ignoring Tocqueville's qualification that the tyranny of the majority had as yet made "itself felt only feebly in political society," they pointed to the frequent newspaper slanders of Old Hickory as proof positive of American freedom of opinion. Others cited the favorable reception of Tocqueville's book among European conservatives and British Tories.[52]

More theoretically minded critiques homed in on Tocqueville's conflation of political majorities with public opinion. A majority, George Sidney Camp argued, was a "political force" composed of constantly shifting coalitions. Public opinion, by contrast, was a "natural force." Though it was exceptionally powerful in America, it was "not that government has made it so, not that majorities have made it so, but that such is the inevitable result of the nature and constitution of man." There could be no tyranny of political majorities, because majorities were "subject to the continual control of public sentiment." But could there be a tyranny of public sentiment? To Tocqueville's charge that the public prohibited the airing of atheistic and anti-republican ideas, Camp asked, "why should it not?" If public opinion could suppress vices, why should it not suppress opinions "generally believed" to "sap the foundations of private morals, of public prosperity, and of political freedom?"[53]

Public opinion was powerful, Democrats argued, because it encountered fewer artificial restraints and felt fewer anti-republican influences than it did in the old world. In the absence royal courts, established churches, hereditary nobilities, and other arbitrary powers, public opinion had assumed what historian and Democratic politician George Bancroft identified as its proper "office" in "art, government, and religion." Because the "the spirit of God breathes through the combined intelligence of the people," it stood to reason that the "best government rests on the people and not on the few, on persons and not on property, on the free development of public opinion and not on authority." If the notion of public opinion as an agent of divine providence seems a bit excessive, some went even further.[54] More importantly, Bancroft's teleological history of democracy allowed him to minimize the role of parties. As Jean H. Baker has astutely observed, Bancroft "was a majoritarian who had moved beyond antipartyism but could not accept the possibility that party conflict contributed to republican society."[55]

Democrats more willing to acknowledge the existence of parties adopted Jefferson and Van Buren's portrait of a struggle between "the Democracy" and a small, refractory minority of Tories, paper aristocrats, and their retainers. While allowing that there "is a great deal of misunderstanding between our parties," John L. O'Sullivan believed that "there does not exist in the people, with reference to its great masses, that irreconcilable hostility of opinions and leading principles which would be the natural inference from the violence of the party warfare in which we are perpetually engaged." Moreover, Federalists and Whigs were largely to blame for this violence. Their complex designs for energetic and extensive government—banks, tariffs, internal improvements, and the like—only served to confuse and alarm the public. These were "the maddening elements which give such violence and acrimony to party strife."[56]

While arguing for the unconstrained influence of public opinion, Democrats subtly incorporated policies of limited government, states' rights, and strict constitutional construction into their rationale for party government. "We are opposed," O'Sullivan declared in the first issue of the *United States Magazine and Democratic Review*, "to all self-styled 'wholesome restraints' on the free action of popular opinion and will, other than those which have for their sole object the prevention of precipitate legislation." He did not offer any examples of "precipitate" or premature legislation. But if *all* legislative branches were made "dependent with equal directness and promptness on the influence of public opinion," he confidently predicted that they would not charter any "self-imposed power" over the sovereign will of the people. O'Sullivan did not, in so many words, explain how all legislative branches—with members elected at different times from different districts and serving terms of various lengths—could simultaneously feel the direct and prompt force of public opinion. But with (in his estimation) at least two-thirds of the presses and most of the learned professions on the side of the "anti-democratic cause," the "present ascendancy of the democratic party" was vital to enforcing a "universal and unrelaxing responsibility" of government to "the vigilance of public opinion." This, O'Sullivan insisted, was "the true conservative principle of our institutions."[57]

A nascent Whig opposition saw nothing conservative in this at all and denounced Jacksonian partyism as a radical and dangerous innovation. Defending his 1835 defection to the Whigs, former House Speaker John Bell of Tennessee asserted that "it is now for the first time in the history of free states solemnly proposed and seriously attempted to give an organized and systematic party action to the government, under the plausible and delusive pretext that it is necessary, in order to preserve the great objects for which the government was formed." In the Jacksonian system of party discipline, Whigs augured a conspiracy to consolidate power in the hands of the chief executive and his party managers through "a process of manufacturing public opinion." The supposed popular and republican nature of party government was nothing more than a ruse designed to draw unsuspecting citizens to meetings and conventions, where "powerful men, hidden behind the curtain, move the wires and secret springs." Party newspapers then broadcasted the results to a wider public, depicting the meetings as "open and unpremeditated" expressions of popular opinion. John C. Calhoun, as was his wont, pushed this argument even farther, taking particular exception to the appropriation of the term "convention" for partisan purposes. A genuine convention was a "meeting of the people in the majesty of their power" in "which they may rightfully make or abolish constitutions." Political conventions—"self-created meetings"—confounded popular sovereignty with party, compelled men to sacrifice their opinions to the majority, and would "eventually supersede the authority of law and constitution."[58]

Whigs frequently likened the eighteenth-century struggle against George III, Robert Walpole, and ministerial influence to their own campaign against King Andrew, Van Buren, and partyism. Their anti-party arguments often borrowed from Bolingbroke, and they rarely passed on an opportunity to quote from Washington's Farewell Address, but the implied continuities were more cosmetic than substantive. Most Whigs accepted parties as a basic and necessary, if somewhat unpleasant, fact of political life. But they placed particular and unique emphasis on the violence that Jacksonian partyism did to individual conscience. Whigs justified their partisan behavior as a defense of conscience against Democratic manufactories of opinion and incorporated this justification into their policy positions. If Jacksonians could depict corporate charters and Nicholas Biddle's bank as Whig attempts to control public opinion, Whigs could depict the spoils system and Jackson's pet banks as "proscriptive" assaults on the freedom of personal opinion. Likewise, they opposed Jackson's use of the veto and the Democratic doctrine of instruction as threats to the moral independence of legislators.[59]

Whig clergymen echoed these themes, likening the evils of partisanship to sectarianism and the delusive enthusiasm of party meetings to revivals. For Calvin Colton, Jacksonian demagogues and unscrupulous revivalists both contrived "to take the public mind by surprise" and "descend upon it in an overwhelming manner." Party spirit, William Ellery Channing warned, "is singularly hostile to moral independence. A man, in proportion as he shrinks into it, sees, hears, and judges by the senses and understandings of his party. He surrenders the freedom of a man, the right of using and speaking his own mind, and echoes the applauses or maledictions with which the leaders of passionate partisans see fit that the country should ring." While Democrats feared a government that imperiled citizens' political and economic autonomy, Whigs feared processes of manufacturing public opinion that compromised citizens' moral and psychological autonomy.[60]

To distinguish genuine opinion from party opinion—or, for that matter, from majority opinion—Whigs drew on the precepts of Scottish moral philosophy and the "didactic enlightenment." Identifying public opinion with the gradual development of civilization, diffusion of knowledge, and progress of morals, they assigned a prominent role to the leadership of wise and distinguished men (fig. 3.2). "By public opinion we must understand," Francis Lieber cautioned, "that opinion of the community which has been influenced either by the modifying correction of time, or the talent or knowledge of those who are peculiarly able to judge upon the subject in question." Among Whigs, as Lynn Marshall once observed, the "greatest emphasis was placed upon the liberty of the individual to express himself, if he were able and sufficiently educated, in great social theories and high ideals." Whig policies aimed to enhance and extend the influence of such individuals while gently instilling national "feelings," whether through the prudent management of credit by the Bank of the United States, the promotion of communication through the "American System" of internal improvements, or the national

Figure 3.2. Edward Williams Clay, *The Almighty Lever* (New York, 1840). In this print from the presidential election of 1840, "PUBLIC OPINION" lifts William Henry Harrison to the White House. The banner held in the talon of the eagle reads: "With a log cabin and barrel of hard Cider for a fulcrum, public opinion for a 'lever,' with old Tip on the tip end the ball of Locofocoism will be rolled into oblivion and a gallant soldier raised to the White House. March 4th 1841." *Library of Congress.*

university proposed by John Quincy Adams. For the most part, a growing "empire" of benevolent and reform societies manifested comparable aspirations, and shared anti-Jacksonian allegiances.[61]

Not surprisingly, the most unalloyed expressions of Whig anti-party constitutionalism came from members of the legal profession. For the Massachusetts Whig, congressman, and attorney Rufus Choate, the bench and bar was "an element of conservativism in the state," perhaps even as a "portion of the state, an estate if you will." Its "studies and employments tend to form in it and fit it to diffuse and impress on the popular mind a class of opinions—one class of opinions—which are indispensable to conservativism. Its studies and offices train and arm it to counteract exactly that specific system of opinions by which our liberty must die." Choate predicted that it would

one day be written, for the praise of the American Bar, that it helped to keep the true idea of the State alive and germinant in the American mind; that it helped to keep alive the sacred sentiments of obedience and reverence and justice, of the supremacy of the calm and grand reason of the law over the fitful will of the individual and the crowd, that it helped to withstand the pernicious sophism that the successive generations, as they come to life, are but as so many successive flights of summer flies, without relations to the past or duties to the future, and taught instead that all—all the dead, the living, the unborn—were one moral person,—one for action, one for suffering, one for responsibility.[62]

For Choate, something essential to the "studies and employments" of the lawyer, something built into the very structure of the legal mind, counteracted the "sentiments and opinions from which the public mind of America is in danger." But what were these dangerous opinions? At bottom, they sprang from a tendency of "reasoning liberty" to "regard the whole concern [the state] as an association altogether at will, and at the will of everybody," a tendency which would result in a crass system of simple majority rule, and a regard for law "as no more nor less than just the will—the actual and present will—of the actual majority of the nation." To this, Choate opposed the "loftier philosophy" of the lawyer. For "in the language of our system, the law is not the transient and arbitrary creation of a major will, nor any will. It is not the offspring of will at all."[63]

Such high-minded Whig constitutionalism did not, as we might expect, easily translate into a practical program for party organization. When defeated at the polls, they bemoaned their inability to organize while taking solace in the purity of their anti-party principles. When victorious, they struggled to explain the success of their party as a vindication of their anti-partyism. In the "Log Cabin Campaign" of 1840, the election of William Henry Harrison branded the Whig Party with a reputation for expediency, hypocrisy, and campaign mummery that it never quite managed to shed. With President Van Buren weakened by economic crisis and dissension within his own party, a new breed of Whig organizers (several of them former Anti-Masons) sensed an opportunity to "prostrate our opponents, with the . . . weapons, with which they beat us." Their first national convention nominated an aging western military hero with no discernable political views. Whigs circulated tales of Van Buren's depraved, aristocratic taste for wine and French cuisine. They organized "Log Cabin" clubs and militias, staged elaborate parades, and plied voters with liquor and hard cider. As for the sacred Whig principle of liberty of conscience, the chair of the national convention assured delegates

[t]hat in our extended confederacy, fortunate in the great number of distinguished citizens, differences of opinion should exist as to the best choice, is no

matter of surprise—indeed, it is rather a matter of pride, as it indicates that we have the independence to think for ourselves, and the firmness to express our opinion; to that extent personal predilections may be justly indulged, but instantly to be surrendered as a ready sacrifice when that sacrifice is demanded by our country—unanimity, let it be impressed on every mind, is the only pivot on which our hope can rest.[64]

But the Whigs of 1840 remained ambivalent in victory. "If parties in a republic are necessary to secure a degree of vigilance sufficient to keep the public functionaries within the bounds of law and duty," Harrison declared in his inaugural address, "at that point their usefulness ends." Beyond that, "Old Tippecanoe" maintained that parties had a corrosive effect on public virtue and liberty. He did not see parties as popular, extralegal lawmaking bodies necessary to defend the Constitution. In a similar fashion, Whig politician Daniel Ullmann allowed that parties were necessary. "The combination any sympathy of those who have common opinions and common interests, is so natural, powerful, and useful, that the sagacious and the patriotic will never cease to resort to it." But parties necessarily required men to sacrifice their opinions, and the larger the party, the greater "the sacrifices of each individual to the controlling opinions of the whole." As a party organization grew and matured, control would usually fall into the hands of "a few ambitious and corrupt, or misguided leaders," and the individual would be "crushed beneath a huge machinery of faction." Worse still, the "despotism" of party and the "passive obedience" it engendered dampened the "ambitious and active spirit which pervades all classes," extinguished the "restlessness and activity of individual minds" and thereby threatened to bring the "constant progressive movement" of American society to a crashing halt.[65]

To prevent this danger, Ullmann proposed that a "great breaking down of party organizations and party distinctions should occur" every few years, "in order that associations should no longer preserve their forms when the objects of their formation have passed away." With the election of William Henry Harrison—a "triumph of popular will over party dictation"—Ullmann believed that such a moment had arrived.[66] But, of course, it did not: Harrison died thirty days after taking his oath. In funeral sermons across the nation, clergymen cast the devout general's death as a divine rebuke to "our national idolatry" of party and political leaders. In contempt of God's authority, Americans had "trusted in an arm of flesh" (2 Chronicles 32:8) and violated every principle of Christian charity in their rage for party. "WHAT A SEVERE REUBKE DOES THIS SAD EVENT GIVE TO POLITICAL BIGOTRY AND RASH INVECTIVE AGAINST THE MOTIVES OF THOSE

WHO DIFFER FROM US IN OPINION," the Reverend George Bethune of Philadelphia thundered. For the Reverend Samuel Francis Smith of Maine, the first death of a sitting president was an act of God designed to moderate partisan zeal. "It seems to me that GOD has inflicted this judgment upon the nation, by smiting its chief magistrate so early after his accession, not simply for our national sins, as such, but for the sins which an inordinate political excitement engendered and involved. GOD forbid that I should cool an honorable patriotism! But we have exhibited more than that. In the heat of party strife for a few months, every thing, sacred and profane, seemed swallowed up."[67]

While it seems unlikely that Harrison's death did much to moderate party zeal, it reinforced the anti-partyism of the Whigs. And after granting the nomination to the ever-eager Henry Clay in 1844, Whigs fell back on the strategy of nominating popular and ostensibly apolitical generals: successfully with Zachary Taylor in 1848, disastrously with Winfield Scott in 1852. The party continued to denounce Jacksonian partyism as a dangerous constitutional innovation and an imposition on individual freedom of opinion while insisting that Whig partyism was somehow different. "Every man in the Whig ranks, is a MAN—a man that thinks for himself, and acts for himself—an uncompromising *American Democrat*," Calvin Colton insisted. If there was a problem with the Whig Party, it was that "they are *all* leaders."[68]

The absurdity of such statements rankled Democrats and made for easy mockery. Speaking on the floor of Congress in 1848, Representative Howell Cobb of Georgia delivered an unapologetic (and widely reprinted) defense of party organization as "the very corner-stone of our whole political system." Parties were essential to self-government. Indeed, a nation could not have a public opinion without parties: "however just and correct the opinions of the great majority of the people may be, they avail nothing, unless they are enabled to manifest them in the practical workings of the government." Warming to the subject, Cobb turned to examine "the honesty and sincerity of the profession now put forth by some of the organs of the Whig party, of opposition to party organization. It presents at the very outset this strange state of things, that the cry of '*no-party-ism*' is the rallying *cry of a party*. The Whigs, having abandoned all other platforms, have determined to rally upon the 'no-party and no-principle' platform, *an organized party*, whose only principle is, opposition *to party organization*. It needs no comment."[69] While the professions of regard for individual freedom of opinion made by Whig Party organizers were of dubious sincerity, they resonated with more diffuse anxieties about the power and influence of public opinion in American society at large.

The Importance of Having Opinions

And what was worst of all, she no longer had any opinions whatever. She saw objects about her and understood what was going on, but she could not form an opinion about anything and did not know what to talk about. *And how awful it is not to have any opinions!*

—*Anton Chekhov, The Darling (1899)*

People have always had opinions, but in the nineteenth century the possession of opinions assumed a new and distinctive cultural and political salience. Having opinions became, to paraphrase John Stuart Mill, "one of the elements of well-being," a mark of individuality and self-culture, if not self-possession: to not have opinions was to not have a "self" at all. Mill worried that "scarcely anyone, in the more educated classes, seems to have any opinions, or to place any faith in those which he professes to have." Weakened by doubt, distracted by the business of commercial society, and overawed by fear of public opinion, men and women had lost the will and energy to cultivate and express considered and sincere opinions. Mill was not, of course, alone in thinking so. Individual opinions cowered under Tocqueville's "tyranny of the majority," chafed against Bagehot's "cake of custom," resigned themselves to Bryce's "fatalism of the multitude," and in every neighborhood hid from the disapproving glower of Mrs. Grundy. Exaggerated as such fears of a despotic of public opinion may have been, they spoke to deeper concerns about the integrity of the self, or what was then called "character."[1]

To be sure, the tension between individual and public opinion had been a subject of concern well before Mill and Tocqueville. But Poor Richard's maxim that the happiest were "those who are convinced of the general opinion" seemed antiquated by the mid-nineteenth century. It was here, as Jürgen Habermas and others have argued, that universalistic, eighteenth-century fictions of "public opinion" broke down under the "pressure of the street," compelling liberal political theorists like Mill and Tocqueville to take a more ambivalent stance toward the rule of public reason, or more explicitly and exclusively to identify public opinion with the educated middle class. While willing to accept that public opinion should act as a restraint on official power, and eager to believe that it could function as an engine of enlightened progress, liberals developed a strong aversion to the coercive, intrusive, and arbitrary means by which it appeared to exercise its power over individuals.[2]

In the antebellum United States, the identification of public opinion with any particular social class was generally avoided, but anxieties regarding the power of public opinion and the integrity of the self became increasingly pronounced and intense. Indeed, the era witnessed an explosion of what might be called "self-talk"; the "key to the period," as Ralph Waldo Emerson observed, "appeared to be that the mind had become aware of itself." The revivalism and reform movements that emerged from the Second Great Awakening, the widening range of personal choices available in an expanding market economy, and the organizational revolution in politics discussed in the previous chapter focused new attention on the making of private opinions and character. Clergy, educators, academics, and popular lecturers warned Americans away from the "religion of public opinion" and urged them to cultivate their opinions and selves with greater self-consciousness, rectitude, and discipline.[3] The importance attached to having opinions contributed new social and psychological layers of meaning to the concept of public opinion, layers that did not always fit comfortably with its received political and constitutional meanings.

The Will to Opine

Beneath discussions concerning the importance of having opinions lay the question of whether individuals could really *have* opinions—have them, that is, in the sense of willfully acquiring or changing them. While it might, as William James observed in his renowned 1896 lecture "The Will to Believe," seem "preposterous on the very face of it to talk of our opinions being modifiable at will," many early-nineteenth-century philosophers, clergy, and moralists, especially those of a more conservative temperament, found the idea of involuntary opinion unsettling, if not repugnant.[4] Did men and women bear no responsibility for their beliefs? Were opinions nothing more than passive reflections of circumstances and influences that a person could do little to control or resist? If so, what did this suggest about the integrity of the self, much less the stability of public institutions and the social order, in an era when the sway of public opinion seemed increasingly irresistible? The problematic relation between volition and opinion was more than just a conundrum for philosophers; it set the terms for religious disputes over the nature of belief and the "new measures" of revivalism, and it sparked popular interest in new "sciences" of mind, such as phrenology and mesmerism.

The most extensive and widely read argument for the involuntariness of opinion, the British utilitarian Samuel Bailey's *Essays on the Formation and Publication of Opinions* (1821), acknowledged that the idea ran against common sensibilities. But Bailey persuasively argued that British philosophy, whether it be the empiricism of Bacon, Locke, and David Hartley or the common sense faculty psychology of Thomas Reid and Dugald Stewart, agreed: opinions may be creatures of reason, sense, or imagination but not will. "Thus the external circumstances in which men are placed unavoidably occasion, without any choice on their part, the chief diversities of opinion existing in the world." While allowing that the expression of an opinion was a voluntary act, Bailey argued against any restrictions on the discussion or publication of opinions. Because opinions, being contingent products of local and personal circumstance, always contained some amount of error and partiality, subjecting them to "unlimited discussion" provided "the greatest probability which it is possible to have that the truth will be ultimately attained." Restrictions on the free circulation and examination of opinions could only have a "mischievous tendency," which Bailey likened to "the system of forcing the capital and industry of the community into channels."[5]

Positing that legal and ecclesiastic proscription of opinion was both unjust in theory and futile in practice, the notion of involuntary opinion naturally appealed to Bailey's fellow philosophic radicals, religious dissenters, and sundry proponents of "free enquiry" and the "diffusion of knowledge" such as Lord Brougham, who declared that the "Great Truth has finally gone forth to all ends of the earth, THAT MAN SHALL NO MORE RENDER ACCOUNT TO MAN FOR HIS BELIEF, OVER WHICH HE HAS HIMSELF NO CONTROL." To be sure, this "great truth" had long been an important tenet in an Anglo-American "libertarian tradition" forged in frequent and pitched battles over religious toleration and liberties of press, speech, and assembly. Seventeenth-century radicals like the Leveler William Walwyn had insisted that "because of what judgment so ever a man is, he cannot chose but be of that judgment." John Locke's arguments for religious tolerance rested on the assertion that "to believe this or that to be true, does not depend upon will," and the authors of *Cato's Letters* declared, "Men's Thoughts are not subject to their own Jurisdiction."[6]

While libertarian ideas regarding the freedom of the press and religion appealed to many revolutionary-era Americans, this underlying epistemology of involuntary opinion proved less popular. To be sure, the preamble to Thomas Jefferson's 1777 draft of the Virginia Act for Establishing Religious Freedom expressed the theory with his characteristic lucidity: "The opinions and beliefs of men depend not upon their will, but follow involuntarily the evidence proposed to their minds." When members of the Virginia General Assembly eventually passed the act in 1786, they replaced Jefferson's epistemological theory with the more concise and unobjectionable declaration "that Almighty God hath created the mind free." Their rationale for doing so is not entirely clear, but it likely had something to do with discomfort over the claim that opinions were involuntary: a considerable minority had voted to delete the preamble entirely and were only satisfied when the change was made. Indeed, it appears that most American politicians were not as enamored with the theory of involuntary opinion as Jefferson. One searches in vain for the idea in the numerous discussions of religious and expressive liberty that accompanied the debates over the ratification of the Constitution and the Bill of Rights. The preferred argument for freedom of opinion derived from an expanded conception of property that encompassed, as James Madison put it, "every thing to which a man may attach a value and have a right, and which leaves to every one else the like advantage," including "his opinions and the free communication of them."[7]

To assert that men had "property in" their opinions presumed that they willfully acquired them or, at the very least, improved on them by dint of effort. It pushed aside vexing philosophical, psychological, and theological questions about the nature of will and belief and grounded freedom of opinion in the ostensibly natural laws of political economy and the airtight logic of contract. The resulting "political economy of opinion," as I argue in chapter 2, did much to shape the terms of debate over the contestable concept of public opinion in the early American republic. But for some political theorists of the Jeffersonian persuasion, analogies to property rights were not sufficient to secure freedom of opinion, and a dismal science of opinion could not fully comprehend the truly progressive nature of a society animated by a new and unprecedented spirit of enlightened inquiry. The controversy over the Sedition Act of 1798 inspired political writings along these lines. In his treatise on "the uncontrollable nature of the human mind," New York attorney John Thomson hypothesized that "as man individually has no control over his mind, so it must follow of course, that he never could have delegated that to a government, which he did not possess himself." Laws and legislations that aimed to "control public opinion, and prevent its free operation" could only "engender pusillanimity, insincerity, and anonymous assassination of character." Simply put, "no human power" could "prevent the progress of opinion."[8]

Tunis Wortman, another New York attorney of Jeffersonian leanings, developed the concept of involuntary opinion into an even more sweeping vision of intellectual and moral progress. In *A Treatise Concerning Political Enquiry, and the Liberty of the Press*, published in 1800 with the sponsorship of Albert Gallatin, he contended that "freedom of speech and opinion" were indispensible to both personal happiness and "the perpetuation of Civil Liberty."[9] Like Thomson, Wortman held that ideas were "governed by the laws of necessary and irresistible causation," and he assailed "the stupid perversity of that despotism which would attempt to direct the operations of the mind." While allowing that the ability to form reasoned opinions varied considerably, Wortman attributed this to differences in experience, education, and access to information. Truth was available "to the percipient powers of all men," who while not equal in intelligence, remained so in "moral sense" and in their capacity to distinguish virtue from vice. And for Wortman, political questions were essentially moral questions: the "morality which regulates the intercourse of sovereigns, is identical with that which governs the conduct of individuals." Politics being "neither poetry, speculative philosophy, metaphysics, or polemical theology," there could be no legitimate reason to restrict any person's right to participate in public discussion. Indeed, only by encouraging and giving the widest latitude to popular "political enquiry" could Americans hope to preserve their republican forms of government.[10]

For Wortman, the involuntary nature of opinion was more than just an argument against its legal proscription; it was an argument *for* a vibrant public sphere animated by a vigorous and uninhibited exchange of opinion. His *Treatise* offered an interesting yet highly unstable hybrid of Lockean psychology, republican apprehensions of corruption and creeping tyranny, leveling democratic appeals to "common sense," millenarian expectations of social perfection, and the anarchism of William Godwin's *Enquiry Concerning Political Justice* (1793), from which he borrowed heavily.[11] Like Godwin, Wortman believed that the free exchange of opinions would make the oppressive restraints of government and the brutal violence of revolutions increasingly rare and unnecessary. Once unleashed, the force of public opinion could not be restrained, and its progressive tendencies could not be reversed. Wortman invited his readers to imagine an imposing despot, "seated on the throne of Eastern pageantry and splendor," surrounded by flatterers, sycophants, and mercenaries and "habituated to the exercise of unlimited power" until "[a] whisper is heard among the multitude, mysterious and portentive.

Like Dionysus, the tyrant trembles in his throne. Behold the eventful crisis has arrived!—the sovereign voice of public opinion has declared that liberty should be established. In an instant the fairy spell of delusion is dissipated—the tremendous authority of this august and magnanimous despot, like the enchanted castle of the magician, vanished forever."[12]

The rather fanciful language notwithstanding, Wortman made no effort to mystify the nature and workings of public opinion. His individualism and materialism led him to reject corporatist conceptions of public opinion: society did "not constitute an intellectual unity" and could not "resolve itself into one single organized percipient, in which the rays of Intelligence are concentrated and personified." Public opinion thus amounted to nothing more than a "coincidence" of "private understandings," an "aggregation of individual sentiment" that nevertheless added up to more than the sum of its parts. Through public opinion, society had "united the powers of individual intellect into a common bank, and multiplied the peculium of each by a general combination of the whole." Moreover, Wortman's anarchy was by no means disorderly or turbulent. "In proportion as investigation continues free and unrestricted," he predicted that "the mass of error will be subject to continual diminution, and the determinations of distinct understandings will gradually harmonize." Encourage the "incessant habit of independent reflection" and the "establishment of Public Opinion upon a rational and salutary basis" would necessarily (if not paradoxically) ensue. While the opinions of men and women were not voluntary, their voluntary actions originated from those opinions. As the free exchange of opinion produced a progressively harmonious public opinion, Wortman and likeminded democratic radicals could imagine something like a withering away of the state—or, at the very least, a political order that did not require the command of a visible and unitary sovereign.[13]

Despite (or, perhaps, due to) the Jeffersonian "Revolution of 1800," such utopian effusions of democratic enthusiasm for the sweet rule of opinion became increasingly rare in the early nineteenth century, and theories of involuntary belief came to be associated with "foreign" radicalism, "infidel" philosophies, and atheism. If the Sedition Act of 1798 hurt Federalists at the polls, it also encouraged moderate Democratic-Republicans like Jefferson and Madison to distance themselves from the allegedly dangerous and "disorganizing" ideas of Paine, Godwin, and the Jacobins. Regicide, the Reign of Terror, and Paine's *Age of Reason* alarmed conservative politicians, writers, and clergymen, who unleashed a barrage of publications, speeches, essays, and sermons that preached up the grave dangers posed by radical "innovations" and ideologies. Following the lead of Edmund Burke, they mocked the "free enquirer" as that "curious character" who stood "not for the propagation of his own opinions, but for any opinions . . . not for the diffusion of truth, but for the spreading of contradiction." Lamenting the ease with which public opinion could be deceived, they sought to limit popular political activity to elections and a few other carefully circumscribed rituals of consent. Fearful of "infidel" and materialist philosophies that denied moral responsibility for personal action and opinion, they insisted that public virtue depended on private religious conviction and steady habits. Accepting, with varying degrees of disappointment, that in "America *public opinion* must, in a great measure, supply the place of long established precedents, and form the chain which binds together society," they insisted "that the public mind should be correctly informed" but rarely acknowledged that it was.[14]

This new conservatism was especially prominent in New England, where a new generation of Federalists joined forces with clerical defenders of the "Standing Order" of established churches to repel the advancing forces of Jeffersonianism and deism.[15] Daniel Webster, perhaps the most famous product of this milieu, published a scathing review of Wortman's *Treatise on Political Enquiry* that likened it to a "vast Serbonian bog" of "declamation, without genius or spirit, false reasoning, without ingenuity enough to be called sophistry, and an inveterate hostility to the rules of composition and grammar." Such "torrents of nonsense" were unbecoming of "a man, who calls himself a *counselor*" and better suited to "Bedlam, than the Forum." Several years before, Webster had warned his fellow Dartmouth College graduates of the "instability" and "illusions of Opinion" that could "sport with the imbecility of our nature." Without due reverence for authority and tradition, opinion would corrupt the public mind with "the dreams of enthusiasts," especially those "new-fangled rights of men" (and women), which "taught amidst the orgies of a civic feast, and propagated at the mouth of cannon, and point of the bayonet," had "these ten years shaken Europe to its centre." A man who could "stand amidst the turmoil of passion and prejudice, amidst the conflict of the winds and waters of party and opinion" would have "more durable wreaths for his fame, than were ever woven in the schools of the new philosophy"—a man such as Washington, whose "single trait of excellence" lay in his "rejection of the phantasms of Opinion."[16]

Here once again is the language of neo-Stoicism discussed in chapter 1, right down to the equation of opinion with the *phantasi* of the imagination—the most uncontrollable of all mental faculties. While here pressed into the service of New England Federalism, anxieties over the derangement of opinion by imagination were by no means an exclusively Federalist, or even a distinctly American, concern. In an age of democratic revolutions and social upheaval, the disruptive potential of imagination worried observers across the political spectrum. Several years after the American Revolution, Dr. Benjamin Rush classified diseases of the imagination (or "opinionative faculty") as "melancholy," placing them in the larger diagnostic category of *anarchia*. Such afflictions, Rush thought, were endemic to and epidemic in the wake of political revolutions. Sudden changes in the structure of authority upset settled habits of mind and exposed people to the influence of wild, disorganizing theories. While the excesses of the French Revolution (which, as William Ellery Channing recalled, had "diseased the imagination" of his fellow Harvard students) served as exhibit A of such dangers, Americans readily identified numerous domestic causes and consequences of disordered fancy: fustian political rhetoric, frontier revivals, financial speculation, newspaper sensationalism, and novel-reading, which, in Jefferson's judgment, resulted in a "bloated imagination, sickly judgment, and disgust towards all the real business of life." Worse still, the outsized influence of imagination in the collective psyche threatened to level gendered distinctions: if men were assumed superior in the faculties of memory, reason, and judgment, "the province of imagination," as Judith Sargent Murray noted, had "long been surrendered" to women.[17]

But conservatives gave these general concerns over the perils of post-revolutionary imagination a politically potent spin. They hijacked the idiom of "common sense" from Paineite democrats and used it to paint their political enemies as delusional foes of traditional wisdom and impractical prophets of disorder. In so doing, they laid the foundation for what Sophia Rosenfeld has called a "populist critique of democracy, in the name of the people's common sense, that has existed on the underside of democratic politics in the West ever since."[18]

In the satires of Washington Irving, the Jeffersonian faith in free inquiry had ushered in "a pure unadulterated LOGOCRACY or *government of words*," ruled by orators, chatterers, and "slang-whangers." Popular enlightenment had done little more than breed popular discontent and make the people "avaricious after imaginary causes of lamentation."[19] David Everett, a law student and close friend of Lemuel Shaw, wrote a series of newspaper editorials to "introduce uniformity instead of whim," promote "steady habits," and defend a "common sense" opposed to the "writings of Thomas Paine and his deistical colleagues." True common sense was of "peaceable contented temper." A man of steady habits did not keep company with either "the undecided child of chance, who glides down to the grave, with the meanders of fashionable opinion" or "Speculators in ideas," who, "like land speculators," extend "their avaricious views beyond what is useful" and "monopolize the extensive tracts of theory." As to why something so common as sense and steady as habit needed encouragement at all, Everett explained, "There is no country that opens so wide a field for talents and ambition, as our own; and no place, where men experience a greater variety of changes in situation and employment. A frequent change of habits and opinions is of natural consequence. And exchange of a situation tolerably good, for another in itself preferable, is often an injury to him who makes it: And continual alterations of opinion commonly terminate in no opinion at all."[20]

While political conservatives associated the theory of involuntary opinion with dangerous Franco-Paineite radicalism, a more direct assault on the theory came from clergymen and theologians who viewed it as thoroughly amoral or, at the very least, incompatible with the tenets of evangelicalism, which, due to the Second Great Awakening of the early nineteenth century, had come to dominate most Protestant denominations. The evangelical insistence on a new birth, undertaken consciously and voluntarily at a particular moment in response to some measure of divine grace or influence, did not sit comfortably with the assertion that men and women were not responsible for their opinions. If belief was involuntary, what were devout Christians to make of heretics, infidels, and atheists? Why would God allow such persons to believe such things? When an American edition of Bailey's *Essays on the Formation and Publication of Opinions* appeared in 1831, a writer for the Presbyterian *Biblical Repertory and Theological Review* contended that "if men are in no case responsible for their belief or opinions, then there is no such thing as moral responsibility." While allowing that the American publishers and sellers of the *Essays* likely "had no idea that they were putting principles into circulation, the tendency of which is to subvert all sound morality," the reviewer warned that "reception of this doctrine would sanction every kind of persecution, and would open the flood gates to every species of vice— murder and robbery not excepted."[21]

The Reverend Edward Hall, a Rhode Island Unitarian, offered a more liberal perspective on the will to opine but ultimately agreed with the evangelicals. Hall sought a middle ground between two extremes. At one end stood "reasoners," who regarded opinion as "wholly involuntary, subject to no laws of our own making, to no influences which we can control, possessing no moral freedom, and therefore no moral character or responsibility." At the other extreme stood "the great body of Christians," who treated opinions as a form of conduct and for whom "soundness is better than sincerity" and "heresy is worse than immorality." Hall's pragmatic effort to reconcile these two positions anticipated William James's "Will to Believe" by nearly half a century: it was best for people to feel "in their hearts" that their opinions were not entirely involuntary, for this would encourage them to "do much" to "affect that which affects everything—opinion." More importantly, the power of public opinion in the present age demanded some sense of personal responsibility for opinion. Frequent invocations of "the power of opinion" (which Hall thought had become "a matter of wearisome repetition") testified to a "growing conviction of its importance to religion and society." To imagine such a power as "motionless and helpless, like so much dead matter," and "subject to every law but its own" seemed to deny any moral character to society, much less any meaningful or redemptive direction to history.[22]

In a rare instance of theological agreement, Catholics joined evangelical and liberal Protestants in their condemnation of the theory of involuntary opinion. Given Catholicism's emphasis on repentance and good works, this is not surprising; for Cardinal Newman, the theory exemplified "a chief error of the day"—the belief "that our true excellence comes not from within, but from without; not wrought out through personal struggles and sufferings, but following upon a passive exposure to influences over which we have no control."[23] Freethinkers and philosophic materialists such as the New York politician and attorney Thomas Herttell and the South Carolina academic Thomas Cooper continued to rest their arguments for a secular state and freedom of expression on the claim that opinions were "as involuntary and irresistible, as the thoughts from which they are derived."[24] But by the 1830s, such ideas had been pushed to the margins of acceptable discourse by political antiradicalism and a nondenominational Protestant consensus that, having accepted the disestablishment of state-funded churches, continued to advocate a "moral establishment" to promote Christianity and punish infidelity through Sabbatarian legislation, prosecutions for blasphemy, mandated readings from the Bible in public schools, and the exclusion of atheists (and in some states Jews and Catholics) from holding public office and testifying in courts of law. Outside the sphere of law and legislation, a rapidly expanding "benevolent empire" of reform societies aimed to combat infidelity, intemperance, indecency, and an array of other sins both mortal and venial.[25]

Straight for the Soul

The demise of the theory of involuntary opinion signaled a larger shift in the meaning of public opinion. Those who rejected revolutionary radicalism and "materialism," embraced a nondenominational Protestant "moral establishment," and hoped for the reform of manners and morals through revivalism and voluntary associations came to see public opinion as an indispensable instrument of social order and improvement. The relative novelty of this shift should not be overlooked. Spokespersons for the moral establishment imagined public opinion as something different, something more than the political voice of a sovereign people. They saw it as a force of coercion and restraint that could be shaped and directed by an organized minority of righteous and devout men and women seeking to reform public and private morals. Skeptical of political institutions and parties, they envisioned a public opinion that operated through benevolent societies, churches and congregations, revivals, religious publishers, and the force of moral suasion.

This is not to say that the Protestant moral establishment was an apolitical enterprise. Many of its charter members were Federalists who, after seeing their designs for a centralized nation-state scuttled by the Jeffersonian "Revolution" of 1800, redirected their energies and resources to cultural, religious, and phil-anthropic institutions that could cultivate a sense of common nationality and provide an anchor of religious truth and moral consensus in the rough seas of disestablishment, unrestrained theological speculation, and seemingly rampant infidelity.[26] In the aftermath of Jefferson's revolution, Lyman Beecher, a strident yet persuasive defender of Connecticut Congregationalism and Federalism, urged the righteous to form "moral societies" and suppress the rising tide of drinking, dueling, deism, and other vices. Individual righteousness stood power-less against the conspiratorial doings of the sinful, and "the opinion of many in-dividuals in their individual capacity, will avail but little." But "let that opinion be united and formally expressed, and its influence will be great." Once the weight of organized public opinion "laid upon a vicious practice" it would "most inevita-bly sink under it." Although Beecher would likely have preferred that the vicious reform their behavior through sincere Christian conviction, this was beyond the power of "moral societies." By correcting public sentiment, such societies would most likely reach those members of the "respectable class of the community" more influenced "by a regard to character and the public opinion" than "the fear of God and the principle of duty." Beecher aimed to apply the worldly pressure of public opinion in pursuit of more divine plans: the creation (or, in his view of history, re-creation) of a sacred order since lost to an age of democratic revolu-tion, disestablishment, and diversity of religious opinion.[27]

The redemption of individuals was, in Beecher's plan, left to revivals (although the reform of public morals might, he suspected, encourage visitations of the spirit.) Long-standing theological debates as to whether and to what extent gen-uine conversions could be brought about by individual agency and pastoral methods, while analogous to philosophical debates over the will to opine, gener-ated much more controversy. After a series of sensational revivals in western New

York, the "new measures" of lawyer-turned-evangelist Charles Grandison Finney came under intense clerical scrutiny. Critics objected to Finney's use of protracted meetings, his calling out names of the unconverted, his "anxious bench" for the interrogation of penitent, and, worst of all, the public praying of women. Though there was nothing really "new" in such measures (Baptists and Methodists had used them for decades), what troubled critics was how they invaded and upset the small politics of community and family life. Revivalists and their converts would "creep into the houses" of the unconverted and disrupt places of business. Finney prompted children and servants to report on the religiosity of their parents and masters. His "hard language" (Finney at one point exhorted a young Theodore Weld to "puke it up!") and the "audible groaning, violent gestures, and boisterous tones" of his audiences offended polite ministerial sensibilities, and frequent denunciations of "settled pastors" by itinerant evangelists and their converts terrified a good number of clergymen. In an 1827 letter on Finney's revivals, Lyman Beecher warned that "we are on the confines of universal misrule and moral desolation, and no time is to be lost in forestalling and holding public sentiment correctly, before the mass shall be put in motion by fierce winds, before which nothing can stand, and behind which, when they have swept over the land, nothing will remain."[28]

Finney defended his methods as appropriate to both the psychological constitution of man and the character of the times. There were too many excitements and other counteracting influences in society for a sober and reasonable religion to take hold. God had thus "found it necessary to take advantage of the excitability that is in mankind" to "lead them to obey," and the effective revivalist should follow suit. Until the millennium arrived, or until there was enough "religious principle in the world to put down irreligious excitements, it is in vain to promote religion, except by counteracting excitements." Worse still, Christianity had to compete against a "religion of public opinion." No genuine Christian, in Finney's estimation, came to religion from a "mere regard for reputation." The fear of "being considered fanatical" was too strong, and the "public sentiment of the world is all against God." It was thus "a first principle in religion, that ALL THE WORLD IS WRONG!" Only the ignorant and various sects of "FASHIONABLE CHRISTIANS" believed otherwise.[29]

Finney and other revivalists had reasons to feel embattled. Critics of revival methods could be found in almost every denomination and across a wide spectrum of theological persuasions. While Perry Miller's assertion that the "dominant theme" in antebellum intellectual history was "the invincible persistence of the revival technique" overstated the case, debates over revivalism informed larger understandings of mass psychology in ways that contemporary scholarship rarely acknowledges, exposing a deep ambivalence toward democracy. If the revival exemplified the "democratization of American Christianity," it could also illustrate how democracy rendered individuals susceptible to new and powerful methods of persuasion and social pressure. Critics attacked camp meetings and the "New Measures" for their use of excessive emotion and enthusiasm, which threatened to turn worship into just another amusement and to lead people to seek ever more sensational religious thrills from radical sects, cults, and sundry spiritual quacks. They blasted the theatricality of revivalists, at times likening it to Roman Catholic "priestcraft." They warned that the disrespect for order, tradition, and decorum would foster anarchy in both the churches and the state. Some even argued that revivals posed a threat to religious liberty. Calvin Colton (who converted from Presbyterianism to Episcopalianism out of disgust over the "new measures") allowed that the hearts of revival converts had been "subdued to God," but their "minds" had been *broken down by man*," and a "mind reduced to such bondage" could "never afterward be free."[30]

To be sure, "anti-revivalism" (like the anti-partyism discussed in chapter 3) encompasses a wide array of critics, some favorably disposed to revivals but wary of excesses, others more inclined to dismiss the practice as fundamentally misguided. Colton, for example, started out as a supporter of revivals, whereas Lyman Beecher had, by 1831, come to accept the New Measures, sensing perhaps that his squabbles with Finney had only served to strengthen their common "Fashionable Christian" opponents, also known as "Unitarians." Having jettisoned "supernatural" beliefs in the divinity of Christ, the corporeality of God, and the material operations of the Holy Spirit, Unitarians did not need to parse out the respective roles of human and divine agency in revivals. Believing with Channing (insofar as Unitarians believed together) that God approached man "as a pure intelligence, an unmixed and indefinite Mind," they could steer clear of the old vexing Edwardsean conundrums regarding free will and divine agency and judge revivals on psychological, social, and political grounds.[31] Unitarians and their liberal-minded allies repeatedly charged that the new "system" of revivals could only work to "enslave" the human mind. Writing in the guise of an "English Traveler," Orville Dewey reported on the manifold ways revivals set into motion "plans and combinations for getting possession of the public mind" and "operating upon" individual minds. Indeed, the "whole system of Revivals" appeared to reduce religion "into a set of passive impressions." Revival preachers induced feelings that were "not active, nor self-wrought" and thus neither "effectual" nor "habitual." And in many instances, awakenings had less to do with genuine religious conviction or feeling than a desire to conform and a fear of ostracism. In this regard, Dewey proposed that "there never was a people in the world who had less true religious freedom of thought and feeling, than the congregation over whom this brooding incubus of a Revival has settled itself heavily down."[32]

Attacking the new system of revivals also afforded Unitarians another opportunity to take a few shots at Calvinism. In theory, Calvinist doctrines of divine sovereignty and unconditional election did not appear consistent with anxious benches and laughing exercises. But in practice, the harsh austerity of the doctrine invariably led to the orgiastic excesses of the revival. For James Walker, clergyman, professor of moral philosophy, and future president of Harvard, the Calvinist revival functioned as an "opiate to the consciences" of the lazy and the improvident. Convince them that grace was awarded solely by divine arbitrary fiat, and they would naturally allow "their passions to be acted on and wrought up to any pitch" by some peripatetic shouter and submit to his peculiar tenets "as a substitute for plain practical religion—to anything that shall relieve them from the difficult and endless task of establishing and preserving an upright character."[33]

Appalled by the intrusive excesses of the revival, and uncomfortable with the harsh denunciatory practices of reform societies, liberal clergy and their congregants often fell back on the vague hope of exerting some form of moral "influence." In a discussion of the growing presence of Roman Catholicism in America, Channing pondered these problems with his distinctive mix of liberal optimism, candid curiosity, and conservative cautiousness. Catholicism posed no genuine threat to America, for it stood motionless against the progress of civilization and the diffusion of knowledge. Although some might fall prey to their ostensibly time-honored claims of infallibility, the only real advantage Catholics held in their war with Protestant sects was the confessional, an instrument "much more powerful" than the Protestant pulpit or revival, for it gave the Catholic priest special "access to the individual mind" and the "secrets" of the laity's "hearts." Insisting that "nothing too bad" could be said of the confessional, Channing then went on to wonder whether Protestant ministers might find some other point of entry into the hearts and minds of their parishioners. Sermonizing alone could no longer suffice, for "the press now preaches incomparably more than the pulpit." Even women, when unable to speak in church, could "speak from the printing room." The diffusion of knowledge and the march of mind might in the end prove no less friendly to the Protestant pulpit than it had been to the Catholic papacy: "I imagine that our present religious organizations will slowly melt away, and that hierarchies will be found no more necessary for religion than for literatures, science, medicine, law, or the elegant and useful arts. But I will check these imaginings."[34]

Catharine Beecher also addressed the growing Catholic presence in America, and the contrast is instructive. While Channing could only (and half-heartedly) advise opposing Catholicism by preaching, Beecher looked to institutions. Although Beecher agreed that the great principle of Protestantism was "INDEPENDENCE OF MIND," she bemoaned the "dangerous extreme" to which it had recently been taken and asserted that it worked to the advantage of the Roman Church. Religious inquirers driven to doubt and distraction by the multitude of Protestant sects and creeds would increasingly seek refuge in the "infallible priestly dictation" of Catholicism. Only the "preventive benevolence" of a "right system of mental training" taught in Protestant common schools and academies could counter the Catholic Church and its expanding network of parochial schools.[35]

Although not anti-institutional to the same degree as many transcendentalists and radical abolitionists, a persistent suspicion toward institutions accounts for much of what Channing and his liberal colleagues had to say about public and individual opinion.[36] Channing's 1830 Election Sermon—perhaps the first significant discussion of the "despotism of public opinion" in American literature—may be read as a template for much of what was subsequently said on the subject. Standing before an assembly of state officials, Channing called attention to a "deeper" foundation of public prosperity than constitutions and political administration: "Inward, Spiritual Freedom." The "highest end" of man was "indefinite spiritual progress," and political relations were but a means toward that end: "the individual is not made for the state, so much as the state for the individual." Thus the chief purpose of free institutions was to promote free minds that rose above sensual and material concerns, guarded their "intellectual rights and powers," were not "passively formed by outward circumstances," and did "not cower to human opinion." Unfortunately, the present age made these tasks increasingly difficult:

> The advantages of civilization have their peril. In such a state of society, opinion and law impose salutary restraint, and produce general order and security. But the power of opinion grows into a despotism, which, more than all things, represses original and free thought, subverts individuality of character, reduces the community to a spiritless monotony, and chills the love of perfection. Religion, considered simply as the principle, which balances the power of human opinion, which takes man out of the grasp of custom and fashion, and teaches

him to refer himself to a higher tribunal, is an infinite aid to moral strength and elevation.

This religious principle had much to contend with. The "slavish love of lucre" and the division of labor, which condemned many minds to "an unceasing round of petty operations," distracted men from higher things. Religion itself, organized into hostile sects, squelched freedom of mind. "One of the strongest features of our times," Channing noted, "is the tendency of men to run into associations, to lose themselves in masses, to think and act in crowds, to act from the excitement of numbers, to sacrifice individuality," and to "identify themselves with parties and sects."[37]

Channing's liberal colleagues echoed these themes. Associations artificially magnified the already overwhelming power of public opinion and enabled the "timid and faint-hearted" to lose themselves in the crowd. Party politics in general, and political newspapers in particular, exacted an oppressive toll on individual conscience. Even without these formal organizations, public opinion found a way to go, as Alexis de Tocqueville famously put it, "straight for the soul." In public opinion, the Unitarian Henry Ware saw

> a tyrant, sitting in the dark, wrapped up and vague terrors of obscurity; deriving power no one knows from whom; like an Asian monarch, unapproachable, unimpeachable, undethronable, perhaps illegitimate, but irresistible in its power to quell thought, to repress action, to silence conviction,—and bringing the timid perpetually under an unworthy bondage of mean fear to some impostor opinion, some noisy judgment which gets astride on the popular breath for a day, and controls, through the lips of impudent folly, the speech and actions of the wise.

American public opinion, in Orville Dewey's curious formulation, was "the aggregate of universal opinion," a force that pressed against individuals on every side while leaving them "unconscious of its power." Men (and only men—Dewey thought women to naturally "susceptible" to the influence of public opinion) had to train themselves to become aware of its subtle power. Like Theodore Parker, they had to become aware of the way in which the opinions of other men "fool me away from myself, and divulse me from my soul," how "public opinion takes my free mind out of me."[38]

What are we to make of such anxieties over the "despotism" of public opinion and the corresponding preoccupation with the integrity of individual opinion? To be sure, what the French sociologist Pierre Bourdieu has called the "petit-bourgeois pretension to 'personal opinion'" tends to be pronounced among "individuals whose whole past and whole projected future are oriented towards individual salvation, based on personal 'gifts' and 'merits,'" and who privilege the "private and the intimate, both at work and at home, in leisure and in thought," over "the public, the collective, the common, the indifferent, the borrowed." It is not surprising that having opinions became more important during a period that social historians have long identified with the formation of an urban middle class characterized by nonmanual work for men and "domesticity" for women.[39] While middle-class culture certainly laid heavy emphasis on "personal opinion," we should be careful not to think of it as an exclusively bourgeois preoccupation. Talk of the despotism of pubic opinion and its dangers to the moral and mental independence of individuals could easily find its way into the discourse of the wealthy or the working classes. Free African Americans certainly felt the force of public opinion arrayed against them and worried extensively over how it diminished men and women's self-worth. In almost every corner of antebellum American society, the growing power of public opinion appeared to foster widespread insincerity and hypocrisy that could ultimately lead the unreflective to lose their sense of self.

Phrenology Surveys the Public Mind

For many antebellum moralists, the key to preserving the autonomy and integrity of the self lay in what William Ellery Channing called "self-culture," something more commonly referred to as the formation of "character." Alongside the expected list of virtues—honesty, sobriety, thrift, decency—having opinions appeared as an essential element of character. The act of freeing "ourselves from the power of human opinion and example, except as far as this is sanctioned by our own deliberate judgment" was, for Channing, an "important means of self-culture." In spiritual matters, the equation of freedom with solitude and privacy became even more pronounced. For Ware, the formation of a genuinely Christian character required persons to "be free from the interference of every human mind," to accept no "secondary knowledge," and to become "as absolutely subjected to God as they are freed from man."[40]

This was by any measure an exacting, if not unattainable, standard for sincere conviction, religious or otherwise. Fortunately, less demanding and more ostensibly practical programs for self-culture became available, and they focused on the human body and the materiality of thought and character. In August 1832, the celebrated Austrian phrenologist Johann Gaspar Spurzheim arrived in the

United States, hoping to find a receptive audience for his scientific philosophy of mind. Phrenology originated from the late-eighteenth-century researches of Viennese anatomist Franz Joseph Gall, who hypothesized that the functions of the brain were localized. He assigned particular propensities ("murder" and "theft," for example) to twenty-seven distinct organs of the brain and argued that their relative influence on an individual's character could be determined by measuring corresponding bumps on the surface of the skull. Spurzheim, his favorite pupil, coined the term "phrenology" (or "mind discourse") and contributed a more elegant nomenclature to the whole scheme: "murder" became "destructiveness"; "theft," "acquisitiveness." Teacher and student ventured across Europe to promote their findings, eventually settling in Paris. When differences surfaced between the two in 1813, Spurzheim relocated to Britain, discovered eight more organs, gained innumerable converts, and issued a steady stream of publications, many of which had found their way to American bookshelves before his arrival.[41] But his American tour would be brief: after several demanding months of public lectures, social calls, and school, asylum, and prison inspections throughout the Northeast, he took ill and died. Over 3,000 Bostonians turned out for his funeral, which included the singing of a special "Ode to Spurzheim," a eulogy by Charles Follen, and the laying of a headstone in the new Mount Auburn Cemetery. But there was no head beneath the stone: Spurzheim's skull had, appropriately enough, been donated to Harvard Medical School.[42]

Spurzheim's untimely death ignited widespread interest in phrenology, especially among young members of (or aspirants to) to the middling and professional classes who, faced with agonizing choices among possible careers and mates, proved particularly receptive to a science that promised to read aptitude and character. For example, when the Amherst College Debating Society assigned Henry Ward Beecher to argue a case against phrenology, Orson Squire Fowler won Beecher over to his side. Looking back on the debate years later, Beecher remained firm in his conviction that phrenology was "far more useful, practical, and sensible than any other system of mental philosophy which has yet evolved." Laying questions of its scientific validity to the side, the most famous preacher of his time insisted that phrenology had at the very least "introduced mental philosophy to the common people."[43]

After graduating from Amherst College in 1834, Orson Fowler and his brother Lorenzo went on to found the most successful phrenological firm in the United States. Had the Fowlers attempted such an enterprise ten years earlier, they would have probably failed. But by 1834, the communications and transportations "revolutions" had achieved critical mass. New printing technologies, cheaper paper, and more cost-effective means of marketing and distribution conspired to create a mass market for the "popular" reader. The proliferation of lyceums and mechanic's institutes, improved roads, and the growth of rail travel led to the emergence of a profitable lecture circuit, where luminaries like Emerson shared the podium with phrenologists, temperance speakers, water-cure advocates, and sundry curiosities.[44] The Fowlers and other commercial science entrepreneurs exploited these new means of organization and persuasion with the methodical energy of a revivalist. Champions of the rapid diffusion of "practical" knowledge, they marketed other promising new educational technologies. For example, they took keen interest in "phonography," a system of shorthand that promised a shortcut to literacy for poor laborers and slaves.[45]

The rapid diffusion of phrenological texts and lecturers in the 1830s thus appeared as something novel, unprecedented, and, for critics of phrenology, alarming. In a scathing 1834 review of Spurzheim's work, Frederic Henry Hedge reported that "heads of chalk, inscribed with mystic numbers, disfigured every mantelpiece" and a "general inspection and registry of heads took place." Phrenology "obtained a speedy and signal triumph, and all the higher principles of our nature were in danger of being entombed in the little *tumuli* of the brain."[46] Years later, Hedge immodestly claimed that his attack on phrenology marked the first distinctive expression of New England transcendentalism. But many transcendentalists took a more charitable view of phrenology. Theodore Parker thought its popularity did much to weaken the "power of the old supernaturalism" and inspired Americans to "study the constitution of man more wisely than before." While put off by the coarse and "impudent knowingness" of phrenologists, Emerson believed the science had "much truth in it. It felt connection, where the professors denied it, and proved it by modifying the language, and forcing its phraseology into universal use."[47] Indeed, the influence of phrenological language and ideas on nineteenth-century writers and artists—Walt Whitman, Edgar Allan Poe, Harriet Beecher Stowe, Lydia Maria Child, Sarah Josepha Hale, Herman Melville, William Rimmer, Hiram Powers, and William Sidney Mount, to name but a few—has been extensively documented.[48]

At first glance, phrenology seems antithetical to romanticism: a deterministic, materialistic, reductive, and brazenly empirical science of bumps that strip-mined the deep mysteries of mind with charts, measuring tape, and calipers. Indeed, numerous antiphrenologists made such arguments. But in the main, phrenology is better understood as a species of romantic morphology, built as it was on the key romantic doctrine of correspondence between matter and spirit. Phrenology was also a science of individuality, revealing to every man and woman a mental and moral composition as unique in its infinite combinations and gradations as a fingerprint. Of course, such revelations came with a small fee. Phrenology was what James Secord has called a "commercial science." Its rapid emergence casts light on some significant ways that democratization and the market revolution conspired to upset and redefine the meaning of scientific practice, intellectual authority, and "mind" itself. Democratic resentments against "aristocratic" monopolies of knowledge upset inherited equations of scientific inquiry with the "disinterested" scientific pursuits of gentlemen. When married to the tangible opportunities presented by the market and communications revolutions, scientific enterprise opened itself to venturesome men (and, to a lesser but notable degree, women) whose teachings resonated with the anxieties and aspirations of their customers. Phrenologists and mesmerists marketed their wares to a nascent middle class ready to lay down their dollars in protest against aristocracy, partisanship, feckless "theoretical" speculation, and the tyrannies of majority opinion and fashion.[49]

Academic and professional elites initially greeted phrenology with approval or, at worst, ambivalence. Channing wrote a British correspondent to solicit her opinion on the recently deceased Spurzheim. While Channing thought him "eminently liberal in his views," some passages in his lectures had been used "to press him into the ranks of Calvinism." Channing's confusion is understandable: phrenology could easily appear to argue that biology is destiny, and its enumeration of "bad" faculties mirrored Calvinist notions of innate depravity. But most phrenologists insisted that self-knowledge was power and that a phrenological reading offered a road map for self-improvement.[50]

The confusion quickly settled, and the majority of academics and clergy rallied to the standard of antiphrenology. The *North American Review* warned readers against a mental philosophy no different from the "infidel" materialism of Voltaire, Diderot, and Thomas Paine. Phrenology blasted all notions of moral responsibility, advancing doctrines that depended "more upon the imagination than the judgment of their disciples." Like most American academics, the *Review* advised its readers to hold fast to the sound principles of Scots moral sense philosophy. Orestes Brownson, who had rejected Scots philosophy as materialist and infidel and embraced the romantic psychology of Samuel Taylor Coleridge and Victor Cousin, warned his readers that the phrenologist "recognizes no self, no ME, but some thirty or forty faculties that have no common spiritual center." Christianity rested on the fundamental virtue of ascetic self-denial, and phrenology offered no self to deny. Brownson stood on firmer philosophical ground.

Phrenologists could easily reply that their conception of moral responsibility was no different than that proffered by the Scots commonsense philosophers. If anything, phrenology had simply made legible the faculties enumerated by Scots metaphysicians. Indeed, 70 percent of the "organs" that Spurzheim "discovered" had already been named as distinctive "faculties" by Scots moralists.[51]

For these reasons, the debate between phrenologists and their opponents represented less a clash of incommensurable scientific theories than a debate about the relationship between science, commerce, and the public. Yet even this may be too charitable a characterization. Contestants traded personal aspersions at a high volume. When not blasted as infidels, phrenologists stood accused of "the most pitiful facts of deception" and were branded as "public nuisances" who "filch from every town, hundreds of thousands of dollars." Antiphrenologists supplemented such ad hominem attacks with copious personal endorsements. It was not uncommon for authors to append notices to their books, but Thomas Sewall's *Two Lectures on Phrenology* stands out: ten pages of antiphrenological diatribes from the likes of John Quincy Adams, Daniel Webster, John McLean, and the *North American Review*. The "pretensions" of phrenology were, by contrast, petit bourgeois pretensions, its converts drawn largely from the ranks of those "that have risen a trifle above the vulgar in knowledge" and now wished to impose on the credulity of "their former associates." As Emerson dryly remarked: "*Le Bourgeois Gentilhomme* delights to classify."[52]

Phrenologists happily conceded that their constituency was not built of "college lumber." Their publications invariably described the audiences for phrenology lectures as "respectable" folk drawn from all the productive classes: young clerks, improving artisans, concerned mothers, and sturdy Christian farmers seeking education and self-culture. Who would mock such a gathering? Who would continue to defend the useless metaphysical theories propounded from college lecterns and pulpits?

> The men in our towns, upon whose opinions (in matters of supposed discoveries) the least reliance should be placed, are the very men most listened to, namely, the middle-aged professional men of the place. The present system of collegiate and professional instruction is calculated, in and of itself, to trammel the minds of pupils—to make them move within prescribed orbits, not to expand them, and prepare them to perceive and love universal truth. I would not condemn every lawyer, and doctor, and minister; but, as a class, those commonly called learned men are generally half a century behind the age, in all discoveries, in all forward advances in society.[53]

In contrasting the narrow minds and provincial authority of local professionals with the universal advance of society and the diffusion of knowledge through the popular podium and press, phrenologists frequently invoked statistics. Like the emerging penny press, phrenological publications made much of their circulation and sales statistics. (Fowler's vehicle topped 50,000 by the late 1840s.) Along the same lines, in 1836, British botanist and phrenologist Hewett Watson published his compilation of *Statistics of Phrenology*, an exhaustive survey of publication data, periodical subscriptions, and society membership rolls. American versions soon followed. Antiphrenologists appealed to authorities, phrenologists appealed to numbers. Hewett Watson is today better known (insofar as he is known at all) as one of the first authors of a statistical rationale for randomly sampled public opinion surveys.[54]

Starting from a desire to make the mysteries of the individual mind measurable and legible, phrenologists soon sought to do the same for the public mind. Letters and numbers offered ready access to the secrets of nature: the masthead of the *American Phrenological Almanac* informed its readers that "Nature's Printing Press is Man, her types are Signs, her books are Actions." Harriet Beecher Stowe likened phrenological terminology to "algebraic signs in numbers." By "demonstrating the primary faculties of the mind and their relations," Elisha Bartlett declared that phrenology

> rendered intelligible the infinite variety of thought and action in individuals. Extending the same principles from the individual to the race—from the one person, thinking and acting to-day, to the many hundreds or millions of like persons, thinking and acting at any time, and all times, in the past—it solves the riddle of history—it interprets the great events of the time. Beautifully unfolding itself in the process of this interpretation, we shall find, everywhere, Law. Chance disappears, and we see that, throughout all that multitudinous thought and action of humanity . . . there [is] nothing fortuitous, nothing accidental, nothing anomalous.[55]

If "character"—a word both typographical and psychological—could be read, the practical and political utility of phrenology was clear. To demonstrate this, the phrenological press devoted considerable space to cranial profiles of prominent political and cultural figures. Not surprisingly, Webster's impressive head garnered rave reviews, and the crania of Henry Clay and John Calhoun passed phrenological muster. The skulls of the founders comprised a virtual Golgotha of greatness. Applying the same standards, the propensities of less eminent politicos could be readily assessed: "Ye liberty-lovers! study Phrenology. But, until you do, take a hint from one who has studied it: Get close behind your candidates while they are shouting freedom from the caucus-stump, and if the back of their heads keeps your zenith out of sight, then you may respond, 'Fiddle-stick!' for they are merely playing on the popular chords; they don't care a squeak for anything but their own music and the coppers that may be coming: the people are mere catgut to them."[56] Phrenological lectures dramatized the power of head reading. After a brief discourse on the principles and utility of their science, phrenologists often challenged their audiences to produce subjects of particularly inscrutable character. Some even offered to conduct examinations blindfolded. When the residents of Worcester County, Massachusetts presented "Dick Williams," a "dirty-looking man covered in coal and soot," phrenologist Nelson Sizer determined that he was "one of God's noble men." An "Esquire Jones," followed, and Sizer concluded, as politely as he could, that he found the gentleman both morally and mentally decrepit. "Dick Williams" was, in truth, Esquire Jones, an esteemed local judge; "Esquire Jones" was really Dick Williams, village idiot.[57]

Tales in which the traps set by skeptical locals are avoided and the truth of phrenology vindicated were a staple of phrenological folklore. While reassuringly demonstrating (at least in this case) that the natural order was in fact the social order, such tales also identified scientific authority with the act of reading. Implicitly rejecting long-standing conceptions of science as a heroic "hunt" for the "secrets of nature," phrenology redefined science as an everyday activity, the equivalent of opening the morning newspaper. Indeed, popular interest in phrenology peaked at a moment when, as David Henkin has argued, print assumed a new and confounding cultural authority. Phrenology coincided with the appearance of penny newspapers and the wide circulation of paper money and offered solutions comparable to those promised by "independent journalism" and counterfeit detectors, allowing the informed reader to more safely navigate the dodgy landscapes of politics, commerce, and society. Phrenologists stressed the practical applications of reading character. Businessmen could better assess prospective employees, partners, customers, lenders, and borrowers. Lawyers could better select and read juries. Protestant preachers could use phrenology to assess the character of a congregant in ways superior, as Henry Ward Beecher argued, to the Catholic confessional.[58]

Phrenology claimed particular relevance to the cause of education and its reform. Emerson surmised that its chief value was "not as a science but as a criticism on the Church and School of the day." Phrenologists railed against the teaching of "useless" classical languages in colleges and criticized the Lancasterian (or "monitorial") system in common schools as insensitive to the individuality of students. Horace Mann enlisted phrenology in his pleas for education reform, praising the science for its "analytical knowledge of the faculties of the human mind" and contrasting it to literary and metaphysical "works of the imagination," which "assumed the existence of spiritual laws such as man never knew." Phrenology also provided critics of the revival with fresh ammunition. Samuel Gridley Howe used the science of criticize the strong and damaging excitements aroused by revivalists. Other phrenologists cited the high rates of "religious insanity" in revival-struck communities to call for a more sober and scientific Christianity.[59]

Phrenology attracted many religious "come-outers," and a good number of other souls wearied and confounded by the proliferation of sects and revivalist excitements. Consider Deiadamia Chase of Cortland, New York. Profoundly distressed by the "rancor and hypocrisy of churches," and alienated by her husband's baffling devotion to Millerism, she "found the food for which her soul had so long hungered" in the pages of the Scots phrenologist George Combe's *The Constitution of Man*. A "lifetime agency" from the Fowler brothers followed, and with it came the attendant knowledge of homeopathy, mesmerism, water cures, temperance, and Graham crackers sufficient to practice medicine in Michigan. And a successful practice it was: in the cholera epidemic of 1848, she won over a prejudiced "public opinion" by killing far fewer patients than the local (male) practitioners of "heroic" medicine.[60]

Such were the narratives of phrenological progress: the power of practical, inductive science, communicated through the medium of print, discredits academic, religious, and medical orthodoxies and embarrasses the pretensions of social (and, every now and then, gendered) hierarchies. If there is a common nemesis here, it is "public opinion," a crude amalgam of mindless prejudice, local oligarchy, newspaper politics, and partisan wire pulling. Accordingly, phrenologists valorized individual opinion. "Call no man lord over your opinions," Fowler counseled. "Why is not the deliberate opinion of a private citizen as good as that of a king, provided both are equally informed, talented, and moral?" The reason why, one could object, is that the private citizen can only deliberate publicly. Not so with phrenologists, who imagined "Debates in Cranium," deliberative assemblies in which arguments between "amativeness" and "philopropogenitiveness" rose to levels of eloquence surpassing Webster and Hayne.[61] One journal reported on a subject who had been mesmerized to debate the topic "public opinion" with himself:

Approbation: "If I believe this what will my friends say, and, what will the public
  think? I had better wait till public opinion turns in its favor."
Self-Esteem: "I don't care for public opinion."
Combativeness: "I'll defend it."

Better this imaginary, solipsistic exercise, Fowler implied, than the realities of
partisan politics, in which men "submitted like whipped spaniels, and even lick
the hand which brandishes the rod in their faces! Fools and cowards all! Have you
no wills, no souls, no opinions of your own!"[62]

Phrenology gave its adherents the tools to understand, shape, and read character. But did this "technology of the self" work? Or did phrenology fail to deliver, as Brownson argued, a self, a "ME"? If "self" means a deep and mysterious
yet wholly integrated sense of personal identity accessible only through painful
and rigorous introspection, it certainly did not. But phrenology did give people
an embodied self: its emergence was part of a burgeoning popular interest in
physiology and health, interests once again identified as "middle class."[63] Phrenology also gave its believers a way of talking about themselves in a more accessible and "middling" language than that found in philosophy books. And, as "debates in crania" suggest, phrenology gave people a way of reflecting on their
characters and opinions. This was Emerson's point: phrenology diffused its terminology, but it did not alter commonsense understandings of will and moral
responsibility.[64]

Phrenology and other commercial sciences of mind posited a self more malleable and receptive to methodical, "scientific" manipulation. After 1840, phrenology became increasingly intermingled with various doctrines and practices
of mesmerism. Phreno-mesmerism, a "new demonstrative school of metaphysics," resulted. On its own, mesmerism was merely a science of "sympathy"; when
combined with phrenological truths, it became a science of "impressibility," a
technology of control in which "the will of the magnetizer became the law of the
magnetized."[65] Impressibility, "the power of being affected by surrounding influences," represented the "widest field for the exploration of science," revealing
truths perhaps "too grand and incredible to be recognized by the people of the
present time." But not for long: the "progress of the human race in education and
refinement," Joseph Buchanan theorized, increased this power. As this "susceptibility to delicate and impalpable agencies" became more general, "society would
be more harmonious" and "public opinion would be more unanimous." Such
Lamarckian evolutionary theories were quite common in the literature of pre-
Darwinian mental science. Believing (conveniently) that less civilized races had

smaller cranial capacities, phrenologists assumed that Anglo-Saxon brains would expand still more with the progress of civilization and that larger brains would lead to greater social and political harmony.[66]

Phreno-mesmeric demonstrations suggested as much, appearing to open a doorway to a universal spirit of the age. Magnetized subjects underwent remarkable transformations. They sang and spoke in foreign languages. Men became women, whites became blacks, and vice versa. One white male subject was induced to deliver "a patriotic Indian effusion, denouncing the white man's oppression." Yet in practice such demonstrations simply reinforced extant hierarchies. Phreno-mesmerists agreed that the women and uneducated young men were the most easily magnetized subjects. Fearful that a public audience might compromise the susceptibility of their subjects, phreno-mesmerists often conducted "private" demonstrations for local juries of public figures and journalists. And so we find Democratic editors William Cullen Bryant and John L. O'Sullivan sitting in a private apartment in 1843 while Dr. Joseph Buchanan (who had just invented the new science of "neurology") conducts a series of experiments on Mrs. R., a "lady of intelligence and respectability." When Buchanan excited her organs of self-esteem, combativeness, and firmness, she proceeded to argue that "she was qualified for a higher station in life than she had occupied, and that she possessed intellectual powers sufficient to exert a controlling influence over public opinion." Having heard enough, Buchanan instructed his assistant to excite her organs of humility and relaxation. She promptly dropped the subject. Buchanan then magnetized Mr. M., a "workingman." He quickly launched into a "harangue against party politics and party editors, advising Mr. Bryant to confine his attention to literature."[67]

The "Great Mesmeric Mania" reached its peak in 1850. In February of that year, six members of the U.S. Senate, among them Daniel Webster and Henry Clay, summoned John Bovee Dodds, the "inventor" of "electrical psychology" to Washington to reveal his sensational scientific discoveries in a series of lectures. Or so he claimed. Though I have found no hard evidence that Webster and Clay did in fact invite Dodds, much less attend his lectures, they had reasons to do so.[68] After all, Clay's Omnibus Compromise bill—the Compromise of 1850—had just been introduced. Could the science of impressibility come to its aid? There is a famous engraving of Clay speaking on behalf of the bill. In it, he appears to have mesmerized the Senate.

Or is Clay simply charismatic? By 1850, it had become difficult to tell the difference. In many respects, popular sciences of mind engaged in what Max Weber once called "the routinization of charisma" (though Weber had different things in mind). Popular mental scientists staged seemingly magical demonstrations of discernment into the character, and power over the wills, of their subjects and then offered (for a small fee) to share their knowledge and technique. Their publications claimed to explain how the charisma of the preacher and the politician *really* worked.[69] Much of this was, of course, "humbug." But humbug was a democratic, middle-class art, perpetrating frauds and impostures while inviting the audience to detect them. Moreover, the humbugs of mesmerism had, as all effective humbugs do, some truth in them. "Orthodox" scientists had begun to uncover and manipulate layers of unconscious nervous reflexes in the human psyche. Their findings, as Alison Winter has argued, led to new understandings of "consensus," both biological and social. In the former sense, "consensus" simply referred to unconscious coordination between mind and body. In the latter sense, "people would become part of a consensus, healthily coordinated with each other, immune to dangerous influences yet sensitive to proper leadership."[70]

While willing to tolerate the "impudent knowingness" of the phrenologist, Emerson viewed the mesmerist with alarm and disgust. The prophet of self-reliance saw mesmerism as a lazy attempt to cheat nature and "raise the state of man to rare and transcendent degrees." The mesmerist robbed his subjects of their autonomy, their selves, their opinions, and, worst of all, their consciousness of being robbed. His art was an illiberal humbug: it did not allow subjects to actively participate in their own deception. Emerson's aversion to mesmerism is in these respects a nineteenth-century equivalent of present-day anxieties over the narcotic effects of mass media.[71] Like Emerson, we are not Stoics. We cherish a self that is receptive to social influences without being subject to them. Modernity has often been characterized as "self-reflexive." This is one way of saying that modernity is rife with humbugs, shot through with the ceaseless and pervasive influences of the commercial marketplace and the mass media, cluttered with technologies and techniques for molding opinions. Antebellum Americans wrestled with the problem of how to form reflective selves and opinions in such an environment, and they did so in ways that resonate with our own efforts to do the same. It is important to have opinions, and it is difficult.

CHAPTER 5

The Fatal Force of Public Opinion

Public opinion! How shall I describe that invisible guardian of honor—
that eagle eyed spy on human actions—that inexorable judge of men
and manners—that arbiter, whom tears cannot appease, nor ingenuity
soften—and from whose terrible decisions there is no appeal?

—*William Crafts, Jr., "An Oration on the Influence
of Moral Causes on National Character" (1817)*

In addition to diffusing useful and interesting knowledge, publishing legislative proceedings and government records, and organizing political parties, antebellum American newspapers functioned as a staging ground for violence. Nearly half of the duels fought between 1787 and 1860 involved newspaper editors. Add to that sum affairs brought to a point of honor by newspaper articles, and it can be safely said that journalism was the favored muse of the antebellum duelist. Newspaper offices were also a frequent target of mobs, and the location of countless other incidents of battery, gunplay, and mayhem. The much-vaunted American "march of mind," it would seem, was as much a military as a civil procession. Colorful tales of horsewhipped printers, pistol-packing editors, and pugilistic paperboys were a staple of nineteenth-century literature. Yet surprisingly few of these stories depicted newspaper combat as a grave danger to press freedom or an affront to norms of rational, civilized discourse. Unlike today, violence against (and by) the press was a familiar and frequently accepted feature of the political landscape.

If a man took personal offense to harsh words in the public prints, he could physically attack or demand honorable satisfaction from the responsible party. Even if he committed murder—and actually went to trial for it—he had good reason to anticipate acquittal from a jury of his peers. With the aid of an adept attorney, he could claim that "public opinion" had compelled him to shed blood.

Based on research into over 150 duels, assaults, and affrays involving newspaper editors, contributors, and readers, this chapter scrutinizes that claim. The use of violence to protect the honor of public men and police the boundaries of public discourse was not an aberrant exception to the otherwise peaceful rule of public opinion. Sentiments of honor and practices of violence were in many respects essential to American understandings of public opinion. A common presumption that there could be no public opinion without honorable public men to articulate it made the maintenance of honor an essential prerequisite of representative government and deliberative democracy. But a reticence to protect personal honor through courts or legislation (the course taken in many European and Latin American nations) left American men at liberty to pursue their own violent, self-help remedies.[1]

It would be impossible to understand what public opinion meant to antebellum Americans without taking into account that unstable compound of ideas, emotions, desires, and rituals known as "honor." For William Crafts Jr., a Harvard-educated South Carolina lawyer, poet, and newspaper editor, public opinion was first and foremost an "invisible guardian of honor" that (when properly enlightened) rewarded virtue and punished vice with irresistible force and irrevocable finality.[2] This "public opinion" was something more than an aggregate of privately held opinions, and something quite different from the political voice of a sovereign people that emanated from a public sphere of communication and deliberation. These varieties of public opinion changed with the times and were susceptible to reform. The public opinion that guarded honor was resistant to change, and it compelled men and women to obey its dictates or suffer shame and ostracism. This, at least, was the theory. In reality, antebellum Americans never managed to devise a stable conception of honor for public opinion to enforce. The leveling impulses of democracy and evangelical religion made traditional notions of honor appear "aristocratic" and unchristian, while a deeply partisan political culture eroded restraints against attacking the honesty and dignity of public figures. To be sure, differences between Southern and Northern conceptions of honor became increasingly evident as political tensions between the sections intensified. But Southerners and Northerners continued to agree that newspapers posed the greatest danger to the reputations and "usefulness" of public men.

This chapter begins with an analysis of the peculiar configuration of economic circumstances, political practices, and social animosities that set the stage for newspaper violence. A close reading of a particular case—the 1840 St. Louis homicide trial of William P. Darnes for killing a newspaper editor—illustrates how anxieties over the power of the press to destroy reputations could be used to excuse such violence as necessary, if not involuntary, responses compelled by the force of public opinion. The final third of the chapter examines the how the relationship between newspapers, honor, and violence went in different directions in the North and South after 1840, and how this schism contributed to increasingly divergent conceptions of public opinion.

Why the Fighting Editor Fought

Acts or threats of violence against the press are today roundly denounced as something more than attacks on individuals; they are assaults on "our" civil liberties. The body of the journalist has in this way come to embody our abstract constitutional rights. It can perform such a metonymic function because "the media" (tellingly, a term now acceptable to use in the singular) is seen as a distinct institution, a "fourth estate." But no such "press" existed in the antebellum mind; Americans "seemed to view the press as an extension of other institutions."[3] Most courts agreed and quickly dismissed the contention that newspapers enjoyed any constitutionally incorporated role as a "watchdog" over public affairs. If the "editors of newspapers" did not, in the estimation of the New York Supreme Court, "have any other rights than such as are common to all," their communications could claim no special privileges or protections from libel or defamation suits. Editors had to be held strictly liable for the content of their newspapers, "otherwise the press, which now often teems with gross licentiousness, might easily be made the vehicle of the most wanton approach and vile calumny, without the possibility of correction; and this palladium of liberty would thus become a hateful curse."[4] Lest they be misunderstood, judges often furnished their opinions and treatises with lamentations on the low state of journalism. Chancellor Kent's *Commentaries on American Law* bemoaned a rising "current" of popular "opinion" regarding libel law that threatened to "diminish or destroy altogether every obstacle or responsibility in the way of the publication of the truth." The increasing use of truth as a defense in libel cases—a doctrine written into numerous state constitutions after 1815—led the chancellor to complain that "the tendency of measures in this country has been to relax too far the vigilance with which the common law surrounded and guarded character."[5]

For these reasons, it is difficult to regard antebellum "journalism" as a profession. Indeed, the term did not enter the English language until the 1830s (from the French *journalisme*). Nor did it catch on quickly, as there appeared to be no distinct set of skills, specialized knowledge, or vocational ethics that distinguished newspaper work from anything else that dealt in paper, ink, and politics. In an era when over 80 percent of newspapers relied on partisan support—government printing contracts, postmaster appointments, favorable loans from politically oriented banks, or outright grants from wealthy notables—it was difficult to imagine "the press" as an independent fourth estate. Neither a distinct institution nor a profitable commercial enterprise, the antebellum newspaper is best described as a circuit of partisan patrons, elected officials, subscribers, and contributors "conducted" (as common parlance aptly put it) by either a printer, an editor who oversaw the printer's work and contributed an occasional piece, or a "proprietor" who performed some important but ambiguous role.

Outside of basic literacy, the only skills necessary to the production of a newspaper were those of the printer, and his fortunes had diminished since the days of Benjamin Franklin. From the 1780s onward, republican ideals of a nonpartisan and "open" press steadily gave way to practical political realities, and newspapers became increasingly instrumental to the management of parties. Printers abandoned their eighteenth-century identity as impartial "meer mechanics" and defined their work in more explicitly political terms.[6] But the politicization of newspaper work also opened the field to aspiring politicians of more genteel pedigree. Printers resented the encroachment of "hireling editors" into their craft but could not claim for themselves any greater measure of economic or political independence. Despite generous tax abatements and postal subsidies, subscription rates remained beyond the means of most Americans, leaving the survival of a newspaper dependent on the patronage of the wealthy and politically influential. Though it took little in the way of economic capital to start a newspaper, the art of sustaining one required quantities of sociopolitical capital beyond the reach of most printers. With a line of credit and the right political connections (in antebellum America, the two usually went together), an aspiring lawyer-politician or ex-military officer could vault himself into the editorial chair of a local paper.[7]

The emergence of a partisan press coupled with the influx of more bold editorial voices (many of them recent refugees from the radical British press) added considerable rancor to the already tumultuous politics of the early republic. In Philadelphia and New York, factional and ethnic animosities ensnared many notable printers and editors in affairs of honor.[8] Newspaper combat did not confine itself to major coastal cities. In Pittsburgh, editorial belligerence persisted well into the 1830s, though aristocratic pretensions were eschewed in favor of random gunplay, fistfights, and canings. The problem, as local jurist, novelist, and former newspaper editor Hugh Henry Brackenridge saw it, lay in a popular Jeffersonian distrust of the legal system. Fearing that pettifogging attorneys and judges would rob them of justice, men opted to conduct their disputes in print. To those "of the opinion that it would be better to argue all matters of *meum*, or *tuum*, in the public papers, or in hand-bills posted upon the trees," Brackenridge's fictional "Captain Farago" warned "that the suitors waxing warm in the controversy, would call one another names and come to blows. A great deal of ill-blood between neighbours might shew itself. How could you keep lawyers from writing in the gazettes, any more than from speaking at the bar? And here, their jargon reduced to paper, would spread wider, and have more permanence than floating on the atmosphere with which their breath had mixed it in the first instance." Jurists and lawyers were thus the natural allies of editors and other opinionated citizens, for only the law could protect them from the "cudgelist, or pugilist."[9]

Brackenridge's "cudgelist" likely alluded to one of the first and most widely read justifications of newspaper violence—authored, ironically, by Benjamin Franklin. In a 1789 newspaper essay entitled "An Account of the Supremest Court of Judicature in Pennsylvania, viz., The Court of the Press," he proposed that abuses of the press against public decorum and private reputation be corrected with the occasional exercise of the "liberty of the cudgel." If Franklin wrote in jest, the joke soon came at the expense of his nephew, Benjamin Franklin Bache of the *Philadelphia Aurora*. In the heated political conflicts of the 1790s, Bache and other printers became the common flogging property of military officers and elected officials.[10] Cudgel liberty might strike the modern reader as a rather un-Franklinesque idea. But it neatly joined two cornerstones of the American Enlightenment: a fear of unchecked power and a faith in civility. If the unlicensed exercise of the former tempted a printer to violate the latter, a solid beating would remind him of the difference between barbarism and civilization.[11]

Conspicuously absent here is the notion that violated *honor* demanded violent satisfaction. Convinced that the "feudal" code of honor would never take root in an enlightened republic, Franklin could not have foreseen that it would soon insinuate itself into the culture of partisan politics—and the press. After all, duels had been scarce in the colonies. Even Virginia cavaliers rarely resorted to arms. With the (somewhat reluctant) exception of Alexander Hamilton, the "founding fathers" did not duel. Washington, Madison, Adams, Jefferson, Franklin, and Paine never made or accepted a challenge. Adams declared that dueling transgressed the "great Distinction between Savage Nations and polite ones . . . that among the former, every Individual is his own Judge and his own Executioner; but among the latter, all Pretensions to Judgment and Punishment are resigned to Tribunals erected by the Public." Respect for the rule of law would progressively "exterminate" the "revengeful Sentiments and Tempers" of mankind—but only if "no romantic or cavalier-like Principles of Honour intermix[ed]" with its operations. Paine believed that courts of honor could prevent duels; Jefferson proposed the public "gibbeting" of fallen duelist's bodies. Neither expected that a republic founded on the principles of antiquity would allow the sort of barbarous private combats unknown among the Greeks and Romans.[12]

But the Revolutionary War taught Americans to duel. When not fighting the British, Continental Army officers spent a disconcerting amount of time bickering over rank, commissions, and credit for victories. Dueling proliferated, as Charles Royster has argued, because it settled such disputes "in a distinctive, gallant way for men newly self-conscious about their uniqueness and their proper public inviolability." And as dreams of liberty turned to dreams of empire, duels became as much a part of military life as rancid food. Looking back on his youth, William Henry Harrison estimated that "there were more duels in the northwestern army, between the years of 1791 and 1795, inclusive, than ever took place in the same length of time, and among so small a body of men as composing the commissioned officers of the army, either in America or any other country at least in modern times." More alarming still was the spread of dueling among civilians north and south, the rapid infection of the res publica with *rage militare.* Politicians, planters, gamblers, merchants, artisans, students, and (most disturbing of all) lawyers took to the field of honor to settle disputes in growing numbers. There was, one essayist lamented, "not a single district upon the whole earth, where duelling is so much tolerated and honoured as it is in the United States."[13]

The proliferation of dueling was less a departure from revolutionary republicanism than its democratic extension. It only seemed aberrant if one genuinely believed Montesquieu's claim that "virtue" was the motivating principle of republics, and "honor" that of monarchies—an emotionally dishonest piece of political taxonomy if there ever was one. For how could virtue be cultivated if it was not honored, and what was honor but an inducement to virtue—and civility? Not quite an aristocracy but not yet a democracy, the political culture of the new nation came to resemble the ancient category that stood betwixt the two: timocracy (from the Greek *timē,* or "honor"), the rule of the ambitious.[14] Virtue, honor, and ambition depended equally on the approbation of the public, and that public required newspapers. Enlightened hopes that the diffusion of printed knowledge would progressively cultivate civility and political tranquility gave way to more dire forecasts. As early as 1790—the year of Franklin's death—John Adams worried,

The world grows more enlightened. Knowledge is equally diffused. Newspapers, magazines, and circulating libraries have made mankind wiser. Titles and distinctions, ranks and orders, parade and ceremony, are all going out of fashion . . . Are riches, honors, and beauty going out of fashion? Is not the rage for them, on the contrary, increased faster than improvement in knowledge? Does not the increase of knowledge in any man increase his emulation; and the diffusion of knowledge among men multiply rivalries?[15]

"Emulation" provided a convenient culprit for critics of dueling, who attributed its proliferation to a mindless aping of European fashion. But the most influential anti-dueling sermon—Lyman Beecher's 1804 *Remedy for Duelling*—identified a domestic source: republican politics. The very "genius of our government favors, not only the descent of the practice, but multiplies to an unlimited extent the occasions of duelling." By "genius of government," Beecher meant faction, and the essence of faction was combat. Dueling was but one example of how factions could both isolate themselves from public opinion and misrepresent it. In what political scientists today call a "polity of courts and parties," the path of public ambition ran through the partisan worlds of the courthouse and the newspaper office. With "what views can a Christian parent look to the law as a profession for a son," Beecher implored, "where, if he rise to fame, he must join the phalanx of murder, or, if he refuse, experience their united influence against him?" What newspaper editor could "investigate the conduct of rulers, and to scrutinize the character of candidates for office . . . when the duellist stands before him, with pistol at the breast?" In all likelihood, the only editors would be "duellists themselves," sufficiently "mad with ambition" to "brave the danger."[16]

History soon fulfilled Beecher's prophecy. Timocratic politics subordinated the cudgeled printer to the dueling editor, shunting aside ink-stained proles in favor of prospective gentleman with liberal, legal, or military educations. Genteel credentials notwithstanding, the demands of conducting a newspaper on a day-to-day basis could reduce an editor to a stature scarcely distinguishable from that of a competent printer. Nothing was more precious to a man of honor than his word, and nothing more shameful than to not own it, to be a "hireling" whose words were purchased for a few dollars or came at the command of others. By this fact alone would newspaper work have been shameful, but there was more. Debt shamed a man of honor, and the newspaper proprietor was continually forced to beg for money from patrons, government officials, and the many delinquent subscribers who resented paying for public information. And finally there was the verbal and physical abuse from disgruntled readers. All told, newspaper work could be a disgraceful way to make a living. As one New York editor put it:

> The editor who wills to please
> Must humbly crawl upon his knees,

> And kiss the hand that beats him;
> Or if he dares presume to walk,
> Must toe the mark that others chalk,
> And cringe to all who meet him.[17]

One need not delve too deeply into psychological theory to surmise that the action of shame on the editor could provoke an equal and opposite reaction. And if antebellum newspaper lore is any indication, it often did. Brandished weapons, heavy drinking, gambling, foolhardy boasts of courage, and seemingly unprovoked insult and violence against the powerful and powerless alike were stock in trade. All of this established an air of blasé nihilism around a newspaper office, as Mark Twain parodied in his *Journalism in Tennessee*. Appointed as associate editor for the *Morning Glory and Johnson County War-Whoop*, Twain is informed of his responsibilities thusly:

> Jones will be here at 3. Cowhide him. Gillespie will call earlier, perhaps—throw him out the window. Ferguson will be along at 4—kill him. That is all for today, I believe. If you have any odd time, you may write a blistering article on the police—give the Chief Inspector rats. The cowhides are under the table; weapons in the drawer—ammunition there in the corner—lint and bandages up there in the pigeon-holes. In case of accident, go to Lancet, the surgeon, down stairs. He advertises—we take it out in trade.

Editorial combat made for good parody because a predilection for verbal and physical violence was one of the first and few distinguishing characteristics of this nascent profession. Indeed, editors (like Twain) did most of the parodying themselves—and it was, I should emphasize, parody, not satire. Satire would have played on ironic discrepancies between principles of press freedom and practices of press violence. Though parodists may have hoped to mock editorial dueling into nonexistence, this could easily backfire. When *Harper's Magazine* published Virginia editor George Bagby's sketch of the "Virginia Editor" as "a young, unmarried, intemperate, pugnacious" man "escorted to a premature grave" by "drink and dueling-pistols," Bagby received challenges from two Virginia editors.[18]

Was the antebellum press as violent as these anecdotes suggest? Was it violent enough to instill expectations of continued violence and sustain the legend of the "fighting editor?"[19] At this point, it seems necessary to gauge the incidence of actual or threatened press violence. Although incidents were, as a matter of course, more likely to be reported in newspapers, this does not make the task much easier. Given the extremely local and decentralized nature of the antebellum press,

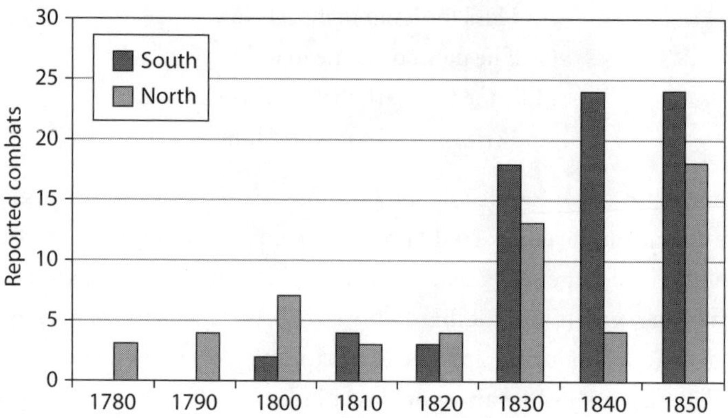

Figure 5.1. Editorial combats by region, 1780–1860.

there are simply too many newspapers (nearly 600 titles as early as 1820) for the mortal researcher to survey. Lacking any centralized repository of statistics, I have relied on histories of dueling and journalism, biographical dictionaries, editors' memoirs, local histories, and selective samples of several major urban dailies.[20] This admittedly limited search turned up over 150 newspaper combats between 1783 and 1860—considerably more than previous studies have estimated (fig. 5.1).[21]

Incidents varied considerably over time and by region. Following Twain and Bagby, historians generally treat the "fighting editor" as a character native to the chivalrous old South and the Wild West. But the history of editorial combat begins in the North. I have found only six incidents of newspaper violence in the Southern states between 1780 and 1820, compared to more than twenty above the Mason-Dixon line. Of course, more newspapers were published there. After 1820, Southern editorial combat progressed at a rate comparable to the expansion of newspapers, but Northern incidents did not regress in a linear fashion. After fallow periods in the 1820s and 1840s, Northern editors and readers revived the deadly arts in the 1830s and 1850s. Several factors account for the Northern spikes. Party realignments and an upsurge of anti-abolition violence factor into the equation, as do the pronounced effects of these tensions in border states and territories such as Kentucky, Missouri, and California. Finally, newspaper editors appear to have had a particular proclivity for dueling, involving themselves in over one-third of a roughly estimated 350 duels fought during this period.

It should be acknowledged that these sums appear negligible when set against figures reported in recent studies of late-nineteenth-century Latin America and

Europe. Between 1880 and 1893, Cubans fought 164 duels, and Italians fought close to 2,000—a rate that Germany, France, and Spain probably matched. The Great War effectively put an end to European dueling, but Argentina (nearly 100 incidents between 1904 and 1927) and Uruguay (around 50 between 1914 and 1920) soldiered on. But beneath these considerable discrepancies of scale a common historical agent operates: the proliferation of newspapers. Journalism accounted for more than half of the Italian duels, and there are good reasons to suspect that comparable proportions prevailed elsewhere. Studies of political honor and violence in nineteenth-century Europe and Latin America strongly suggest that the introduction of a liberal constitution, the rule of law, and an ostensibly free press—a "public sphere," if you will—precipitated fresh waves of political violence among the professional classes: politicians, lawyers, military officers, and journalists in particular.[22]

Newspapers did much to aid and promote duels. The frequent editorial use of "fighting words"—"poltroon," "blackleg," "dog," "insect," "villain," and so on—made it difficult to distinguish newspaper criticism from the giving of the lie. It was hardly "news" to learn that the editor of the *Philadelphia Independent Gazetteer* was a "blasted, posted, loathsome coward," or that his counterpart at the *Savannah Republican* was "a hired, pitiful slanderer, picked up from a dunghill, an outcast of creation brought to Georgia so that he may compete with gentlemen," but this was the stuff of partisan newspapers. Editors combed the exchange papers for dueling stories, and many allowed the placement of "posts" and "cards" in their columns. Despite often promising to eschew attacks on "private character," no hard and fast rules of journalistic ethics restrained them from printing open letters of personal malediction by their readers, or from descending to that level themselves.

Davis and Darnes: A Case Study in Club Law

Consider the story of William Darnes and Andrew Jackson Davis, two young men who had migrated to St. Louis in the late 1830s.[23] Darnes had come from Maryland by way of Virginia, seeking a higher wage for his carpentry. Davis, a novice attorney, hoped for better prospects than those available in the overcrowded bar of his native Massachusetts. Both (as Davis's name suggests) were Democrats, and they soon became political friends. Darnes quickly won recognition as a representative of the local "mechanics interest." Davis, finding little success with the law, became "Proprietor" of a Democratic newspaper, the *Missouri Argus*, in 1839. When divisions over banking policy split the Missouri

Democratic party in half during the "Log Cabin" campaign of 1840, the friendship of Davis and Darnes ended abruptly and violently. As Davis and the *Argus*
continued to advocate the hard-money policy of Senator Thomas "Old Bullion"
Benton, Darnes joined a local faction composed of Whigs and anti-Benton "soft"
money Democrats. The *Argus* and its editor, Colonel William Gilpin, immediately attacked Darnes as a "Catiline" betrayer, a tool of the "Federal-British-
Whig-United-States-Bank-Hard-Cider-Tippecanoe-Gourd-Convention-Party"
and a man of "dunghill breed." Worse still, they "put him in small letters" (printed
his name in lower case). Darnes responded by publishing a disjointed essay on
Gilpin's character in the Whig *Saint Louis Commercial Bulletin*, denouncing the
colonel as an "insect" of indeterminate sex, a "sprig of aristocracy" descended
from "old John Gilpin, of race-riding fame," and a coward in battle, who boasted
of his courage—but only to "gemmen ob colour."[24]

Darnes then appealed to the code of honor. His "second," Captain Thornton
Grimsley, delivered a note to Davis declaring that Darnes intended to hold Davis
personally responsible for his personal attacks. Davis informed Grimsley that the
low "character" of Darnes set him beneath the recognition of gentlemen. In the
next day's *Argus*, Colonel Gilpin related the incident and suggested that Darnes,
though a "common street loafer and vagabond," could receive satisfaction from
him. Instead, Darnes purchased an iron cane, confronted Davis outside of the
National Hotel, and endeavored to club him over the head. As Davis tried to
shield himself with a broken umbrella, Grimsley (who owned the hotel) discouraged spectators from intervening. This was "a fight between two political friends,"
he warned, "let it be a fair fight." After beating three holes into Davis's skull,
Darnes walked away unharmed. Davis died five days later.

Despite resistance from local law enforcement officials, two Democratic
attorneys—Thomas Gannt and Peter Engle—managed to secure a third-degree
manslaughter indictment against Darnes. The prosecutors knew that the simple
fact that Darnes had beaten Davis to death in front of as many as forty witnesses
would not suffice. They would have to establish that Darnes had acted dishonor-
ably. After all, Darnes knew that Colonel Gilpin wanted to fight him but instead
attacked Davis—who, the prosecutors revealed, had intended to duel Captain
Thornton Grimsley all along. The contention that a manslaughter defendant
had prevented the victim from shooting someone else—and thereby robbing yet
another individual of his right to aim bullets at the defendant—is certainly an
unconventional piece of prosecutorial forensics. And just how did the prosecution know that Davis and Gilpin desired a double duel with Grimsley and Darnes?
Because prosecutor Gannt had been the bearer of yet another note to Gilpin (this

one from local attorney Charles Carroll), and learned of it while "smoothing" things over. This put Gannt at some pains to explain why he had volunteered to prosecute a man who had sought only the same satisfaction that Gannt had sought for Carroll.[25]

From there, the prosecution's difficulties mounted. Their witnesses turned out to be an impeachable lot. The physicians of St. Louis used the trial to discredit the famed Dr. William Beaumont by fingering his experimental trephining procedure as the true killer.[26] Finally, it became clear that Gannt and Engle were sitting on some damaging secrets regarding the true ownership of the *Argus*.[27] But the worst thing that happened to the prosecution was Henry S. Geyer, Darnes's lead defense attorney. As Missouri's most prominent trial lawyer, orator, and Whig, Geyer doubtless saw political capital in the case, a rich opportunity to expose Democratic insensitivity to the working man while avowing, in the style of Davy Crockett and "Hard Cider" Harrison, his affinity for "our leather moccasin boys."

The Darnes trial attracted national attention, and Geyer's closing speech to the jury—a two-day-long tour de force of antebellum rhetorical tropes, sentimentalist pathos, just-folks humor, and nationalistic bombast designed to argue a third-degree manslaughter charge down to fourth-degree (or "excusable") manslaughter conviction—was widely circulated in pamphlet form.[28] Geyer began by telling the jury,

> You are now called upon to decide whether the people of this country are to be exposed to the arbitrary tyranny of the press—the defenseless victims of its relentless cruelty . . . Whether we shall foster and protect in our midst, a vampire gnawing at the very vitals of social order and assailing with remorseless cruelty our most cherished possessions. Whether in this country a man may be struck to the dust, by merciless assaults upon his character and honor, or, wounded to the heart, through his domestic relations, the cherished objects of his fondest affection, without a remedy; for over all these a licentious press asserts its usurped jurisdiction, and all are equally exposed to its blighting and withering influences, all equally unprotected. You will determine then, whether these are not injuries for which the law affords no redress, abuses against which it interposes no shield to protect us, wrongs which we must resent, or be dishonored and disgraced, dangers against which we not only may, but must protect ourselves.[29]

Darnes had become "the unfortunate and unwilling actor" in a journalistic game, one in which enemies were insulted on points of honor but denied opportunities for honorable redress. Contrary to the prosecution's double duel theory, the *Argus* had singled out Darnes in its columns because he could be refused satisfaction on the field of honor. These games of editorial brinkmanship had several variations. Geyer believed it "an established rule among editors . . . that however flagitious the libel, the name of the writer will not be given up, but upon terms which require that the injured party shall either challenge him to fight a duel, or prosecute him; and when these terms are submitted to, it often happens, that the name given up belongs to a man without character or responsibility, who can neither be challenged nor prosecuted, without giving him importance, to which he is not entitled."[30] With this argument, Geyer shifted the onus of cowardice away from Darnes and onto the "prostituted press." At the same time, it stressed the forced necessity of Darnes's actions, the extent to which he had little choice but to publicly and violently "chastise" Davis. Even a successful libel suit only would have made matters worse by rebroadcasting the libel to a wider audience, making a martyr of the editor, and yielding only a few spare nickels from his barren pockets. This was not simply a practical consideration owing to some defect in the administration of justice. It was an inherent shortcoming of law itself. Assaults on personal reputation were *damna absque inuria*: injuries for which law supplied no remedy.

For this reason, justification for violent redress could not to be found in common or statutory law but in a "law of higher origin, and of more enduring nature, the law of your own hearts, written there by your Maker, in indelible characters"— namely, in "the instinct of self-defense and self-protection." American society, Geyer argued, had nurtured this instinct from the start—even Benjamin Franklin advocated the "liberty of the cudgel"—and carried it westward. Indeed, it was "the law of the West, approved and sustained by an enlightened public sentiment, to resist and resent indignities upon the spot where they are offered." Boys were taught "never to suffer themselves to be dishonored, by allowing a slander upon their character to pass with impunity," and from this grew a "feeling of self-respect and self-dependence" that "pervades society everywhere."[31]

When put together, the power of the press, the weakness of law, and American traditions of masculine self-defense formed an extenuating circumstance that Geyer called the "irresistible law of public opinion," a law that "required Darnes to inflict chastisement" on Davis under penalty of dishonor.[32] Darnes had acted in a state of "moral duress, more potent over the will than physical torture," for

> [i]n this country, public opinion exerts a powerful influence over the actions of all men, who are not wholly lost to virtue. It is the concentrated power of many minds, acting upon each one individually; it forces the will more readily, than

any duress or torture of the body. It cannot be disregarded, without danger of a penalty, more dreaded than loss of life—the loss of character. It is right, it should be so. It belongs to the nature of our civil institutions, and the constitution of society. The general character of every community depends on the conduct of individuals composing it. Society cannot, without reproach to itself, allow its members to disgrace themselves. All have an interest in the conduct of each. Everyone is bound for the common good, for the security of his own privileges, social and political, to aid in forming and sustaining a public sentiment, which shall make it the object of chief solicitude in all to maintain by their deportment, a character worthy of high station as members of a community of freemen. Public opinion, thus formed and sustained, acquires a moral force over the mind as resistless, as the power of the Mississippi over matter.[33]

Even those jurors who did "not concur in the prevailing sentiment of our people, which authorizes, and in some cases commands, a forcible redress of private grievances," would surely not wish to punish "those who yield to the existing force of public opinion." They would have to recognize that "public opinion, whether they approve it or not, gives law to society, and there are few who can disobey it with impunity." Moreover, they would have to appreciate the "great and momentous" consequences of the Darnes case. An acquittal would "serve as an admonition to all profligate editors, and will improve the general character of the press." A conviction "would serve as a new license, and an encouragement to new aggression" at a time when the "characters of our public men are already scarcely worth anything."[34]

To the prosecution, the "club law" arguments of the defense "foully slandered" the citizens of St. Louis, implying that "they approved the killing either beforehand or after it was over." As evidence against this supposition, they reminded the jury that mob action against Darnes had been threatened. And if there was such a "mystical something" as "public opinion" here, Gannt thought it "required an attack upon Gilpin and not Davis." If Darnes "would have been dishonored by not attacking, in obedience to 'public opinion,' and so rescuing himself from the imputation of cowardice, he is still dishonored by having attacked a man [Davis] with whom no one imagined he would have a collision." Simply put, "deference to 'public opinion' was not his motive." Judge James Bowlin's instructions to the jury agreed. But the jury did not, returning a verdict of fourth-degree manslaughter. Darnes paid a $500 fine for killing his friend and left the St. Louis County Courthouse a free—and honorable—man.[35]

There was nothing unique about the trial and defense of William Darnes, except that cases of this sort rarely went to trial in the first place. When they did, juries heard similar arguments and delivered comparable verdicts. If a war of words devolved into an exchange of blows and bullets, antebellum courts usually demonstrated lenience. As precedent, Darnes's attorneys cited the well-known acquittals of Thomas Selfridge in Massachusetts (1806) and Judge Edward C. Wilkinson in Kentucky (1839).[36] Selfridge, a Federalist politician, shot Charles Austin (the son of the Democratic *Independent Chronicle* editor, Benjamin Austin) after a heated newspaper exchange over the payment of a tavern bill for a Fourth of July celebration. If men could not defend their reputations against journalistic "calumniators," Selfridge's attorney Samuel Dexter argued, they could not be "useful." Because a "man daily beaten on the public exchange, cannot retain his standing in society, by recurring to the laws," it was

> more dangerous for the laws to give security to a man, disposed to commit outrages on the persons of his fellow citizens, than to authorize those, who must otherwise meet irreparable injury, to defend themselves at every hazard. Men of eminent talents and virtues, on whose exertions, in perilous times, the honour and happiness of their country must depend, will always be liable to be degraded by every daring miscreant, if they cannot defend themselves from personal insult and outrage. Men of this description must always feel, that to submit to degradation and dishonour is impossible. Nor is this feeling confined to men of that eminent grade. We have thousands in this country who possess this spirit; and without them we should soon deservedly cease to exist as an independent nation. I respect the laws of my country, and revere the precepts of our holy religion; I should shudder at shedding human blood; I would practice moderation and forbearance, to avoid so terrible a calamity; yet, should I ever be driven to that impassable point, where degradation and disgrace begin, may this arm shrink palsied from its socket, if I fail to defend my own honour.[37]

Wilkinson, a Mississippi judge on the way to his wedding in Bardstown, Kentucky, had stopped in Louisville for a proper matrimonial suit. When a local tailor produced an unflattering jacket, Wilkinson and his groomsmen beat him and, Bowie knives drawn, threatened worse. Before the tailor could obtain a writ against the judge and his band, news of the attack spread among Louisville workingmen, who confronted the out-of-state "aristocrats" in the tavern of their hotel. Wilkinson's party proclaimed their unwillingness to fight men of such low status. A lethal brawl ensued, resulting in murder indictments against the Mississippians for the murder of a bartender and a butcher. Wilkinson retained the services of

Samuel Smith Prentiss, Mississippi's most renowned courtroom orator. In the face of considerable local prejudice against the murderous bachelor party, Prentiss contended that passive submission to "personal degradation by personal chastisement" would have reduced these honorable men to the level of a "Negro slave." He reminded the jury that "Kentucky has no law which precludes a man from defending himself, his brother, or his friend. Better for Judge Wilkinson had he never been born, than that he should have failed in his duty on this occasion. Had he acted otherwise than he did, he would have been ruined in his own estimation, and blasted in the opinion of the world." The jury found Wilkinson and company not guilty.[38]

Darnes's attorneys could have easily cited another Kentucky precedent: the 1829 murder trial of Charles Wickliffe, who had killed the editor of the *Kentucky Gazette* in an argument over the anonymous authorship of an article castigating Wickliffe's father, a candidate for the state legislature. In a two-and-a-half-hour stem-winder delivered before a Lexington jury on July 4, Wickliffe's defense attorney, Henry Clay, equated the natural right of self-preservation with the principles of the Declaration of Independence and the bullets Wickliffe had pumped into the unfortunate editor with the shot heard round the world. Wickliffe was acquitted but was killed several years later in a duel with George Trotter, the succeeding editor of the *Kentucky Gazette*. Trotter was committed to an insane asylum shortly thereafter.[39]

Historians generally categorize *Wickliffe*, *Selfridge*, and *Wilkinson* as three early cases in a developing American doctrine of "excusable" homicide. From the early nineteenth century onward, juries, judges, treatise writers, and legislators considerably modified the common law requirement that potential victims pursue all available avenues of retreat before fighting back against an assailant.[40] By the 1870s, jurists could confidently declare that one had "no duty to retreat." Requirements that one flee from an assault not only violated the spirit of a "true man" but also ran counter to the "tendency of the American mind." This tendency drew on significant influences: a post-Darwinian conception of manliness as an essential instinct, a widespread concern with the feminizing influence of urbane "over-civilization," and a consequent valorization of "true" American manliness as a product of bumptious frontier individualism. Oliver Wendell Holmes Jr. put the matter succinctly: "a man is not born to run away."[41]

When making self-defense arguments, antebellum attorneys made much of manhood and the American mind, but they did so in a decidedly different manner. Retreat from an assault did not so much contradict a "true" man's natural instincts as denigrate his social standing and public duties as a man. By constructing "manhood" as a quality defined by the exercise of political rights and social responsibilities, antebellum legal culture had more freedom to parse out the rights of men as circumstances dictated. When the man on trial happened to be publicly prominent and engaged in law or politics, his public stature necessarily rendered him more susceptible to the "irresistible influences" of public opinion and gave him more latitude to act in defense of his public "usefulness."[42]

The disproportionate involvement of politically prominent men in antebellum "self-defense" precedents suggest that cases like *Wickliffe*, *Selfridge*, and *Wilkinson* tell us more about the rights to (and rites of) political violence than they do about attitudes toward violence in general. If they were indeed self-defense cases, why would Henry Geyer cite them as precedents in favor of Darnes, who had clearly been the aggressor? By deftly conflating the grievances of the political libel plaintiff with the mitigating circumstances of excusable homicide, Geyer managed to turn a libeler into the moral and legal equivalent of an assassin. If, *pace Wilkinson*, threatening insults shouted in a barroom justified lethal self-defense, printed provocations and affronts could be regarded as equally, if not more, exculpatory. Geyer equated the "doctrine that a libelous publication will in no case justify or excuse the smallest battery" with the doctrine of a duty to retreat: both reflected English feudal law's "degrading theory" that men were "*subjects*, not sovereigns." Warning the jury to prevent English principles and precedents from controlling "the administration of justice here," he portrayed the clubbing of a licentious editor as an enlightened exercise of personal and popular sovereignty. That the founders had freed the press from prior legal restraint necessarily implied that they expected abuses of the press to be remedied by "public opinion" and the individual "redress of private grievances." Liberty of the cudgel was the necessary corollary to liberty of the press.[43]

If American law was in fact premised on the personal sovereignty (of men), it could not oblige a man to subject himself to public humiliation at the hands of private persons. The written law could require men neither to beat shameful retreats from assailants nor passively to bear public insults and provocations. "Man," "public," and "private" are, of course, the operative terms here—as much in unwritten as the written law. Nineteenth-century liberalism's distinction between public and private law had a gendered rationale: that which might shame a man came to be defined as a matter of "private" law. In this way, as William Reddy has argued, "personal honor and personal liberty became intertwined. The 'private' in the sense of freedom from government interference and the 'private' in the sense of family secrets, male authority, and the management of family name, were merged."[44] Written law alone could not seamlessly effect such a comprehensive merger. Far from contradicting written law, unwritten law patched the inevitable gaps in this larger gendered (and, in many cases, racial) edifice, allowing (some) men to go beyond the written law in defense of their honor.

The patchwork task of unwritten law entailed many clumsy confrontations with logic and fact. Henry Geyer had to argue that "public opinion" compelled the "private" and "personal" actions of Darnes. To paper over this inconsistency, he shoehorned gendered ideology and domestic imagery into his argument, asserting that the virtue of women and the tranquility of the hearth were in some way implicated in a fight between two bachelors. Exactly why he did not say. Nor did he need to. When antebellum lawyers appealed to unwritten laws, twelve men good and true did not need to have the implications spelled out for them. In a club law argument, mere allusion to the "honor" (that is, the chastity and fidelity) of the fair sex equated libelers with libertines and the licentious editor of newspapers with the lecherous seducer of wives. The "unwritten law" arguments used to acquit husbands who killed seducers bore many similarities to club law defenses. Attorneys justified editor-clubbing and libertine-killing as means toward the greater end of maintaining social and civic propriety without the unwieldy intervention of the state.[45]

While the difference between third- and fourth-degree manslaughter might seem trifling, most observers viewed the Darnes verdict as an unmitigated triumph for Henry Geyer and his Missouri Whigs. A favorable verdict over a minor point of law gave them a much larger moral and political victory. They had shown that a licentious Democratic press had gone "too far" in its incivility, intemperate language, and impudent disregard for the reputation of public men. And that victory was well timed: the Darnes trial began a few days after election day, but before the results of the hotly contested presidential campaign were known. By the end of the trial (November 14, 1840), Whig candidate William Henry Harrison had emerged as the winner. The unprecedented partisanship of the log cabin campaign inspired, as we have seen, a great deal of post-election editorializing and sermonizing against the evils of excessive party spirit—evils all too vividly dramatized by the "tragic" conflict between Davis and Darnes.[46] In this environment of collective self-recrimination, the jury may have resolved to let fresh civic wounds heal. By assenting to the proposition that "public opinion" had caused the killing, they could deem the act a lamentable but excusable act of transient political fervor.

By rejecting the third-degree manslaughter charge and finding William Darnes guilty in the fourth degree, the jury affirmed that his cane was not a deadly weapon and, more importantly, that he had acted "involuntarily."[47] On the face of things, it is difficult to imagine how his actions could have been so construed. Although he was in the "heat of passion," his actions had not been suddenly provoked. Nor did his defense hazard the relatively novel argument that passion had rendered Darnes temporarily insane.[48] They contended that Darnes had rationally acted in principled defense of public liberty—albeit involuntarily or, at the very least, out of necessity. If public opinion was the voice of reason and exerted a "moral force over the mind as resistless, as the power of the Mississippi over matter," could there be any difference between rational and involuntary action?

"Public Opinion Is Practically the Paramount Law of the Land"

The argument that public opinion could compel a man to murder required an attorney to deftly weave together multiple claims: that a licentious press posed an existential threat to the honor of public men, that libel laws could do little to protect that honor, that libelous and defamatory words were the moral equivalent of a physical attack, and that retreat in the face of either would permanently dishonor the victim. Yet for all the talk about the mighty force of public opinion, Geyer and other purveyors of "unwritten law" defenses rarely offered any empirical evidence as to what public opinion actually was on the question at hand. If, for example, public opinion required Darnes to attack Davis, why did it not require Davis or William Gilpin to attack Darnes for his published insults? Could it really be shown that Darnes would have been diminished in the eyes of the people of St. Louis had he turned the other cheek? Of course not. In an "unwritten law" argument, the "public opinion" that compelled violence was less a collective opinion *about* a matter of public interest than a personal *expectation of public judgment*, a felt apprehension of humiliation and ostracism.

There was nothing new in this peculiar conception of public opinion. The history of discourse on dueling is in many respects a history of discourse about public opinion and vice versa. This peculiar genealogy reaches back as far as Francis Bacon's *Charge Touching Duels* (1614). For Bacon the historian, the origins of dueling lay in a "false and erroneous imagination of honour and credit" imported to England from Italy and France. But even "staid and sober minded" men who saw through the vainglory of the *code duello* were carried onto the field of honor by a "steam of vulgar opinion" that "imposes a necessity upon men of value to conform themselves; or else there is no living or looking upon men's faces." For Bacon the reformer, dueling posed an intractable problem because it had less to do "with particular persons, as with unsound and depraved opinions, like the domination and spirits of the air, which the scripture speaks of."[49]

Enlightenment-era reformers took a more hopeful view of the situation: if public opinion caused duels, public opinion could be reformed through law. Jean-Jacques Rousseau proposed the formation of honor courts, which would hear disputed points of honor and mete out nonviolent sanctions and monetary settlements, thereby disabusing the public of the belief that only blood could avenge insulted honor. Jeremy Bentham's conviction that public opinion, the "first and purest" of all tribunals, had been corrupted on the subject of dueling led him to propose a characteristically long and peculiar list of legal reforms. Courts of law could compel men who gave offense to apologize on their knees, don masks ("an adder's head in cases of bad faith, the head of magpie or parrot in cases of rash words or conduct") or, in cases of male insults toward women, dressing the culprit "with the headgear of a woman" and allowing "retaliation inflicted by a woman's hand."[50]

While equally convinced that public opinion was the root cause of dueling, antebellum American reformers possessed less confidence in the efficacy of legal remedies. The earliest criminal statutes of most states had outlawed dueling. In the wake of the Hamilton-Burr affair, many states passed additional laws that punished the sending of a challenge with disqualification from holding public office. In the rare instances in which such penalties were imposed, the guilty were usually pardoned by politically sympathetic governors and soon forgiven by voters—much to the dismay of evangelical reformers like Lyman Beecher, who had hoped to abolish dueling by persuading Christian men to reject duelists and their accomplices at the polls. Given that editors were not elected, none of these measures could deter journalistic dueling. Some lawmakers therefore suggested more drastic measures. Edward Livingston's *System of Penal Law* proposed that "[i]f any person shall use any insulting words or gestures, or make an assault upon another with intent, either to provoke any one to give a challenge to FIGHT A DUEL, or as an alternative, to dishonor him, he shall be fined not less than fifty, nor more than three hundred dollars, or imprisoned not less than five, nor more than thirty days, in close custody." Such a measure, if passed into law, would have criminalized countless columns of newsprint.[51]

The seeming impotency of anti-dueling laws led many to conclude that American public opinion was simply too powerful and immobile to be reformed by mere acts of legislation. Indeed, on the subject of dueling, public opinion could appear to be the law. Here, for example, are the words of Congressman William Graves, spoken before the House of Representatives as he defended his murder of fellow congressman Jonathan Cilley in an 1838 duel:

> I am not, and never have been, an advocate of the anti-social and unchristian practice of dueling. I never up to this day fired a dueling pistol; and until the day I went to the field, I never took any weapon in my hand in view of a duel. Public opinion is practically the paramount law of the land; every other law, both human and divine, ceases to be observed, yea, withers and perishes, in contact with it. It was this paramount law of this nation and of this House that forced me, under penalty of dishonor, to submit myself to the code which impelled me unwillingly into the tragical affair. Upon the heads of this nation and the doors of this House rests the blood by which my unfortunate hands have been stained.

The New York nabob Philip Hone copied this "touching" passage into his diary as a "glowing portrait" of "the absurdity of the tyranny which is exercised by public opinion over the minds and consciences of the people of this country."[52]

Graves, a Kentucky Whig, had fatally shot Cilley, a Maine Democrat, on the point of honor of whether Whig editor James Watson Webb of the *New York Courier and Inquirer*, was a "gentleman." The "martyrdom" of Cilley gave Democrats an opportunity to affirm their oft-questioned commitment to Christian morality and civilization. Even Democratic duelists like William Leggett, Thomas Hart Benton, and Andrew Jackson could now decry dueling and implore Congress to "wash out the stain of the murdered blood of Cilley from its walls." Countering Graves's contention that public opinion had forced him to kill Cilley, the *United States Magazine and Democratic Review* predicted that the Kentuckian faced certain doom at the hands of public opinion, "which, springing spontaneously and unanimously from the moral sense of all society, without distinction of classes or parties, may without presumption be called the Voice of God arising out of the depths of the human heart." In less lofty language, a decidedly pro-Democratic House committee report on the duel called for the expulsion of Graves and the censure of the "seconds" of both Graves and Cilley (Congressmen Henry Wise and George Wallace Jones), leaving James Watson Webb to "the chastisement of courts of law and public opinion." The proposed punishments broke with the congressional tradition of ignoring duels. Moreover, the report intimated that Whigs utilized the barbaric "code of honor" as a weapon in their "scramble for undue advantages." All of this caused House Whigs to close ranks and attack the report—an assault led by John Quincy Adams, who contended that the duel committee had committed a greater breach of House privilege than "those whose hands were imbrued with blood."[53]

The ensuing debate over a bill to outlaw dueling in the District of Columbia initially followed along partisan lines, but it soon hinted at the sharp sectional differences over the meaning of honor and its relation to public opinion. When Senator Perry Smith of Connecticut characterized the measure as a "law to defend the Northern people from the attacks of the Southern," Southerners took immediate exception. William Preston of South Carolina declared that "the whole business of dueling is an appeal to public opinion." Like law, this "institution" had "originated in, and was sustained by, public opinion," functioning as "a mode by which public opinion regulates and restrains the exercise of that wild justice, as Lord Bacon calls it, which the infirmity of our own nature prompts us to take beyond the justice of the laws." If Northern public opinion was truly set against dueling, he reasoned, Northern congressmen needed no legal protection and could decline challenges without fear of popular dishonor. Southern Senators who favored the bill nonetheless worried that house rules alone could neither restrain nor properly punish insulting language. Several suggested that a law allowing juries to consider "abusive words" as "justification" for physical assaults would promote more civil debate. Yet another member proposed to exempt duels fought at a distance of less than six feet.[54]

Following a series of amendments and delays, the anti-dueling bill passed in 1839. But in some respects, the following decades proved Senator Preston right. Northern public opinion had appeared to turn against dueling and to become increasingly antipathetic to other forms of political violence. Southern politicians and editors, by contrast, fought almost twice as many duels in the following twenty years as they had in the previous forty. What accounts for this divergence?

The increasing rarity of dueling in the Northern states was not part of a more general downturn in violence. The decline of dueling went largely unnoticed amid a seeming epidemic of mob violence that reached its peak in the late 1830s, when hundreds of mobs allegedly speaking for "public opinion" targeted brothels, theaters, Roman Catholic convents, gambling dens, abolitionist meetings and presses, and free African American neighborhoods.[55] From the 1820s onward, duels progressively fell out of fashion for a variety of reasons: the success of legislation and evangelical campaigns against the practice, a greater willingness to take offending parties to court, and a growing distaste for violence and aristocratic pretension. To make a long story short, reformers attributed the decline of dueling to "public opinion," and the same explanation sufficed to explain why it persisted in the South. The stock story of a Yankee visitor to the South pushed onto the field of honor by the force of local opinion found its way into numerous works of antebellum fiction, which generally treated affairs of honor as a foolish custom of sham-etiquette that tragically robbed young men of their lives. When Northern men removed themselves from the influence of civilized public opinion—as in gold rush California—they appeared to revert to old ways, recreating the bloody alliance between political faction and newspapers, with editors reassuming their station as the preeminent instigators and organizers of political violence.[56]

Back East, a gradual commercialization of the press had weakened such alliances. Urban growth and rising literacy rates created a demand for newspapers that traditional six-cent partisan dailies (such as James Watson Webb's *New York Courier and Inquirer*) could not satisfy. A more enterprising breed of editor-proprietors introduced new economies of scale to newspaper production, distribution, and advertising, creating the first genuine mass-circulation dailies. While "penny papers" such as Benjamin Day's *New York Sun* and James Gordon Bennett's *New York Herald* exemplified this "revolution," other newspapers adopted some of these innovations, and in doing so gained some measure of independence from partisan patrons.[57]

Commercialization allowed editors to claim that they were in the business of making money, and that the measure of a newspaper's influence on public opinion could be measured in the hard numbers of circulation, not vague notions of character and reputation. James Gordon Bennett did not edit a newspaper to demonstrate his valor, virtue, or loyalty to a political faction. Neither a hireling nor a man of honor, he was a businessman, and he put the occasional humiliations of newspaper work in proper business perspective. Consider his 1836 account of one of the many beatings he received from his rival and former employer, James Watson Webb:

> My damage is a scratch, about three quarters of an inch in length, on the third finger of the left hand, which I received from the iron railing I was forced against, and three buttons torn from my vest, which any tailor will reinstate for sixpence. His loss is a rent from top to bottom of a very beautiful black coat, which cost the ruffian $40, and a blow in the face, which may have knocked down his throat some of his infernal teeth for anything I know. Balance in my favor is $39.94.

The profit margin may have been even greater; legend had it that Bennett's circulation doubled every time Webb beat him. Though impossible to confirm, the legend suggests that the perceived locus of newspaper competition had shifted from the editorial board to the circulation department.[58]

This commercial revolution in journalism did not completely sever ties between newspapers and political parties. While partisan patronage mattered less, businessman-editors proved no less partisan than politically subsidized editors. Commercialization inspired an ideology of "independent journalism" long before delivering such a product (if, indeed, it ever has), and this ideology had significant legal corollaries. The more newspapers promoted their independence from parties, their role as civic boosters, and their status as a distinct "fourth estate," the more jurists agreed. After the Civil War, courts declared what before had been denied: that newspapers had a privileged "watchdog role" over public affairs. An antebellum "nuisance" became "one of the necessities" of postbellum "civilization." As such, newspapers now required more protections than those afforded by the mere absence of prior restraint and the use of truth as a defense in libel. Jurists and legal scholars (Thomas Cooley foremost among them) formulated a common law doctrine of qualified or conditional privilege with an explicit free-market rationale. News was a commodity in the marketplace of ideas, and as its common carrier, newspapers could not be unreasonably hindered when gathering and retailing their wares.[59]

In the South, dueling—especially among newspaper editors—increased dramatically after 1840, with nearly twice as many incidents of newspaper violence in the following two decades as in the five previous decades. To be sure, some of this was simply due to an increase in the number of newspapers published in that region, and some it can be attributed to the failure of anti-dueling campaigns. Southerners often lamented the prevalence of dueling and frequently fingered public opinion as the culprit. But when reformers proposed tougher laws or aggressive campaigns to reform public sentiment, waffling and backtracking generally ensued. Although "the mass of our intelligent community do not approve of dueling," one Southern reviewer observed that "neither do they positively and earnestly disapprove it, nor speak out boldly against it." In Kentucky, a proposed constitutional amendment against dueling met with worried objections that "ambitious persons" would more readily insult public figures once protected from challenges by law. Thomas Hart Benton complained that the District of Columbia anti-dueling act of 1839 "did not look to the assassinations, under the pretext of self-defense, which were to rise up in place of the regular duel," seeing this as proof that "passions of the mind, like diseases of the body, are liable to break out in a different form when suppressed in the one they had assumed."[60] Benton's remarks on assassinations under the "pretext of self-defense" may have been a dig at the man who had deprived him of his Senate seat in 1852: Henry Geyer.

Viewing dueling as a lesser and necessary evil, many Southerners held to the traditional nostrum that it promoted civility. In his *Code of Honor*, an 1838 handbook of dueling rules, former newspaper editor, duelist, and South Carolina governor John Lyde Wilson offered a pointed justification of this custom: Northern newspapers "teeming with abuse of private character, which would not be countenanced" in the South, testified to the social benefits of dueling.[61] Senator Louis Wigfall of Texas believed that duels "engendered courtesy of speech and demeanor" and "had a most restraining tendency upon the errant fancy." In his popular novel *Beauchampe*, South Carolina writer William Gilmore Simms remarked,

> In our country, a great many crimes are committed to gratify public expectations. Most of our duels are fought to satisfy the demands of public opinion; by which is understood the opinions of that little set, batch, or clique, of which some long-nosed Solomon—some addle-pated leader of a score whose brains are thrice-addled—is the sapient lawgiver and head. Most of the riots and mobs are instituted by half-witted journalists, who first goad the offender to his crime, and, the next day, rate him soundly for its commission!

Pessimistic as this might seem, Simms preferred Southern customs to the "social laws" that prevailed in Northern cities, where the "vital soul-blood" of an "untainted reputation" was shed and sullied with impunity and men were not "brave enough to bring the guilty to punishment."[62]

In the South, newspapers remained dependent on political factions. But even with partisan patronage, few could access telegraph wires or afford steam-powered presses and gathered most of their news by waiting for Northern papers to arrive in the mail. Any Southerner with a subscription to a Northern daily had news-gathering resources equal to those of an editor. Due to their limited resources and readerships, most Southern newspapers carried on with the uninviting layout, style, and content of traditional, eighteenth-century journalism: seas of small type, dense columns, exhaustive reprints of government documents, and prolonged political essays laden with classical allusions and formulaic partisan malediction.[63] By 1850, Northern newspapers more closely resembled those of 1900; Southern newspapers, those of 1800.

In addition to the financial, commercial, political, and logistical obstacles facing Southern editors, they also had to contend with a vague suspicion and general devaluation of their product. The exceptional value attached to personal communication—to a man's word—taught many to take anything printed in a paper personally, and instructed them to hold someone personally responsible for it. Thus did the most trivial provocations give readers and editors cause to reach for their pistols. John M. Daniel of the *Richmond Examiner* and Edward C. Johnston of the *Richmond Whig* exchanged shots to settle an argument over the aesthetic merits of Hiram Powers's statue *The Greek Slave*. Similarly, newspaper debates regarding the authenticity of P. T. Barnum's "Fiji Mermaid" led to several challenges when the exhibit visited Charleston in 1843. And when the *Charleston Courier* prematurely published news of a costume ball he was hosting, James Johnston Pettigrew challenged the entire editorial staff. Even the more mundane aspects of managing a newspaper were fraught with danger. The cudgel taught several editors not to dun errant subscribers in their columns (a common practice in the North) or misprint advertisements.[64]

Like war, dueling was politics by other means. As it had in the case of Darnes and Davis, the duel tested and publicly displayed factional loyalties. In the South, these loyalties were especially personal ones of kinship, clientage, and patronage. For example, sons demonstrated their loyalties to fathers by calling offending editors to the field of honor. When John Hampden Pleasants of the *Richmond Whig* cast some mild aspersions on Thomas Ritchie Sr. of the *Richmond Enquirer* in 1846, Thomas Ritchie Jr. accused him of abolitionism (the Southern equivalent of giving the "lie direct"), proposed a duel, and killed him. So grateful and proud was the elder Ritchie that he made his son a full partner in the family business. When the family business was politics, sons often took the helm of a newspaper to defend the family name. Obadiah Jennings Wise, son of Virginia governor Henry A. Wise, fought eight duels in his two years as editor of the *Enquirer* (1858–1860). Some political opponents complained that the father was using his designing murderer of a son as a "professional bully for political gain." Others sought out their own professional bullies—crack-shot editors willing to fight "Obie" Wise. Indeed, it appears that editors were occasionally hired for the express purpose of fighting a particular rival editor. When a group of nullifiers in Greenville, South Carolina, recruited Turner Bynum to edit the *Southern Sentinel*, Benjamin Perry of the unionist *Mountaineer* suspected him of being "a desperate adventurer without home or reputation, a Swiss who will fight for anyone." Whether prescient or merely self-fulfilling, the prophecy turned out to be true. Perry killed Bynum in a duel several months later.[65]

It was not common practice to recruit such mercenary editors, for an abundance of ambitious young men eager to impress local elites was usually available. James Henry Hammond, son of a lowly South Carolina schoolmaster who would become a governor and senator, began his political ascent as editor of the *Columbia Southern Times*. Nullifiers appreciated Hammond's harsh rhetoric against "submissionists," but it was his affair of honor with congressman General James

Blair that won him the gratitude of Hayne, Calhoun, and Governor James Hamilton. By most standards a states' rights man, Blair had expressed support for President Jackson after Calhoun had turned against "The Democracy." In the interest of party discipline, Hammond mocked the sophistication of Blair's rural constituents and accused him of "reeking foulness." When Blair retorted by calling him a "blackguard," Hammond, assured by political allies that public opinion was on his side and that Blair was a poor shot, requested a duel. Though an amicable adjustment was reached, Governor Hamilton complimented Hammond for the "early and powerful exhibition which you have made of public spirit and Talent" and rewarded him with a militia title. Thus emboldened, the new lieutenant colonel made a journey to the country to bludgeon, kick, and bite C. F. Daniels of the *Camden Journal*.[66]

It is no coincidence that nullification, state's rights, and abolition served as the pretexts for many editorial duels, as these issues were regarded as indices of a Southern man's capacity for loyalty and virtuous self-sacrifice. A duel manifested these implied meanings by demonstrating a willingness to die for one's section and its principles. However, duels of this sort were more common to the "old" and aristocratic seaboard South of Virginia and the Carolinas than to the middle and deep (or "Cotton") South. As politics moved farther south and west, issues of economic development—land, banks, canals, and railroads—exerted a stronger influence over the dynamics of factional alliance and animosity. As a result, the networks of political affiliation that made up a newspaper were (as we have seen in the case of Davis and Darnes) more closely tied to economic institutions, enterprises, and interests. But the rhetoric of honor did not so readily acknowledge or adapt to such changing political and economic realities. Politicians and editors continued to speak of their virtue and "disinterestedness," but such claims had become increasingly transparent and open to dispute. Charges of corruption and challenges to duels proliferated.

Mark Twain's burlesque on "Journalism in Tennessee" seems only a slight exaggeration when compared to journalism in Arkansas, Alabama, Louisiana, Texas, or Mississippi in the decades prior to the Civil War. When not busy promoting filibusters into Mexico, editors and readers acted out their martial fantasies on one another. The example of Vicksburg, Mississippi, can suffice here. In June 1843, James Hagan of the *Sentinel* was murdered on the street by Daniel Adams. When club law acquitted Adams, Hammet of the *Vicksburg Whig* rejoiced. The new *Sentinel* editor, James Ryan, challenged him and was shot dead in February 1844. Ryan's replacement, Walter Hickey, murdered a local doctor in April and was killed in an 1848 duel. The next editor, John Jenkins, did not go a year before falling prey to a local attorney. Jenkins's successor, Franklin Jones, threw himself into the Mississippi, leading one local wag to conjecture that Jones "preferred drowning to the apparent certainty of being killed as Editor of the *Sentinel*." Instead of indulging in gallows humor, some Vicksburgers had actually tried to put a stop to the killing. In May 1844, they formed the Mississippi Anti-Dueling Society, pledging to "cordially sustain" anyone who refused to challenge or accept a challenge to a duel, report all rumors of impending duels to authorities, and boycott newspapers that gave "publicity to articles involving private character and calculated to arouse the angry feelings in men." These pledges aroused the anger of one local. Captain Jefferson Davis mocked the society's charter as "a constitution designed for every body else rather than fighting men."[67]

Davis, as we all know, had some ideas of his own about constitutions for fighting men.

Irrepressible Conflicts,
Impending Crises

He has not analyzed this subject aright nor probed it to the bottom,
who supposes that the real quarrel between the North and the South is
about the Territories, or the decision of the Supreme Court, or even the
Constitution itself; and that, consequently, the issues may be stayed and
the daggers arrested by the drawing of new lines and the signing of new
compacts. The division is broader and deeper and more incurable than
this. The antagonism is fundamental and ineradicable. The true secret of
it lies in the total reversion of public opinion which has occurred in both
sections of the country in the last quarter of a century on the subject of
slavery.

—William Holcombe, "A Separate Nationality;
or, The Africanization of the South" (1861)

It is difficult for a historian to overstate the influence of slavery on antebellum
American politics. Even when the existence or extension of the institution was
not directly in question, slavery threw a long shadow over national politics. In
ways not always subtle, slavery shaped debates and policies regarding taxation,
labor, internal improvements, Native Americans, banking and currency, defense,
and other issues. In addition to the appalling racism that it sponsored, slavery (as
Robert Forbes has aptly put it) "engendered habits of evasive and dishonest public discourse, of hostility to far-reaching legislative responses to national problems, and even of antagonism to basic components of national sovereignty."[1]
From the Missouri crisis of 1819 on, the deepening political conflict over slavery
also prompted Americans to think and talk about public opinion in new and
different ways. Political compromises over slavery roused the indignation of abolitionist agitators. Rejecting conventional political action as a form of complicity
with the evils of slavery, abolitionists invested their hopes in public opinion as the

main, if not sole, instrument of emancipation. Abolitionist publicity campaigns that depicted the manifold cruelties of slavery then prompted Southern and Northern defenders of slavery to identify public opinion as the greatest protector of the slave from mistreatment. Additionally, the suppression of abolitionist publications and speech by law and popular violence exposed deep differences over the openness of the public sphere—differences that increasingly polarized Americans along sectional lines.

By 1860, controversies over slavery had altered the terms and frameworks Americans used to discuss and conceptualize public opinion. If the concept had earlier served to define the political and constitutional differences between "democratic" and "aristocratic" political parties, it was increasingly used to define the political and cultural differences between North and South—differences that further inflamed sectional animosities, limited possibilities for compromise, and enhanced the seeming inevitability of secession and war. To be sure, divergent sectional conceptions of public opinion did not "cause" the Civil War. But a widespread conviction that American government was uniquely and emphatically a "government by opinion" deepened the sense of crisis that pervaded American political culture in the 1850s. Hopes that public opinion could resolve or even mitigate the crisis disintegrated under the pressure of a seemingly irrepressible moral conflict over slavery.

A Wall of Antislavery Fire

Wendell Phillips thought of himself as an agitator. Indeed, he may have invented that job description. The scion of a wealthy and long-established Boston family and a graduate of Harvard College and its recently established law school, Phillips soon discovered that his talents and interests were better suited to the court of public opinion than the court of law. Intrigued by the bold righteousness of William Lloyd Garrison and outraged by the violence of Boston's anti-abolitionist mobs, he shuttered his law practice and embarked on a career as a lecturer and reformer. With a plain and direct style that set him apart from the mannered, fustian oratory of the day, Phillips became one of the most sought-after speakers on the lecture and lyceum circuit. The hefty fees he commanded for his popular and edifying talks on history, the arts, and the diffusion of knowledge subsidized his decidedly less popular speeches on slavery, women's rights, temperance, capital punishment, and most every other cause dreamed up by New England reformers.[2]

But Phillips was first and foremost an abolitionist; he blasted the evils of slavery, the treachery of the slave power, and the perfidy of Northern unionists and doughfaces with a vitriolic force that could exceed even Garrison at his most Garrisonian. Believing with Garrison that the immediate abolition of slavery could only be accomplished through moral suasion and the force of public opinion, he refused to let any standard of decorum moderate his arguments, or any deference to esteemed men temper his words. Phillips's address to an 1852 meeting of the Massachusetts Antislavery Society offers an illustration of this propensity. More importantly, it suggests that the spirit and strategy of reform and agitation led abolitionists to develop a rather novel and expansive conception of public opinion. Taking "Public Opinion" as his theme for the evening, Phillips assured his audience that they lived in "a reading and thinking age . . . when the accumulated common sense of the people outweighs the greatest statesman or the most influential individual." Americans did not live under a government of laws; they lived "under a government of men—and morning newspapers," in which the "penny papers of New York do more to govern this country than the White House at Washington."[3]

For Phillips, the recent history of abolitionist agitation demonstrated that the statesman was no longer "an integral element in the state, an essential power in himself." After all, just twenty years before, the nation's greatest statesmen had "pledged themselves not to talk" about slavery. But thanks to a "regeneration of public opinion"—and the *Liberator*—they had been made to talk. To illustrate just how insignificant statesmen had become, Phillips proceeded to lash the "rhinoceros hide" of Daniel Webster, the eminent Bay State senator who had been driven into retirement after his unpopular defense of the Compromise of 1850. The audience remembered well how Webster had stood on the steps of the Revere House Hotel and ridiculed abolitionism as a "rub-a-dub agitation" stirred up by fanatic sentimentalists and hysterical spinsters. This, Phillips noted, was the same Daniel Webster who had frequently heaped praise on the virtues of free inquiry and the sublime power of public opinion. How could Webster square these declarations with his desire to silence discussion of slavery? Because the "great scoundrel" seemed to think that public opinion was formed "only in Congress, or on hotel steps" by statesmen like himself, not "in the school-houses, at the hearthstones, in the railroad cars, on board the steamboats, in the social circle," and "in the Antislavery gatherings which he despises."[4]

By the 1850s, the notion that Americans lived in a new age of popular intelligence and discussion in which public opinion reigned supreme had become commonplace, a staple of orations and newspapers across the political spectrum. But abolitionists invested more in this notion than most other Americans, and envisioned a public opinion that was at once more broad and inclusive in scope yet more powerful, invasive, and menacing. Abolitionists opened their meetings and lectures to men and women both white and black, printed literature for children as well as adults, and aimed to distribute that literature throughout the public and private spheres—the steamboats, railroads, social circles, and hearthstones—of both the North and South. But Phillips also acknowledged that public opinion was "a dangerous thing under which to live." If Daniel Webster saw public opinion as a means of harmonizing sentiments and solidifying the Union through statesmanship and high-flown eloquence, Phillips saw it as potentially despotic force of conformity, group-think, and idolatry. Taking his cue from Alexis de Tocqueville, he argued that freedom and equality tended to make men timid before an omnipotent public opinion. Only the agitator could prevent the spirit of liberty from being "smothered in material prosperity" and teach men to not be "bullied by institutions." Phillips insisted, "Republics exist only on the tenure of being constantly agitated. The antislavery agitation is an important, nay, an essential part of the machinery of the state. It is not a disease nor a medicine. No; it is the normal state,—the normal state of the nation." While integral to the machinery of the state, the agitator was also necessarily an outsider; "the moment he joins the government, he gravitates against that popular agitation which is the life of a republic." The agitator raised questions that the public was reluctant to hear, and institutions were reticent to address. The newspaper editor might wield more power than a statesman or clergyman, but he too remained largely subservient to the whims of public opinion and "might well shoot his reader with a bullet as with a new idea."[5]

Agitators were not legislators, jurists, or political scientists; they sought to arouse the moral indignation that would lead to reform, leaving others to work out the details. This was especially true of abolitionist agitators. Having rejected gradualist approaches to emancipation, "immediatists" like Phillips and Garrison focused their energies on the immorality of slavery, brushing aside questions concerning the practicality of immediate abolition as morally obtuse temporizing. At the same time, their pacifist, "non-resistance" principles led them to insist that abolition could and should be accomplished without violence. A conviction that slavery had fundamentally corrupted politics, courts of law, and other public institutions led them to reject voting, partisanship, and (with the notable exception of petitioning) other conventional forms of political action. The only remaining tactic lay in direct appeals to public opinion. Had the concept of public opinion not existed, abolitionists would have had to invent it to explain how emancipation would be brought about without resort to violence or the force of law. Put another way, abolitionism would not have been possible without a belief in the pervasive and irresistible power of public opinion.[6]

In the moral imagination of abolitionism, public opinion was both the force that sustained slavery and the agent of its impending destruction. Frederick Douglass hoped to see "the slaveholder surrounded, as by a wall of anti-slavery fire, so that he may see the condemnation of himself and his system glaring down in letters of light," until "stunned and overwhelmed with shame and confusion, he is compelled to let go the grasp he holds upon the persons of his victims, and restore them to their long-lost rights."[7] Before that could happen, Northern opinion would have to be roused from its indifference and, in the words of a Vermont abolitionist, "set right." Public opinion would "then spread with irresistible sway over the South."

> Public opinion cannot be walled in. The people of the South cannot shut it out from their borders. It knows no barriers—it is not arrested by geographical boundaries—is not hemmed in by state lines or imprisoned by state legislation. It is a moral atmosphere that spreads itself noiselessly throughout the domains of intellect and intelligence. Like electricity, it mingles itself with all the elements of the moral world and imperceptibly becomes a part of the mental constitution. Neither its progress nor its power can be stayed.[8]

In retrospect, the abolitionist belief that slavery could be ended through the force of public opinion alone might seem extraordinarily naïve, and to many of their contemporaries it seemed wildly impractical, if not counterproductive and dangerous. But abolitionists could look to the triumphs of British antislavery campaigns and anticipate (albeit with some wishful thinking) comparable success in mobilizing American public opinion. They could look to the history of post-revolutionary New England, where slavery, according to the influential interpretation of Jeremy Belknap, had been "abolished by *publick opinion*."[9] Predominantly evangelical in their Protestantism, they could look to the more recent history of what would later be called the Second Great Awakening, wherein countless men and women had been brought to an awareness of their own sinfulness through the work of revivals, circuit preachers, and tract societies devoted to spreading the gospel. Animated by perfectionist and postmillennial beliefs that mankind could be purged of sin, and that the government of God would then supplant the government of men, abolitionists had their reasons to believe that history, both secular and divine, was on their side—and that public opinion would be its agent of revolution and redemption.[10]

In addition to believing themselves in the right, abolitionists also believed that they possessed the tools to move public opinion in their direction, if not dramatically convert it to their cause. They could put no small number of eloquent men and women—Phillips, Douglass, and Lucretia Mott, to name a few—on lecture podiums. They invested considerable resources and a seemingly unlimited faith in the persuasive force of the printed word: "Those who can be induced to Read," announced the frontispiece to Maria Weston Chapman's *Right and Wrong in Massachusetts*, "will most assuredly be abolitionized, and THOROUGHLY converted." And they understood the value and used the power of voluntary association as well as any other group of reformers or politicians. In 1838—five years after its founding—the American Anti-Slavery Society had 1,350 auxiliary local societies; employed 38 traveling agents and 75 lecturers, collecting petitions with over 415,000 signatures; circulated 646,502 publications; and counted a national membership approaching 250,000—nearly 2 percent of the national population. Given these figures, abolitionists were not entirely unreasonable in their hopes to transform public opinion, or unusual in their methods.[11]

Yet no one regarded the power of abolitionist agitation with greater awe than the anti-abolitionist, something made all the more curious and surprising by the fact that "antis" greatly outnumbered abolitionists. Daniel Webster's dismissal of abolition as a harmless "rub-dub agitation" was a decidedly minority opinion. In both the North and South, critics denounced abolition societies as dangerous agents of sedition equipped with potent technologies of organization and persuasion. Alarmed by the "amazing power of its vast political machinery," they feared that groups like the American Anti-Slavery Society would boldly assail "the Constitution and the laws of the country, with no rival influence to counteract it." Beneath the veneer of abolitionist benevolence, anti-abolitionists saw foreign conspiracies, secret plans for disunion and racial amalgamation, the deliberate instigation of violence, and a strategy more reliant on humiliation and coercion than rational argument and moral suasion. In their frequent and urgent warnings that public opinion could be abolitionized by a small band of well-organized fanatics, anti-abolitionists articulated several significant and widely shared anxieties about public opinion in the age of Jacksonian democracy.[12]

First, abolitionist agitation exploited opportunities made available by early-nineteenth-century revolutions in communications and transportation, but in ways that many Americans neither anticipated nor desired. The belief that "internal improvements" would necessarily promote national unity became difficult to sustain when abolitionists sought to bombard the slave states with mass-produced literature. In July 1835, the American Anti-Slavery Society (AAS) took advantage of the recently introduced Hoe single-cylinder press and cheap postage to send

175,000 newspapers, pamphlets, and illustrated magazines to postmasters, businesses, public offices, and homes throughout the South, with plans to send close to a million more pieces nationwide over the next year. The reaction was swift and in some places violent. In Charleston, South Carolina, for example, a group known as the "Lynch Men" broke into the post office, stole the AAS mailings, and burned them along with effigies of Garrison and Arthur Tappan. Over 150 Southern towns held public meetings to condemn the mailings, accuse abolitionists of inciting servile rebellion, and demand that Northerners take action, legal or extralegal, to suppress abolition societies and presses.[13]

Congress and Northern state legislatures expressed dismay over the incendiary mailings and made a show of solidarity with the South, but they took little concrete action. Northern mobs appeared to oblige with at least thirty-five separate incidents of violence against abolitionists over the next four months, but on closer inspection, many of the mob actions appear unrelated to the mailings. In fact, the AAS mailing campaign of 1835 was neither as unprecedented nor as prodigious as is often asserted: major evangelical and temperance organizations distributed considerably more literature, and the output of AAS presses at their peak was around half that of the major New York City dailies. The significance of the 1835 campaign was primarily symbolic. It provided anti-abolitionists with the vivid image of a growing and powerful antislavery menace, financed and directed by a small and irresponsible band of wealthy fanatics and British agents using cheap print and even cheaper government postage to abolitionize slaves, free blacks, women, and children; assault private property; disrupt public tranquility; and ultimately destroy the union.[14]

Of course, the claim that an association could employ superior financial means, technologies, or organizational acumen to unfairly influence or manufacture public opinion should be familiar to us by now. In the age of Jackson, the Bank of the United States, Masonic lodges, the Roman Catholic Church, numerous evangelical and reform societies, the legal profession, and every political party (including the Anti-Masons) became the target of comparable allegations. While most anti-abolitionists accepted that associated action and mass persuasion were necessary features of the present age, they argued that abolitionism exemplified its tendencies toward extremism (or what was often called "ultraism"), incivility, and coercion, and did so on highly volatile subject. Even those sympathetic to abolitionist ends worried over its means. The abolitionist "system of agitation" comprising "affiliated societies, gathered, and held together, and extended, by passionate eloquence" was, as William Ellery Channing observed, "the common mode by which all projects are now accomplished."

The age of individual action is gone. Truth can hardly be heard unless shouted by a crowd. The weightiest argument for a doctrine is the number which adopts it. Accordingly, to gather and organize multitudes is the first care of him who would remove an abuse or spread a reform. That the expedient is in some cases useful is not denied. But generally it is a showy, noisy mode of action, appealing to the passions, and driving men into exaggeration; and there are special reasons why such a mode should not be employed in regard to slavery; for slavery is to be opposed as not to exasperate the slave, or endanger the community in which he lives.[15]

Anti-abolitionists contrasted the "showy, noisy" means of mass agitation with the virtues of reasoned discussion and deliberation. According to New York physician David Reese, it was "the *spirit*" of abolitionist "*bitterness, wrath, censoriousness*, and *calumny*," not abolitionist "arguments and facts," that had upset the peace of the community. Like his fellow Unitarian Channing, Orville Dewey thought slavery a moral evil but repudiated "utterly the too common language of abuse adopted by the abolition societies." For Dewey, such language usually resulted when men and women resorted to associations and "combination" to remedy social injustice and neglected "the grand modern instrument of Reform": peaceable "*discussion*." Abusive language also invariably led to violence, making the abolition society and the anti-abolitionist mob two sides of the same coin of incivility. Both Reese and Catharine Beecher floated the theory that abolitionists deliberately provoked violence to garner sympathy for their cause. Beecher thought it "unchristian" to "tempt" men to violence with harsh words in this way: "It is not so much by exciting feelings of pity and humanity, and Christian love, towards the oppressed, as it is by awakening indignation at the treatment of Abolitionists themselves, that their cause has prospered." She found the progress of abolitionism all the more troubling because of the threat it posed to individual conscience and moral agency. If Christianity was "a system of persuasion, tending, by kind and gentle influences, to make men *willing* to leave off their sins," then abolitionism operated as a meddlesome "system of *coercion* by public opinion" that sought "not to convince the erring, but to convince those who are not guilty, of the sins of those who are."[16]

While most critics assailed abolitionists for their allegedly harsh language, preference for emotional appeals over reasoned argument, and eagerness to employ public opinion as a coercive force of humiliation, otherwise antislavery Northerners with Whig political inclinations pushed these points with greater urgency. Antislavery Jacksonians, being less concerned with politeness and more comfortable with collective political action, found other faults with the tactics of abolitionists. Northern "doughfaces," Southern Democrats, and Cotton Whigs would increasingly meet them head-on with more full-throated defenses of slavery and no small measure of vicious race-baiting.[17] But the hand-wringing of avowed antislavery Northerners over civility, reason, and coercion proved particularly vexing to abolitionists. To the advice that he should "argue more and denounce less" and "persuade more and rebuke less," an exasperated Frederick Douglass asked, "What point in the antislavery creed would you have me argue? On what branch of the subject do the people of this country need light?" The year was 1852, and Douglass thought that the "time for such argument is past." Like Wendell Phillips, he believed that what Americans needed to hear was "scorching irony, not convincing argument."[18]

Put another way, Douglass and Phillips did not necessarily equate public opinion with what we today call "deliberative democracy." Driven by an unshakeable conviction of the sinfulness of slavery, they had little patience for civil and reasoned public debate: "where all is plain," Douglass insisted, "there is nothing to be argued." In this light, calls for more discussion could seem like little more than a ploy to evade real moral choices and forestall reform. Indeed, nineteenth-century ideals of deliberation often went hand in hand with a conservative aversion to popular opinion and democracy.[19] Moreover, abolitionists recognized that the power of public opinion did not derive solely from discussion and reason, and they were not as troubled as their critics by what social scientists today call the "latent function" of public opinion: the power to isolate, ostracize, and shame individuals.[20]

Calvin Colton was not an agitator. In fact, he may have been the most dogged, and certainly the most prolific, critic of the "spurious and unhealthful excitements" inflicted on the public by the many "enthusiasts" and "fanatics" espousing sundry "wild projects of reformation." In this he was not, as his biographer observes, an especially original or eloquent voice for conservatism—and Colton possessed a thoroughly conservative temperament—but his writings enjoyed wide circulation and, presumably, readership.[21] For our purposes, Colton is of particular interest because he repeatedly identified public opinion—or what he alternatively called "the dynasty of opinion"—as both the distinguishing feature of American political culture and the greatest danger to the good order provided by constitutional government and statesmanship. And not surprisingly, he viewed abolitionism as organized sedition: a "grand political organization, aiming, by the use of political agencies and powers, at a radical and great change in the American political fabric."[22]

Born in Massachusetts and educated at Yale and Andover Theological Seminary, Colton served for a decade as a Presbyterian minister in upstate New York amid the religious fervor of the "burned over district." In 1826, just as the famed Finney revivals began, Colton left the ministry due to health problems and the death of his wife. Turning to a career in writing, he authored several sympathetic accounts of the Native Americans of the Great Lakes region. Relocating to England in 1831, he filed reports for the *New York Observer* and published works that defended his homeland from the aspersions of Frances Trollope and other English travelers, promoted emigration to the United States, and justified American-style revivalism. Witnessing the rigid class system and cold, formal religion of the English, Colton found many reasons to praise the openness of American society and the enthusiastic religiosity of its people.[23] But after returning to America in 1836, he reversed course. Appalled by the loud and coarse egalitarianism of both evangelical reformers and Jacksonian Democrats, he joined the Episcopal Church and the Whig Party and proceeded to churn out an impressive volume of books, pamphlets, and essays promoting the virtues of both. While unable to persuade the American people to provide state support to his church, Colton became a very successful Whig publicist, authoring the widely circulated *Junius* pamphlets and becoming the authorized biographer of Henry Clay.

While certain that public opinion exercised unusually extensive power in American society, wielding a "secret and invisible influence" that "operates on every mind, and modifies everyone's conduct," Colton admitted that it was "too ghostly, too impalpable, to be made a subject of definition." He was nonetheless convinced that a broadly shared adherence to Christianity and a general spirit of harmony between the classes pervaded American public opinion. But the openness of American society, and the absolute freedom of speech, press, assembly, and religion enjoyed by its citizens left it vulnerable to "the perpetual iteration of extravagance" and excitement "urged on by an organizing corps of itinerating, artful, everywhere-present empirics"—Colton's term of choice for "reformers." Just as the popular medical theory of the day identified overstimulation as the root cause of disease, Colton regarded the "high stimulation" of the moral world as the origin of most social ills. The "new measures" of Finneyite revivalists that Colton had earlier defended now appeared as the source and inspiration for agitating reforms. While most Americans had tolerated the *"forcing* methods" of revivalists in the hope that they would win converts and "make better citizens" of them, revivalism had also "infected" the "popular mind" with "a love and determination for excitement" that religion could never satisfy. Seeking a "wider scope of action," evangelicals turned to temperance reform and abolitionism. Just as they had undertaken "to convert sinners by force, so they undertook to reclaim mankind from their vices by force; and as they had adopted various new inventions and machineries for their former operations, so they did for the latter."[24]

It is not entirely clear what Colton meant by "force," or what "forcing methods" actually entailed, but it involved, at least in part, the use of social pressure and ostracism. Abolitionists, he alleged, were especially adept at employing "all the power of associated influence to destroy the characters of those who differed from them in opinion." As a publicist and agent for the American Colonization Society, Colton no doubt took umbrage at the fierce abolitionist assaults on colonization as a racist scheme intended to remove free African Americans from the country. As a Whig, he suspected all "political" associations (excepting, naturally, those associated with the Whig Party) of trampling over individual conscience in their quest to install a permanent and unconstitutional "*imperium in imperio*." Colton found it "astonishing to observe, how that gem of society, independence of private character, and the right of private opinion, has been marred and prostrated before the authoritative edicts of these high and formidable Associations, the most extravagant of which were concocted in caucus, and forced upon the public, by those very men who will generally be found in the Abolition ranks." This went a good way toward explaining how temperance reformers or abolitionists could carry their "unreasonable, unphilosophical theory by storm, against the sobriety and good sense of the community." And it demonstrated that "the interests of moral and religious reform" were "in the hands and under the control of a few small combinations of individuals" who were not duly elected public officials responsible to public opinion.[25]

In *The Age of Jackson*, Arthur Schlesinger Jr. identified Colton (somewhat caustically) as a "Neo-Jeffersonian Whig." Along with *New York Tribune* editor Horace Greeley and Daniel Barnard, a leader of the proslavery wing of the party, Colton aimed to "stage a boarding party against Democratic principles and rally the business community under the stolen banners." But beneath the log cabin fanfares for the common man a deeply conservative political philosophy remained in place. Barnard, for example, desired to see a more "settled and solid opinion on fundamental questions, to keep the body of the public mind at ease and at rest," and resist "all the shocks which the restless, the speculative, the bigoted or the fanatical may direct against it."[26] Try as Colton might to paint abolitionists as a small, antidemocratic band of fanatics, he could never fully suppress his own profound discomfort with democracy and public opinion. In his 1839 *A Voice from America to England*, published anonymously in London, Colton depicted the brief history of his country as a "great struggle" between "the Constitution and the Democracy." Taking his cue from Alexis de Tocqueville's recently published *Democracy in America*, he contended that American society, lacking any vestige of the "ancient institutions" and monarchical or aristocratic principles still found in Europe, had become "a dynasty of opinion." Popular education and the "march of mind," though laudable, had the "necessary evil" of making "every man, woman, and child … a politician." The Constitution provided the only settled institutions and principles in American life, but these too seemed increasingly subject to modification by public opinion, leading Colton to despair: "The Constitution is the bulwark of the nation's safety; but the dynasty of opinion is perpetually assailing it; and whether the Constitution will yet give way altogether, and totter, and fall to the ground, remains to be proved."[27]

Public Opinion, North and South

Antebellum Americans saw dangers to the Constitution and public order more tangible than Colton's "dynasty of opinion," chief among them being the ostensibly popular "justice" violently enacted by mobs. In his celebrated 1838 address to the Young Men's Lyceum of Springfield, Illinois, a young Abraham Lincoln identified "the increasing disregard for law which pervades the country; the growing disposition to substitute the wild and furious passions, in lieu of the sober judgment of Courts; and the worse than savage mobs, for the executive ministers of justice" as the greatest threat to the "perpetuation of our political institutions." Yet Lincoln's insistence that Americans should make obedience to the law "the *political religion* of the nation" required them to forget the violent history of their own revolution and the vengeful passions that animated it. "Passion has helped us; but can do no more," he concluded. "Reason, cold, calculated, unimpassioned reason, must furnish all the materials for our future support and defense." Nothing less could rescue the heroic efforts of the "founding fathers" to transform a violent politics of revolution into a peaceful and routine politics of consent. Simply put, the republic was in crisis.[28]

While Lincoln insisted that "outrages" against the rule of law were not "confined to the slaveholding, or to the non-slaveholding states," the three instances of mob violence he highlighted came from the South. In Mississippi, mobs had recently hung five gamblers in Vicksburg and five other white men and at least a dozen slaves for their suspected role in a slave insurrection. In Missouri, a St. Louis mob had lynched Frank McIntosh, a free African American boatman accused of killing a sheriff. After a mob wrested McIntosh from his jail cell, chained him to a tree, and burned him to death, a grand jury assembled to consider indictments. Luke E. Lawless, the appropriately named presiding judge, delivered the following charge to the jurors:

> If, on the other hand, the destruction of the murderer of Hammond [the sheriff] was the act, as I have said, of the many, of the multitude in the ordinary sense of those words—not the act of numerable and ascertainable malefactors, but of congregated thousands seized upon and impelled by that mysterious metaphysical and almost electrical frenzy which in all ages and nations has hurried on the infuriated multitude to deeds of death and destruction—then, I say, act not at all in the matter. The case then transcends your jurisdiction, it is beyond the reach of human law.

The jurors agreed and refused to issue any indictments.[29]

Having exonerated the lynch mob, Judge Lawless proceeded to condemn abolitionism as the true enemy of public order. Frank McIntosh "was, morally speaking, only the blind instrument in the hands of abolitionist fanatics" whose doctrines (in Lawless's overheated imagination) incited blacks to murder "their white brethren." The judge singled out Elijah Lovejoy, editor of the *St. Louis Observer*, as the chief local instigator of race war. Lovejoy, while not a full-fledged abolitionist, had reprinted abolitionist materials in his newspaper, prompting mobs to destroy his printing press on three separate occasions. When Lawless delivered his instructions, Lovejoy saw the writing on the wall and relocated across the Mississippi River to Alton, Illinois. The free state, however, proved no more accommodating. While defending his fifth press from a mob in November 1837, Lovejoy was shot and killed.[30]

Lovejoy's death gave abolitionists one of their first martyrs. In some respects, it did the same for Northern newspaper editors. While the Lovejoy mob had its share of Northern defenders, many editors—while disavowing any abolitionist sympathies—denounced the killing as a grave affront to press liberty. "If an abolition editor is murdered with impunity to-day," the *Philadelphia Commercial Herald* predicted, "an Anti-Masonic or Masonic editor may be murdered tomorrow—a Jacksonian or Van Buren or a Whig editor the next." Timing contributed to Lovejoy's martyrdom. National controversies over the suppression of abolitionist mailings and the "gagging" of abolitionist petitions to Congress had sensitized the Northern public to issues of expressive liberty. In a larger sense, the controversial emergence of abolitionism prompted Northerners to think and talk about the nature and role of public opinion in new ways. Abolitionists and other reformers embraced the possibilities suggested by an expanding public sphere and improved means of communication to envision public opinion as an engine, if not *the* engine, of radical social transformation. While many anti-abolitionists reacted by simply reasserting, often violently, the racial, gendered hierarchies that governed access to the public sphere, others of a typically Whig and conservative bent looked on the concurrent rise of abolitionism and Jacksonian democracy as indicative of a deeper crisis of political order and sought security in constitutionalism and religious orthodoxy. For other Northerners, the violent suppression of abolitionists, the censorship of the mails, and the "gag rule" on antislavery petitions in Congress "led to discussion of the nature of free speech and its relation to other interests, to seeing private suppression as a violation of free speech, to discussion of access to public discourse, and to discussion of the press as a defender and violator of free speech"—what Michael Kent Curtis has called the "popular free speech tradition."[31]

In the South, reactions to abolitionism and the resulting rethinking of public opinion proceeded along more uniform lines. Libertarian traditions of expressive liberty were discarded in favor of legal and extralegal forms of repression: laws prohibiting incendiary publications and teaching slaves to read or write, grand jury charges against public speakers and preachers suspected of exhorting slaves to revolt, lynch mobs and other acts of violence and intimidation directed against alleged agitators. A growing belief among Southerners that they lived in a distinctive, isolated, and politically embattled region went hand in hand with an increasingly unabashed defense of the peculiar institution as a positive good. In this light, the concept of public opinion performed two distinct yet complementary tasks. First, it was deployed to identify, demonize, and expel "outside" threats to Southern institutions and traditions. Second, it helped proslavery publicists to imagine and describe a home-grown, paternalistic, slaveholding humanitarianism in which public opinion protected slaves from cruelty without infringing on the rights of the master or diminishing the subordination of the slave.[32]

During the 1835 outcry against abolitionist mailings, Southerners repeatedly expressed fears that abolitionist literature would incite violent slave uprisings. In most instances, they did not bother to explain how the literature would fall into the hands of slaves, much less achieve wide readership among a largely illiterate population. It was enough simply to assert that abolitionist doctrines would somehow infiltrate the slave quarters through the medium of public opinion. More problematically, the fear of an abolitionist-inspired servile insurrection did not sit comfortably with the Southern dogma that slaves were the contented beneficiaries of a civilizing and Christian institution. How could a few AAS pamphlets stir such a happy people to bloodshed and destruction? More discerning observers saw the real purpose of the abolitionist campaign, and feared that it just might work. The greatest threat to Southerners, the Jacksonian editor Duff Green feared, was not servile insurrection but "the gradual operation of public opinion among ourselves." Should it fall under the sway of "insidious and dangerous invaders" determined to "persuade us that slavery is a sin, a curse, an evil," Green worried that the "morbid sensitivity of our own people" might lead them to agree and thus "make them the voluntary instrument of their own ruin."[33]

To justify the suppression of abolitionist presses and speech, Southerners had to acknowledge, at least implicitly, the potential persuasiveness of the abolitionist appeal, be it to slaves, free blacks, or whites. Such acknowledgments were, however, usually qualified with an insistence on the "foreign" character of abolitionist ideas and the "insidious and dangerous invaders" intent on propagating them. The South Carolina politician and planter David James McCord saw an

> invasion of the public opinion of other people, and of foreign nations, more sensible to our improvement and amendment than to their own, alike ignorant of our institutions, as indifferent to our feelings and to our interest, which through the power of the press and the unkindness of our neighbors, is brought to bear against us—to excite and divide our people, to weaken or destroy our system, and in the end, if not arrested, to end in revolution and bloodshed . . . Are we to allow, then, this foreign public opinion to mingle with our principles, and to control and alter our American institutions?

For McCord, writing in 1849, the "principles and feelings of Wilberforce and Clarkson" had come to exercise an unrivaled dominion over the public mind; the "daily press, the periodicals, the works of political economy and of fiction, the whole mass of literature" were "filled and reeking with abolition." Antislavery and a "morbid sensibility for the African" now seemed to set the agenda for all public discourse, and every event and "topic which can arouse attention, or inflame the imagination" could be "perverted" to advance the abolitionist cause.[34]

Northerners, to be sure, also worried over the susceptibility of American opinion to foreign (especially British) influence, exhibiting a sensitivity to foreign criticism every bit as prickly as that found in the South. But many Southerners believed, with good reason, that British opinion held greater sway in the North and that what Senator William Preston of South Carolina called "an immense and immediate sympathy" bound Old and New England together. This made the growing population, political power, and economic might of the Northern states all the more worrying, as did Northern dominance of the publishing industry. Boast as they did of the superiority of their refined literature, Southern presses could never hope to match the output of the North, and the frequent calls for an "intellectual blockade" of Northern writings were only partially heeded at best. As late as 1861, the *Southern Literary Messenger* complained that "if the angel Gabriel had gone into the very heart of the South, if he had taken his seat on the top of the office of the *Charleston Mercury* and there proclaimed the immediate approach of the Day of Judgment, that would not have hindered the hottest secessionist from buying the *New York Herald* and subscribing to *Harper's Magazine*." The influx of Northern journals cut into an already limited potential readership, for cities remained small and the Southern distaste for publicly supported education had left the region far behind in terms of literacy: 20.3 percent of native-born white men could not read, compared to only 3 percent in the mid-Atlantic states and 0.42 percent in New England.[35]

Southerners often responded to such unflattering facts by making them into virtues, or asserting that print and literacy were unnecessary to Southern society. As Edward J. Pringle, a young, Harvard-educated attorney argued:

> They tell us, in South Carolina, of 20,000 men who cannot read and write; we do not care for reading and writing as first of all things. If our 20,000 untaught men are daily imbibing a public opinion which teaches them, intelligently and mercifully, to perform the duties which any man in South Carolina may be called upon to perform; if the education they pick up in the thousand high places of instruction for the people, leads them to a thorough comprehension of the position they occupy, then reading and writing may come at any time thereafter.

Southerners, as Louis T. Wigfall told an English traveler, were a "peculiar people," primitive but civilized, proudly rural with no need for cities or their cultural institutions: "We have no literature—we don't need any yet. We have no press—we are glad of it. We do not require a press because we go out and discuss all the public questions from the stump with our people." Many Southerners shared Wigfall's faith in the stump as a superior medium of persuasion and believed that theirs was the "region of eloquence." Even Southern *writers* made much of this "myth of the Southern orator" and built it into a distinction between a speech-ifying South and a newspapering North. After observing a Gotham election, a character in William Alexander Carruthers's novel *The Kentuckian in New-York* (1834) lamented the impersonality of Northern campaigns conducted with "little bits of paper," in which "stump speeches" are not heard and citizens "never personally know, or even see their representatives." As sectional hostilities intensified, Southerners grew agitated at "intemperate" Northern newspapers and their faceless editors, whose "love of the almighty dollar and the plaudits of the rabble" led them to fill their columns with "senseless detraction" against the slave states. Southern orators, it was said, subdued the rabble for the sake of honor; Northern newspapers pandered to it for money.[36]

The sentiment of honor and the ideal of mastery colored Southern conceptions of public opinion, and much of what Southerners wrote and said about the vox populi mingled a haughty planter class contempt for popular ignorance with a romantic, if not gothic, dread of its power. Time and time again, public opinion appeared as omnipotent, irresistible, and fateful, yet arbitrary, instable, and fickle. A "Southern Gentleman," Daniel Hundley insisted in his survey of the region's social relations, "would rather stand in the shoes of the meanest slave on his plantation, of the laziest and most ignorant gumbo whose back was ever made to bleed under the overseer's lash, than to become that thing—that most emasculate and miserable mockery of a man—the SLAVE OF PUBLIC OPINION."[37]

But public opinion did have a constructive, albeit conservative, role to play in Southern society as a keeper of tradition, community cohesion, and "the people's peace." Take away the force of "Public Opinion, with its ostracism, its mobs, and its tar and feathers," George Fitzhugh warned, and "many good citizens would shoot, like fiery comets, from their spheres, and disturb society with their eccentricities and their crimes." This, in Fitzhugh's estimation, was exactly the problem in the North, where the "laxity of public opinion" failed to restrain "the right of private judgment," leaving a band of "Infidels, Skeptics, Millerites, Mormons, Agrarians, Spiritual Rappers, Wakemanites, Free Negroes, and Bloomers" to "disturb the peace of society, threaten the security of property, offend the public sense of decency, assail religion, and invoke anarchy."[38] Viewing public opinion as civil society's defense against fanatics and libelers, Fitzhugh did not shy away from the implication that force ultimately made opinion, that aggression was as essential to a salubrious state of public opinion as enlightenment. Many Southern intellectuals indulged in an imaginary identification of writing and debating with fighting and dueling. "Southern thought," Fitzhugh asserted, was distinctively bold, energetic, and fearless, a reflection of the exceptional "strength of will" and bodily power of men "accustomed to command from our cradle." A Southerner did not simply debate a rival; he "challenged" him. Indeed, by the 1850s, secessionists had become known as "fire-eaters," a term originally applied to the dueling societies of eighteenth-century Ireland.[39]

As an enforcer of community values, public opinion was also thought to protect the slave from mistreatment. Slavery apologetics almost never failed to mention this. Clergy, politicians, scholars, and other Southern intellectuals frequently asserted that the ongoing progress of Southern civilization would continue to soften master-slave relations. The Reverend Thomas Thornton of Mississippi confidently declared "in the sight of heaven and earth, that the cases of *cruel* and *bad* masters, on account of public opinion, are comparatively rare, because it is directly against it, and public law, which protects the slave." James P. Holcombe, a professor of law at the University of Virginia, informed members of the State Agricultural Society that a "public sentiment, growing in its strength and increasing in its exactions, covers the slave with a protective shield, far less easily broken through, than those feeble barriers of law which in our Free States, are interposed between the degraded and outcast black man, and his white brother." Public opinion would do more to protect slaves than legislation could, as it was concerned with "the whole range of their happiness and improvement," especially as it related to religious instruction and the "disruption of family ties." Another law professor, Nathaniel Beverly Tucker of the College of William and Mary, agreed, noting that the "moral coercion exerted by public opinion in this enlightened and moral age" failed to offer similar protections to the "the peasantry of the old continent and the laboring class of Great Britain." Only in the American South did public opinion operate to lessen the hardships of those condemned to physical labor, and it would continue to do so unless "retarded by the efforts of (Northern) fanaticism, which cause the master occasionally to tighten the chains of servitude."[40]

Many Southerners went so far as to claim that public opinion was too sensitive to the welfare of the slave and that this tempted masters to refrain from exercising necessary and salutary discipline. But such indulgence could have its advantages. In his widely circulated 1837 address on slavery, South Carolina state chancellor William Harper argued that "public opinion, should, if possible, bear down even more strongly on masters who practice any wanton cruelty on their slave," for it would lessen "the odium which is so industriously excited against ourselves and our institutions" by abolitionists and improve the reputation of the South in the larger "civilized world." But the claim that public opinion protected the slave was too riddled with theoretical contradictions and practical problems to achieve even these modest objectives. Would the gentleman planter who adamantly refused to be a "SLAVE OF PUBLIC OPINION" permit it to regulate his behavior toward his own slaves? How could public opinion actually supervise and regulate the ostensibly "private" relations between masters and slaves on thousands of isolated farms and plantations across the South? The most ardent and eloquent proslavery ideologues struggled for answers.[41]

Believing slavery to be inherently sinful, abolitionists had no patience for the argument that public opinion mitigated its evils. They denied that public opinion was a friend to the slave, argued that slavery polluted every other aspect of Southern society, and discovered plentiful documentation for both claims in Southern newspapers. Theodore Dwight Weld devoted nearly one-third of his *American Slavery as It Is* to refuting the "fiction" that "Public Opinion is a Protection to the Slave," filling sixty-seven pages of small print with excerpted advertisements for runaway slaves, notices of slave auctions, speeches and editorials celebrating the profits earned through slave breeding, and eyewitness accounts of the cruelties daily visited on slaves and free blacks alike. If public opinion really frowned on such things, why would masters and mistresses advertise that their runaway slaves had been whipped, scarred, and branded? Weld's book (which provided much of the raw material for Harriet Beecher Stowe's *Uncle Tom's Cabin*) sought to document not only the "absolutely diabolical . . . *inhumanity* of slaveholding 'public opinion' toward slaves" but also the more general climate of opinion it fostered, an "omnipresent public sentiment reckless of human life" that came as the "natural result of their daily habit of plundering and oppressing the slave." In Weld's estimation, the recklessness and "savage ferocity" of lynch mobs, eye-gouging, duels, gunfights, and practices of Southern violence took their cue "from the downright ruffianism of the slaveholding *spirit* in the 'highest class of society.'"[42]

Such Northern depictions of the South as a violent, lawless, backward society degraded by slavery and ruled by a "Chivalry" and the poor, illiterate whites who gave them their votes would become increasingly common, especially by the 1850s. So, too, would Southern depictions of the North (especially the Northeast) as a coarse and disorderly society dominated by mercenary capitalists, wild-eyed fanatics, and partisan wire-pullers. Both depictions were, of course, gross oversimplifications, but they played a foundational role—as gross oversimplifications often do—in the formation of sectional identities and, ultimately, the Northern and Southern nationalisms of the Civil War era.[43] As I have suggested, these stereotypes also reflected divergent conceptions of public opinion. After 1840, the relatively clear and consistent differences between the parties that I discuss in chapter 3 eroded as new and different issues shifted the dynamics of political argument. The issues of slavery and sectionalism were of particular importance: as they consumed more oxygen, distinctions between "democrats" and "aristocrats" were replaced by distinctions between North and South, slave and free, and a politics of mass persuasion versus a politics of chivalric violence.

No incident better illustrated this new polarity than the 1856 caning of Senator Charles Sumner of Massachusetts by Representative Preston Brooks of South Carolina. Infuriated by Sumner's "The Crime against Kansas" speech, with its depiction of his uncle, Senator Andrew Butler of South Carolina, as a Don Quixote engaged in a "chivalrous" and delusional defense of "the harlot, slavery," Brooks beat Sumner severely with his walking cane on the floor of the Senate. Republican newspapers readily characterized the incident as a demonstration of the ultima ratio of the South: a resort to violence against arguments they could not answer. "The logic of the Plantation, brute violence and might," the *Albany Evening Journal* opined, "has at last risen where it was inevitable it should rise to—the Senate of the United States." For the *Richmond Enquirer*, Sumner's speech was an abuse of senatorial privilege and decorum that illustrated the "daily abuse of liberty of speech and of the press, and of freedom of religion," that Northern fanatics "habitually employ for greater mischief and crime." It would be far better

> that man were without the gift of speech, than to use it as they do. Better that he could neither read or write, than have his head and heart perverted, by the foul and filthy stuff that oozes from the abolition press. Better, that his religion were prescribed by a priest and enforced by the inquisition, than that he should become an habitué of Greeley's philansteries, of Andrew's gorgeous salons of Free Love, of Mormon dwellings, or of Oneida dens. Better that the cut of his coat and the number of his buttons were fixed by statute and enforced by penalties, than that women should defy public opinion and parade the streets in unfeminine apparel. The liberties of America are safe so long as they are not abused. They are not worth preserving when abuse becomes general.[44]

It is not surprising, but nonetheless worth noting, that Preston Brooks had expressed a similar theory several years before he caned Sumner. Speaking on the floor of the House in 1854 during the debate over the Kansas-Nebraska Act, he declared that the institution of slavery had been "the greatest blessing to the country" by acting as a "safety-valve" through which all the "fanaticism, communism," and "secretions of morbid sentimentality" of Northern society could be harmlessly vented. Take away slavery and all its imagined evils and "presumed immorality," Brooks argued, and Northerners would soon turn on themselves in a "social explosion" of violent discontent and ultraism.[45]

A New and Important Element

As the concept of public opinion became another point of contestation through which Northerners and Southerners could more sharply define their differences, the sentimental project of achieving national unity through national "feeling" became increasingly untenable. Likewise, hopes that the union could be maintained through appeals to the heroic sacrifices of the Revolution and the "genius" of the Constitution became more difficult to sustain as sectional disputes over slavery, the territories, tariffs, and an array of smaller yet no less divisive issues eroded the national character and composition of both major political parties. Improvements in communication and transportation, which had once promised to bind the union together, increasingly appeared to have the opposite effect. As Americans received more news of how Americans from other regions seemed to think, feel, and live, an expanded sense of nationality did not necessarily result. In many respects, the emergence of a national network of communication in the mid-nineteenth century produced, as Trish Loughran has put it, "an ever more entrenched sectionalism" and "a nation whose differences could no longer be contained in constitutional language" and its thin fictions of sovereignty and public opinion.[46]

Ironically, the emergence of a more integrated national public sphere led some to question whether the United States could really be said to have a public opinion. Such doubts resonated with a more general climate of skepticism toward public opinion that developed in the mid-nineteenth century. Influential British and European political theorists and philosophers attacked the allegedly liberal faith in public opinion as a progressive, unifying, and civilizing force as hopelessly naïve in an age of mass politics. While acknowledging the merits of a free press and holding to the principle that governments should take public opinion into account, "Aristocratic liberals" such as John Stuart Mill, François Guizot, and Alexis de Tocqueville grew increasingly concerned with the despotism of majority opinion. Other liberals worried over the diminishment of professional and genteel authority in a public sphere overrun with charlatans, demagogues, and purveyors of sensationalism. George Cornewall Lewis, an English Liberal statesman, in his dense and learned, 400-page *Essay on the Influence of Authority in Matters of Opinion*, argued that proper deference to professional and educated opinion was necessary to the progress of society and allowed it to "approach more and more to a state in which opinion will predominate over violence" and "reason will hold the ascendancy over passion."[47]

Such "liberal ambivalence" regarding public opinion was less prevalent among Americans. In some cases, intensifying political hostilities and the prospect of civil war led some political theorists to invest even more heavily in the promise of public opinion as a moderating and civilizing force. Frederick Grimke's *The Nature and Tendency of Free Institutions*, the most extensive treatise on American politics produced during the antebellum era, identified public opinion as the "great preventative check of civil society." A reclusive Ohio jurist and son of a wealthy South Carolina planter, Grimke believed that the exceptional strength of public opinion in American society made the sort of heavy-handed intrusions employed by European states unnecessary. The "moral force of public opinion" quietly introduced reforms that "would otherwise have disturbed the whole order of society." It also worked to mitigate the evils of party spirit. Although the "journals of no country surpass those of the United States in ribaldry and abuse," Grimke believed that "what we term public discontent is in reality only private discontent in disguise" and that American public opinion rested on a broad consensus of shared political and moral principles. Better yet, public opinion would inevitably work to promote political agreement and social cohesion:

> What we term public opinion is not the opinion of any set of men, or of any particular party, to the exclusion of all others. It is the combined result of a great number of differing opinions. Some portion of truth often adheres to views and speculations which are apparently the most unreasonable, and it is the true side which they present that goes to swell and make up the sum of public opinion. Not that that is always the case—not that it is the case in any particular instance—but the tendency is constantly in that direction.[48]

Grimke's optimistic view of public opinion derived in large part from a conviction that he lived in "the golden age of the republic," where prosperity had diffused wealth and knowledge to an unexampled extent. Despite considerable diversities in the condition of individuals, he believed that the "great bulk" of Americans belonged to the middle class. Yet none of this had produced any leveling effects or diminished the cultural and intellectual authority of what Grimke called "the superior classes." Owing to a basic "principle of human nature," even the most "uncultivated men" aspired to a "standard of excellence," a "feeling so spontaneous and so little under the command of the will that it disposes the bulk of the population to look up to and defer to the opinions of the superior classes." Grimke's happy belief that the moral and material progress of American society was not imperiled by any deep ideological divisions, persistent inequalities, or violent passions is all the more surprising in light of his two more renowned sisters, the abolitionists Sarah and Angelina Grimké. While remaining close to his sisters, Frederick avoided discussing slavery with them: he had no use for abolitionism and little faith in the power of moral suasion, and he viewed the African race as naturally inferior and incapable of assimilation into white society. Moreover, he defended the right of secession but believed that the "superior classes" of the South would never be so foolhardy as to exercise that right. The events of 1860 proved him wrong, but he continued to believe that his political science would be relevant to future generations. Upon his death, in 1863, Grimke's will instructed that a final edition of his work be deposited in both the Library of Congress and the Library of the Confederate States.[49]

Celebrations of the wondrous and sublime power of public opinion remained a staple of Independence Day orations, popular lectures, and college addresses, but they were increasingly accompanied by warnings against the dangers of popular agitation and disorganizing theories and by calls for the sober and responsible leadership of educated and virtuous men. Robert Charles Winthrop, descendant of John Winthrop, former Speaker of the House and Daniel Webster's appointed replacement to the Senate, urged his fellow Harvard alumni to engage in public discourse with the highest sense of moral obligation and responsibility. As a consequence of the "inventions, discoveries, and improvements of modern times," the world was "fast ceasing to be governed by any mere material forces" and had "reached a period of which the great characterizing and governing principle is Opinion,—Public Opinion," a phenomenon Winthrop likened to a "subtle and elastic fluid, that infused "itself into every joint of the social system" and penetrated "the mighty mass of human motive and human action." It was "nothing less, and nothing more, than the aggregate of individual opinions: the resultant . . . of all those various concurring or conflicting opinions which individuals conceive, express, and advocate." The rise of public opinion presented a unique and fortuitous opportunity, for the "main instruments by which individual minds, in proportion to their natural or acquired energy, are brought to bear upon Public Opinion, or upon the public mind from which it emanates, are obviously the instruments which belong peculiarly to educated men."[50]

While there had never before been "so many opportunities for the employment of tongues and types," there had never been "so many temptations to abuse them." To appreciate the enormity of this problem, Winthrop urged his audience to "calculate the pernicious effect upon the community of a single, corrupt, licentious newspaper, coining slanders like a mint, changing phases like the moon, with three hundred sixty-five opinions in a year upon every subject which it treats, splicing its daily and its nightly potions with every variety of obscene and sensual stimulant." Given this, the need for "upright, intelligent, independent, and conscientious men" to take up their pens and espouse "neither wild fanaticism nor a bigoted conservatism" was self-evident. The vast machinery of public opinion had woven "one all-pervading nervous system over the whole range of civilized society" that transmitted ideas and sentiments true and false, sacred and profane, moral and immoral. To Winthrop and other self-identified "moderates," the conflicting and contradictory influences that suffused public opinion required the stabilizing influence of "the best men."[51]

But the fact that public opinion was rife with conflict and contradiction, much of it manufactured by purveyors of sensationalism and partisan propaganda, could just as easily suggest that there was really no such thing as "public opinion" at all. Preaching to his students in 1856, Harvard president James Walker allowed that "public opinion, in its place and degree, is a legitimate principle and rule of human conduct." But what was its place and degree? On "simple questions resting on a direct appeal to common sense and the moral sentiments," public opinion was usually right; on most anything else, it was not. A small number of "active spirits" ran the "whole machinery of party and popular agitation" and could easily make themselves "sound like the public voice." A "small knot of philosophers" had managed to do this during the French Revolution. Could the present age, with its steam-powered machinery of agitation, be any different? To the notion that public opinion expressed the reasoned judgment of the people, Walker replied, "whoever supposes a multitude of persons can really think, and yet think exactly alike, has yet to learn what thinking means." Simply put, there was no such thing as public opinion: "Take away what early education has done, and what mere authority has done, and what sympathy and imitation have done, and what party spirit and party drill have done, and what addresses to the feelings, and especially to men's fears and jealousies, have done, and what is there left? Public opinion, do you say?"[52]

The lesson Walker intended for his students amounted to little more than the standard New England Unitarian injunction to think for oneself. But in other contexts, skepticism regarding the presence and power of public opinion could have larger implications. By the 1850s, if not earlier, reformers who had once invested their hopes in strategies of moral suasion had grown impatient, if not despondent. The derision heaped on "ultraists" in the press, the violence of anti-abolition mobs, the temporizing of party politicians, and the intransigence of sinners had no doubt taken its toll. Women, who had contributed the greatest share of the early fervor and organizational effort to abolitionism, temperance, and other moral reforms, experienced the most acute disillusionment and saw their influence decline as men assumed control of more "practical" political and institutional reform strategies. Temperance reformers abandoned efforts to awaken the souls of drunkards and dram-sellers in favor of Maine laws. Abolitionists turned from appeals to the conscience of slaveholders to lambasting proslavery politicians and (with some trepidation) joining antislavery parties. The power of moral influence mattered less and less; in America, as Theodore Parker asserted in 1852, "public opinion is controlled by money and numbers."[53]

One need not take this assertion too much further to conclude that "public opinion" signified little more than a process by which money controlled numbers. For the radical German émigré journalist Karl Heinzen, editor of the *Boston Pioneer*, American public opinion was "the mere handmaid of a few intriguers, and its expression the result of an unprincipled party training." In a May 1860 speech delivered to a gathering of fellow German-Americans in New York (and later published in Garrison's *Liberator*), he asked what could be made of a "public opinion that has for half a century discussed the question of whether slavery and freedom fit together, and has not yet come clear on the point," and could "still be made to incline from side to side by every humbugger and knave?" Even when public opinion appeared to reach near uniformity on a question, it often lacked the power to effect any change. For example, every resident of New York City had joined in the "general cry against the corruption of the city government." But "public opinion, armed with the right of assembly, the freedom of the press and popular suffrage, has not yet been able to clean this Augean stable." So what hope could any reasonable person entertain for public opinion to combat great national evils? Far from being the voice of a sovereign people, public opinion was in fact the greatest obstacle to progress, justice, and democracy in America:

> Nothing has become more necessary in this time of loitering, of repetition, of faith in authority, and of party servility, than that the authority of public opinion should be abolished, and individual thought installed in its stead, so that from this public opinion may spring up public judgment, public sentiment, public knowledge, and public justice. Public opinion has become public falsehood and tyranny. Almost everything that is classed under its protection is fraud and falsehood, but it prolongs its life through the faith of the great masses.[54]

Heinzen offered no concrete suggestions as to how public opinion would be abolished. But in the Louisville platform of 1854, a political manifesto co-authored with several other radical German Forty-Eighters, he denounced slavery and advocated equal rights for women and African Americans, penal reform, judicial reform, education reform, free homesteads, and the elimination of the office of the president and the U.S. Senate. Conspicuously absent from this list was a "reform" Heinzen had infamously advocated shortly before he left Europe: political assassination. In his 1849 pamphlet *Der Mord* (Murder), which would influence Mikhail Bakunin and countless other anarchists, he boldly declared that a man "who would not joyously sacrifice his life to decimate a million barbarians is not a true republican"—words that have led historians to designate Heinzen as one of the intellectual founders of modern terrorism. That William Lloyd Garrison would publish Heinzen's work in the *Liberator* suggests how thin his commitment pacifism and nonresistance had become.[55]

In the Deep South, and far on the other the end of the ideological spectrum from Karl Heinzen, stood John C. Calhoun. But when it came to public opinion, both men agreed on several points: like Heinzen, Calhoun saw public opinion as a novel and disruptive force in history, an obstacle to true republican government, although the two men's visions of republicanism differed vastly. And unlike Heinzen, Calhoun's ideas had changed considerably over time. As a younger man and ardent nationalist, Calhoun had rhapsodized about building a "perfect system of roads and canals" that would "bind the republic together." As an older and pessimistic defender of states' rights and the slaveholding interest, Calhoun warned that communication, transportation, popular education and the diffusion of knowledge, and all the other "improvements" that nineteenth-century civilization had to offer would not necessarily instill a sense of national unity or bring about a harmony of divergent interests. In his *Disquisition on Government*, written in fits and starts during the 1840s and published shortly after his death in 1850, Calhoun argued that the progress of civilization would first "unsettle the principles and opinions" on which governments originated, leading to a "period of transition, which must necessarily be one of uncertainty, confusion, error, and wild and fierce fanaticism." It appeared to him that

> [t]he governments of the more advanced and civilized portions of the world are now in the midst of this period. It has proved, and will continue to prove a severe trial to existing political institutions of every form. Those governments which have not the sagacity to perceive what is truly public opinion—to distinguish between it and the mere clamor of faction, or shouts of fanaticism—and the good sense and firmness to yield, timely and cautiously, to the claims of one—and to resist, promptly and decidedly, the demands of the other—are doomed to fall.

But how to perceive "true" public opinion and distinguish it from the clamors of faction and the shouts of fanaticism? The founders had confronted a comparable dilemma in 1787 and responded with a federal constitution that promised to check the power of factions, diminish the damaging influence of "enthusiasm," and protect minority interests from the tyrannies of majorities. Both Alexander Hamilton and James Madison soon realized that this was not enough and posited a "public opinion" that would fulfill that promise, albeit in decidedly different ways.[56]

The Calhoun of the *Disquisition* no longer believed that public opinion, especially as expressed by the press, could offer such a remedy. Partisans and fanatics exerted far more control over the press than any of the founders could have imagined. In many respects, the press and public opinion only served to augment the already overwhelming power of numerical political majorities. Public opinion was not, as was often claimed, "the united opinion of the whole community." Rather, it was usually "nothing more than the opinion or voice of the strongest interest, or combination of interests; and, not unfrequently, of a small, but energetic and active portion of the whole." In saying this, Calhoun did not mean to "underestimate the great power and influence" of public opinion. Rather, he thought it deserved "to be considered a new and important political element" that traditional political philosophy and constitutional theory could neither explain nor account for.[57]

With his proposal for a "concurrent majority," Calhoun attempted to do just that. "True" public opinion could only arise through the practice of compromise among the various and competing interests. Indeed, the guiding "principle, in constitutional governments," was "*compromise,*" in "absolute governments" it was "*force.*" But compromise was something that had to be forced; some "necessity" had to compel "the different interests, or portions, or orders, to compromise." For Calhoun, that necessity was the danger of disunion. Accordingly, "the voice of the people—uttered under the necessity of avoiding the greatest calamities, through the organs of a government so constructed as to suppress the expression of all partial and selfish interests, and to give full and faithful utterance to the sense of the whole community, in reference to its common welfare—may, without impiety, be called *the voice of God.*" In what Richard Hofstadter once called the "intellectual Black Mass" of Calhoun's theories, crisis functioned as a necessary precondition for the formation of true public opinion.[58] In the political reality of the 1850s, crisis pushed the United States down the road toward civil war.

Corn-Pone Opinions

Public opinion is formed relative to a property basis. Therefore, slave-holders battle any policy which depreciates their slaves as property. What increases the value of this property, they favor. When you tell them that slavery is immoral, they rebel, because they do not like to be told they are interested in an institution which is not a moral one. When you enter into a defense of slavery, they seize upon it, for they like justification. The result is, that public opinion is formed among them which insists upon the encouragement or protection, the enlargement or perpetuation of slavery—and secures them property in the slave.

—Abraham Lincoln, "Speech at Hartford, Connecticut" (1860)

For Abraham Lincoln, public opinion did not contain the better angels of our nature. As an aggregation of individual opinions shaped predominantly by material concerns, public opinion appeared to work in favor of Southerners and Northern Democrats who wished to expand and even nationalize the institution of slavery. If newly settled territories were allowed to vote on the slavery question, the property interests of Southern settlers would always overcome the "indifference" of Northern settlers. Moreover, racist justifications for slavery also appeared to be winning out in the court of public opinion. Justice Roger Taney's opinion in the *Dred Scott* case asserted that the humanitarian "change in public opinion and feeling in relation to the African race which has taken place since the adoption of the Constitution" did not alter the document's original intent to exclude people of that race from citizenship. Lincoln, by contrast, believed that "the change between then and now is decidedly the other way" and that Taney and the Supreme Court sought to "appropriate the benefit" of an increasingly racist public opinion to protect slaveholding interests. "If slavery is considered upon a property basis," Lincoln reasoned, then "public opinion must be forced to its support."[1]

There were, however, countervailing forces at work. "Almost every man has a sense of certain things being wrong, and at the same time, a sense of its pecuniary value," and these senses could "conflict in the mind, and make a riddle of a man." Human societies also had a "collective sense of right and wrong," something that Lincoln variously termed "public sentiment" or "the public mind." Public sentiment ran deeper than public opinion; it denoted, as one Lincoln scholar has put it, a "largely unconscious body of habits, received opinions, prejudices, assumptions, allegiances, and dispositions through which we make sense of the political world." Public opinion might, for a time, work in favor of an immoral institution like slavery, but public sentiment would never ultimately accept that human bondage was "simply a matter of dollars and cents." For Lincoln, the Democratic Party represented public opinion, and the Republican Party represented public sentiment. The Republicans "would mould public opinion to the fact" that slavery was wrong and, should they get "control of the general government," prevent its extension. Slavery would then be returned to a place "where the public mind shall rest in the belief that it is in course of ultimate extinction." But without public sentiment, Lincoln and the Republicans could do nothing.[2]

Lincoln's conception of public opinion as an aggregation of individual opinions shaped largely by economic concerns was unusually precise, and somewhat unique for his time. In the decades following the Civil War, the belief that public opinion "was formed relative to a property basis" would become commonplace, while a belief in the moral soundness of "public sentiment" became increasingly rare. This shift helps in part to explain the notably dim view of public opinion prevalent among postwar writers and intellectuals, especially those of a liberal bent—a view that led many toward a more empirical, social-psychological conception of public opinion that anticipated the behaviorism of twentieth-century public opinion research.

In an essay entitled "Corn-Pone Opinions" (written in 1901 but not published until 1923), Mark Twain opened with a childhood reminiscence of Jerry, a Missouri slave who entertained young Twain with mock sermons preached from atop a woodpile. In one especially memorable performance, Jerry advanced the proposition that if "you tell me whar a man gits his corn-pone, en I'll tell you what his 'pinions is." Twain took this to mean that an individual "must restrict himself to corn-pone opinions—at least on the surface. He must get his opinions from other people; he must reason out none for himself; he must have no first hand views." But Twain argued that this did not go far enough. Individuals did not tailor their opinions to conform to majority opinion "by calculation and intention." Indeed, Twain doubted that there really was such a thing as a reasoned, independent, original opinion on any subject: "there are none but corn-pone opinions." In matters of fashion, manners, morals, religion, and politics, social ties and sympathies took precedence over individual reasoning and examination. "We all do no end of feeling, and we mistake it for thinking. And out of it we get an aggregation which we consider a boon. Its name is public opinion. It is held in reverence. It settles everything. Some think it the voice of God."[3]

As an exercise in public opinion theory, "Corn-Pone Opinions" is not worthy of much notice. Neither Jerry's sermon nor Twain's gloss on it would have surprised any reader of Mill and Tocqueville—or for that matter, John Locke, who well understood the influence of social feelings and pressures on the formation of individual opinion. It could be argued that Twain's essay simply reiterated a perennial and characteristic liberal ambivalence toward public opinion: if public opinion assumes a new preeminence in a liberal political and social order, its power can also work to undermine the very individual liberty and individuality to which that order is ostensibly committed. But as a document in the history of the concept of public opinion, Twain's essay is instructive. As the high-minded idealism of the Civil War era appeared to give way to the acquisitive utilitarianism of the "Gilded Age" (a phrase that, if it needs reminding, Twain coined), talk of public opinion as the reasoned righteousness of a sovereign people seemed increasingly out of place. Political-constitutional fictions of public opinion had little explanatory power amid the increasing scale, complexity, and interdependence of economic and social institutions and networks.[4]

An influential cohort of liberal reformers devoted particular attention to the shortcomings of American popular government and public opinion. Many were motivated by a feeling that popular partisan politics had excluded them—the "best men"—from their rightful leadership roles, and they sought to remedy the situation with civil service reform and a system of "educational politics" that would emancipate the ordinary citizen from the mindless rituals of popular partisanship. In other instances, liberal skepticism toward public opinion and popular democracy was tied to a defense of corporate capitalism from meddlesome socialists, Greenbackers, and single-taxers. As their embrace of laissez-faire political economy tightened, their commitment to political democracy loosened. In this respect, liberal appeals to science and the authority of experts went hand in hand with a desire to limit the scope of popular government by removing contentious social and economic questions from the docket of public debate.[5]

At bottom, the liberal critique of American public opinion rested on two frequently reiterated postulates. The first was that the "formation of public opinion" was now "entirely left to the press"—a development that liberals greeted with considerable ambivalence. The second postulate was that "democratic public opinion" was "molded as never before by economic, rather than by religious, moral, or political considerations." The contrast between the (ostensibly) principled public debates of the Civil War era and the labor, currency, and tariff "questions" of the Gilded Age led liberals to question the common citizens' ability to fathom the complexities of political economics, much less to understand where they got their corn-pone.[6]

We can get a good sense of how these two postulates worked together by examining one of the most articulate and prominent journalistic advocates of liberal reform: E. L. Godkin of the *Nation* and the *New York Evening Post*. In some respects, Godkin is not an especially reliable liberal narrator. The story of his conversion from idealistic champion of liberal republicanism to disaffected critic of American democracy is well known, and his indifference to the fate of the freedman, his disdain for the "Chromo-Civilization" of the petit bourgeois, and his unblinking advocacy of laissez-faire economics are well established. But if historians no longer regard Godkin's perspectives on late-nineteenth-century politics as accurate or authoritative, his writings exercised considerable sway among his contemporaries. William James thought Godkin the "towering influence in all thought concerning public affairs," a writer who "influenced other writers who never quoted him, and determined the whole current of discussion."[7]

Although he spent most of his professional life on American soil, it is not entirely accurate to characterize Godkin as an American liberal: James Bryce called him a "European who never became thoroughly Americanized." But his youthful enthusiasm for democracy and liberalism—and his discomfort with the English class system—drew him to the United States. Born in Ireland in 1831 and educated at Queen's College in Belfast, where he absorbed the ideas of Mill, Bentham, and Tocqueville, he abandoned a career in law for journalism. After writing a popular and timely *History of Hungary* and covering the Crimean War for the *London Daily News*, he moved to the United States in 1856 and soon found his way into the liberal-intellectual circles of New York and Boston. He continued to serve as a correspondent for the *Daily News*, and then as an editorial consultant for the *New York Times*.[8]

The politics of the sectional crisis fired Godkin's idealism, and Union victory inspired a confidence in the prospects for democracy that could only lead to subsequent disappointment. Godkin clung to his nostalgia for the Civil War years as a time of "real 'Americanism,' " when "[f]orce was worshipped, but it was moral force: it was the force of reason, of humanity, of human equality, of a good example." Such ebullient optimism was not uncommon among American and English liberals. In an 1865 letter to Godkin, John Stuart Mill predicted that the "great concussion which has taken place in the American mind must have loosened the foundations of all prejudices, and secured a fair hearing for impartial reason on all subjects." In a spirited defense of American democracy against its "aristocratic" European critics, written that year, Godkin deemed the spread of democracy inevitable due to the diffusion of Christianity, which taught the principle of spiritual equality, and the study of political economy, which taught "that men are free and independent."[9]

The Victorian conviction that Western civilization had passed into what Walter Bagehot called an "age of discussion" led liberal reformers to take a keen interest in that mysterious phenomenon known as "public opinion."[10] Excluded (for the most part) from public office and lacking influence within the Republican Party, they devoted their energies to shaping public opinion through "independent" newspapers like the *Springfield Republican* and the *New York Evening Post* (which Godkin edited from 1883 to 1899) and the "higher journalism" of such periodicals as *Harper's Weekly*, the *Atlantic Monthly*, and the *Nation*, which Godkin also would edit from its founding in 1865 until 1899. Originally conceived as a strong voice for Radical Reconstruction, democratic nationalism, and the rights of labor, the first issue announced the "triumph of American democracy"; heralded recent triumphs of the many over the few, equality over privilege, law over power, and "opinion over the sword"; and predicted "the rapid growth of the community in intelligence, experience, and self-possession."[11]

But Godkin would soon lose interest in reconstruction and, if he had ever had any to begin with, the fate of the freed slaves. The violent labor strikes of 1867 and 1873 dampened his sympathies for the worker, and his enthusiasm for democracy came with some significant qualifications. In the same month (July 1865) as the first issue of the *Nation*, an essay by Godkin on "The Democratic View of Democracy" appeared in the *North American Review*. In it, he took aim at the "extraordinary notion" that "majorities are infallible" and "that the general diffusion of an opinion is to be accepted as proof of its soundness," a widespread belief that had, among other things, led to the "exclusion of men of high culture from much share in the management of our affairs." He improbably blamed "foreign-born voters" for the pervasiveness of this notion, which they had "received from the democratic teachings of Europe"—teachings that treated the franchise as a right, not a privilege, and failed to recognize "the most important function of popular government—the education of those who live under it."[12]

From here, Godkin launched into a series of related themes that he would reiterate throughout the remainder of his editorial career. First, he insisted that the newspaper had become the common school of popular political education, and thus the dominant organ of public opinion. Steam-powered presses and news wires brought the "voter in Kansas into almost as close and intimate communion with the voter in New York, as if they met everyday in the marketplace." Pronouncements on the new and unrivaled power of the newspaper press were a ubiquitous feature of Gilded Age public discourse. "Few can fail to see that journalism has already become the first power in this land," declared Samuel Bowles of the *Springfield Republican* in 1875, and "that the pulpit, the platform, and the schoolhouse are all subordinate to it, or of narrower influence." Where antebellum-era press criticism tended to view newspapers as extensions of other institutions (most notably political parties), postbellum critics saw the press as a distinct institution—a fourth estate—and drew on the sociological theories of Auguste Comte and Herbert Spencer to explain its development and influence. In this light, the increasing technical sophistication and complexity of newspaper production would naturally lead to greater impersonality and objectivity in its content.[13]

Yet for Godkin, the emergence of the large-scale urban daily was less a sociological than an economic development, and the prospect of greater impersonality in its editorial policies seemed unlikely. To talk of "news" was to engage in airy abstractions: "to make it a ponderable, merchantable commodity, somebody has to collect it, condense it, and clothe it in language; and its quality—indeed its whole value—depends upon the character of the men employed in doing this." Unfortunately, Godkin viewed the newspaper profession as a "moral and intellectual dunghill." Moreover, the ostensibly declining influence of the pulpit, the orator's platform, and other modes of oral communication drove Godkin into deeper despair. The dominance of the press placed the illiterate at greater disadvantage; those who could not (or did not) read became "the blind tool of an educated few." As proof of this proposition, Godkin cited the recent revolt of Southern "redeemers" and cautiously suggested that literacy tests for the enfranchisement of freedmen had some merit.[14]

Given his active role on the Tilden commission of 1875–1877, which (unsuccessfully) proposed to impose a severe property requirement for the suffrage in New York municipal elections, Godkin's distaste for universal suffrage come as no surprise. And as this measure would have denied the vote to a good number of literate men of small means, there are good reasons to suspect that his support of suffrage restriction had as much (if not more) to do with class formation and consciousness, racial and ethnic prejudice, and the well-known animosity of liberal reformers toward urban political machines than it did with the education of the citizen. That said, literacy was not simply a pretext for Godkin: he was genuinely concerned about the apparent asymmetries of knowledge created by the emergence of the "mass media" and, like other founding members of the American Social Science Association, the problems of social knowledge and authority in an increasingly interdependent society.[15]

But it was not enough for citizens to read newspapers. Like Walter Lippmann in his writings on public opinion in the 1920s, Godkin repeatedly asked if the press "could furnish from one edition to the next the amount of knowledge which the democratic theory of public opinion demands." Like Lippmann, Godkin concluded that the answer was in many instances "no." And like Lippmann, Godkin errantly assumed that such a theory did exist, and that at its center stood a naïve faith in an informed, "omni-competent" citizen. Inasmuch as there was a "classical democratic theory" of public opinion, it did no such thing. For earlier generations of liberals, "public opinion" was primarily put forward as a normative demand that (as Jürgen Habermas has put it) "the exercise of political and social power be subject to publicity." But for Godkin, there were issues that no amount of publicity or public discussion could effectively resolve, or that even the most well-intentioned and informed citizens could hope to understand. And those issues were primarily economic.[16]

Here we arrive at the second postulate: that "democratic public opinion in the modern world" was molded "as never before by economic, rather than religious, moral, or political considerations." For Godkin, the recurring Gilded Age debates over the protective tariff and the "money question" demonstrated the mendacity of politicians, the venality of the press, the futility of public discussion, and the mean selfishness and ignorance of the American voter. Although not a dyed-in-the-wool free trader, Godkin repeatedly vented his outrage at the refusal of the Republican Party to reduce the wartime tariffs and their repeated efforts to raise them further. But he increasingly interspersed his recitations of standard liberal political-economic arguments against protectionism with notes of despair on the incomprehensibility of the issue and the structural faults of American representative democracy. If the maddening array of duties placed on imported goods, and the uncertain effect of those duties on domestic industry, tested the capacities of the most discerning political economist, what chance did congressmen have? Beset by lobbyists and "tariff speculators," they were as helpless as "a band of untutored savages in the presence of a body of skilled riflemen, armed with repeaters." Worse still were the demoralizing political effects of protectionism.

Godkin bemoaned the "practice of telling large bodies of ignorant and excitable voters at every election that their daily bread depends not upon their own capacity or industry or ingenuity, or on the capacity or industry or ingenuity of their employers, but on the good will of the Legislature."[17]

The tariff and the currency questions, Godkin came to conclude, were the real legacies of the Civil War, for they constituted "almost the sum total of our politics." If the tariff question illustrated the lengths to which special interests, Congress, and parties would (and could) go to delude public opinion, the currency question demonstrated the dangers of "letting the public decide." Believing without doubt or hesitation that gold was the only genuine currency—and that every sane and honest man believed the same—Godkin could only explain demands for greenbacks or the free coinage of silver as a mass delusion. The issue had been "so surrounded with clouds of verbiage" and rendered so "hard of comprehension to the majority that it has been almost impossible to form anything like a well-defined public opinion upon it." Indeed, Godkin did not want a public opinion on the issue. "What the 'gold bugs' really demand," he explained in 1896, "is not the gold standard, so much as the assimilation in currency matters to the other great commercial nations, and the absolute abandonment of the currency question as a political issue."[18]

While the victory of William McKinley and the gold standard in the election of 1896 soothed Godkin's nerves, the imperialist jingoism of 1898 soon provided him with fresh reasons to find fault in American public opinion (much as it did for liberals and socialists in England).[19] In that year, he published his last book, *Unforeseen Tendencies of Democracy.* In a chapter titled "The Growth and Expression of Public Opinion," he advanced one of the most incisive yet conflicted critiques of democracy in the literature of late-nineteenth-century liberalism. If its contradictions highlight the limitations of nineteenth-century political liberalism, they also hint at the ways in which liberalism would seek to resolve them in the twentieth century. Godkin began with the problem of how public opinion was expressed in a modern democracy—a problem, he argued, that had received insufficient attention from political philosophers. Yet Godkin himself could identify only two means of expression—elections and newspapers—and found both wanting. "We have not yet," he argued, "hit on the best plan for getting at public opinion."[20] In the absence of any independent and verifiable method of assessing the state of public opinion, invocations of its authority on any question seemed dubious.

Godkin then turned to the problem of how public opinion is formed. Religious and moral authority had ceased, he argued, to have any formative influence on public opinion. Utilitarianism had "fully taken possession of public discussion," and "any writer or speaker on political subjects" had to "show that his proposition will make people more comfortable or richer." Appeals to the authority of tradition, experience, or history carried little weight. The modern world was now "governed mainly by ideas about the distribution of commodities." Such were the unforeseen tendencies of democracy. If the Godkin of 1865 believed that the diffusion of Christianity and the science of political economy would lead to the inexorable triumph of democracy, the Godkin of 1898 believed that democracy had bent the teachings of Christianity and political economy to its own will. Bowing to democratic pressure and seeking to restore their diminished authority in an age of newspapers, the churches had rejected the old theological gospel of consolation and taken to preaching a social gospel to the poor or a flaccid religion of sentimental gush to the prosperous. And the science of classical liberal political economy appeared to command little more authority in the political marketplace.[21]

When his declining health forced him to resign his editorial posts a year later, in 1899, Godkin returned to England for the last three years of his life, believing that a new generation had taken possession of American public life, one that, "fed on a very vile and silly press," knew nothing of history before 1776 and read no books. He complained to James Bryce: "Its morals are very low, and it has no religion to speak of, and no public men who act the part of teachers, or exert any influence or authority. It has a curious Chinese contempt in fact, for the rest of the world, and thinks it can do without Europe, and has a superstitious, medieval dislike of bankers, and dealers in money, and knows nothing about credit."[22]

Bryce himself took a somewhat more charitable view of American public opinion, devoting over one hundred pages of his 1889 opus *The American Commonwealth* to the subject. Like Abraham Lincoln, he recognized a distinction between public opinion and public sentiment but drew that distinction along lines of social class. The "mass" or the "humbler strata of society," on the one hand, could contribute little but "sentiment grounded on a few broad considerations and simple trains of reasoning," the soundness of which had more to do "with their taking their stand on the side of justice, honor, and peace, than any reasoning they can apply to the shifting of the multifarious facts thrown before them." The wealthy, on the other hand, were "more influenced by notions, possibly erroneous, of their own interest."[23]

That said, the great shortcoming of American public opinion lay not in the ignorance of the masses. In Bryce's estimation, the political education of the American voter far exceeded that of his European counterpart, but the great demands that "the theory of American government lays on him," could not be met due to the pressures of time and work, and the paltry diet of information and analysis that the press offered him. Nor did Bryce see any evidence of a "tyranny of the majority" that imposed its will by legal or moral compulsion. Public opinion did not so much tyrannize Americans as foster "a fatalistic attitude of mind" that disposed them to readily "acquiesce in the rule of numbers." Dispiriting as this fatalism might be, and the diminished sense of "personal responsibility and of the duty to battle for one's own opinions" that came with it, Bryce saw it as an inevitable and unavoidable feature of modern civilization. And it was not without its advantages. The fatalism of the multitude before public opinion made public order easier to secure. Questions that had been settled by public opinion were no longer subject to public discussion, and controversy was "confined to minor topics" that would upset "the great matters of agreement no more than a tempest stirs the depths of the Atlantic." And this fatalism did "not fail to produce a sort of pleasure, for what the individual loses as an individual he seems to regain as one of the multitude," and most men were better fit "to make part of the multitude than to strive against it." Much like the "opinion" thought to govern the early modern world, the public opinion of Bryce's *American Commonwealth* American ruled gently, quietly, and invisibly. "Happy those," as Poor Richard had once said, "who are convinced of the general opinion."[24]

Notes

Abbreviations

AHR	*American Historical Review*
AST	*American State Trials*, ed. John D. Lawson (St. Louis, 1914–36)
FP	*The Federalist Papers*, ed. Clinton Rossiter (New York, 1961)
GUS	*Gazette of the United States*
JAH	*Journal of American History*
JER	*Journal of the Early Republic*
NG	*National Gazette*
PAH	*The Papers of Alexander Hamilton*, ed. Harold Syrett (New York, 1981)
PJM	*The Papers of James Madison*, ed. Robert Rutland (Chicago, 1962–)
USMDR	*United States Magazine and Democratic Review*
WMQ	*William and Mary Quarterly*, 3rd ser.

Introduction · Public Opinion and the American Political Imagination

1. David S. Reynolds, *Walt Whitman's America: A Cultural Biography* (New York, 1995), 112; Whitman, *Leaves of Grass*, 1892 ed. (New York, 1982), 381; William Gienapp, "'Politics Seem to Enter into Everything': Political Culture in the North, 1840–1860," in *Essays on American Antebellum Politics, 1840–1860*, ed. Stephen Maizlish and John Kushma (College Station, TX, 1982), 14–69.

2. Whitman, *Specimen Days and Collect* (New York, 1882), 22.

3. Jacques Derrida, *The Other Heading: Reflections on Today's Europe*, trans. Pascale-Anne Brault and Michael B. Naas (Bloomington, IN, 1992), 84. See also Pierre Bourdieu, "Public Opinion Does Not Exist," in *Communications and the Class Struggle*, ed. Armand Mattelart and Seth Siegelaub (New York, 1979), 124–29. In 1924, the National Conference on the Science of Politics advised scholars to avoid using the term: Robert Binkley, "The Concept of Public Opinion in the Social Sciences," *Social Forces* 6 (1928): 389.

4. Jeffrey Alexander, *The Civil Sphere* (Oxford, 2006), 71, 73–74.

5. James Carey, "The Press, Public Opinion, and Public Discourse: On the Edge of the Postmodern," in *James Carey: A Critical Reader*, ed. Eve Stryker Munson and Catherine A. Warren (Minneapolis, 1997), 228.

6. Wilentz, *The Rise of American Democracy: Jefferson to Lincoln* (New York, 2005), xxi. For a similar argument regarding the concept of class, see Martin J. Burke, *The Conundrum of Class: Discourse on the Social Order in America* (Chicago, 1995).

7. Jeffrey Sklansky, *The Soul's Economy* (Chapel Hill, NC, 2002), 10.

8. On this point, see Jason Frank, *Constituent Moments* (Durham, NC, 2010), 6. On popular sovereignty and constitutionalism, see also Edmund Morgan, *Inventing the People* (New York, 1989); Jürgen Habermas, *Between Facts and Norms* (Cambridge, MA, 1996); Larry Kramer, *The People Themselves* (Oxford, 2004); and Christian Fritz, *American Sovereigns* (Cambridge, 2008).

9. See, for example, Sarah Knott, *Sensibility and the American Revolution* (Chapel Hill, NC, 2009), and Glenn Hendler, *Public Sentiments* (Chapel Hill, NC, 2001).

10. John L. Brooke, "Cultures of Nationalism, Movements of Reform, and the Composite-Federal Polity: From Revolutionary Settlement to Antebellum Crisis," *JER* 29 (Spring 2009): 1–33.

Chapter 1 · The Moral Economy of Opinion

1. Jefferson to Edward Carrington, 16 January 1787, in *The Life and Selected Writings of Thomas Jefferson*, ed. Adrienne Koch and William Peden (New York, 1993), 381; Jefferson to Madison, 30 January 1787, ibid., 382–83; *Notes on Virginia* (1784), ibid., 207.

2. *Notes on Virginia*, 198. On these points, see Charles A. Miller, *Jefferson and Nature: An Interpretation* (Baltimore, 1988), 158–59, 177–78; John Chester Miller, *The Wolf by the Ears: Thomas Jefferson and Slavery* (New York, 1977), 67; and Rhys Issac, "The First Monticello," in *Jeffersonian Legacies*, ed. Peter Onuf (Charlottesville, VA), 98.

3. Franklin, "Remarks on the Savages of North America" (1784), in *The Writings of Benjamin Franklin*, ed. Albert Smyth (New York, 1905–7), 10:97–105; Morse, *The American Geography* (1789), quoted in Roy Harvey Pearce, *Savagism and Civilization: A Study of the Indian and the American Mind* (Berkeley, CA, 1988), 79.

4. Colden, *The History of the Five Indian Nations of Canada, Which Are Dependent on the Province of New York in America*, 3rd ed. (London, 1755), 1:15; Sandra Gustafson, *Eloquence Is Power: Oratory and Performance in Early America* (Chapel Hill, NC, 2000), 114–18; Carolyn Eastman, "The Indian Censures the White Man: 'Indian Eloquence' and American Reading Audiences in the Early Republic," *WMQ* 65 (July 2008): 535–64.

5. Jefferson to Madison, 30 January 1787, in *Life and Selected Writings*, 382–83; Jefferson to Carrington, 16 January 1787, ibid., 381.

6. Sophia Rosenfeld, *Common Sense* (Cambridge, MA, 2011); Edmund Morgan, *Inventing the People* (New York, 1988).

7. Arendt, *On Revolution* (New York, 1963), 93.

8. Ibid., 93; Wood, *Revolutionary Characters* (New York, 2006), 249.

9. Peacham, "Of Opinion," in *The Truth of Our Times* (1638; reprint, New York, 1942), 54, 58.

10. Ibid., 57–58; Alan Young, *Henry Peacham* (Boston, 1979).

11. Peacham, *The World Is Ruled and Governed by Opinion* (London, 1641), reprinted in *Tracts on Liberty in the Puritan Revolution, 1638–1647*, ed. William Haller (New York, 1934), 1:i.

12. Peacham, *Square Caps Turned into Round-Heads* (London, 1642), 3, 8.

13. Morris Palmer Tilley, *A Dictionary of the Proverbs in England in the Sixteenth and Seventeenth Centuries* (Ann Arbor, MI, 1950), 515. See also George Boas, *Vox Populi* (Baltimore, 1969).

14. Seneca, *Letters from a Stoic*, trans. Robin Campbell (New York, 1969), 65; *Selections from Epictetus*, ed. Edwin Ginn (Boston, 1896), 225; Charles Taylor, *Sources of the Self: The Making of Modern Identity* (Cambridge, MA, 1989), 125–59; G. Watson, "Discovering the Imagination: Platonists and Stoics on *phantasia*," in *The Question of 'Eclecticism': Studies in Later Greek Philosophy*, ed. John M. Dillon and A. A. Long (Berkeley, CA, 1988), 208–33; Maryanne Cline Horowitz, "The Stoic Synthesis of the Idea of Natural Law in Man: Four Themes," *Journal of the History of Ideas* 35 (January–March 1974): 3–16.

15. Richard Tuck, *Philosophy and Government, 1572–1651* (Cambridge, 1993), 347; Dominique Colas, *Civil Society and Fanaticism: Conjoined Histories* (Stanford, CA, 1997); Gerhard Oestreich, *Neostoicism and the Early Modern State*, ed. Brigitta Oestreich and H. G. Koeningsberger, trans. David McLintock (Cambridge, 1982).

16. Hobbes, *Behemoth; or, The Long Parliament*, ed. Ferdinand Toennies (Chicago, 1990), 16, 23; Hobbes, *Leviathan*, ed. C. B. MacPherson (London, 1968), 185; Hobbes, *Elements of Law Natural and Politic*, ed. J. C. A. Gaskin (Oxford, 1994), 105; Christopher Pye, "The Sovereign, the Theater, and the Kingdome of Darkness: Hobbes and the Spectacle of Power," *Representations* 8 (Autumn 1984): 84–106; Corey Robin, *Fear: The History of a Political Idea* (New York, 2004), 34.

17. Sir William Temple, "An Essay upon the Original and Nature of Government" (1672), in *Miscellana, the First Part* (London, 1792), 17, 25. On Hobbes as an opinion theorist, see Stephen Holmes's introduction to *Behemoth* and S. A. Lloyd, *Ideals as Interests in Hobbes' Leviathan* (Cambridge, 1992), 40–41.

18. Samuel Mintz, *The Hunting of Leviathan* (Cambridge, 1962); J. H. Plumb, *The Origins of Political Stability: England, 1675–1725* (Boston, 1967); Kathleen Wilson, *The Sense of the People* (Cambridge, 1995); H. T. Dickinson, *The Politics of the People in Eighteenth Century Britain* (London, 1995); Lois G. Schwoerer, "Liberty of the Press and Public Opinion: 1660–1695," *Liberty Secured? Britain before and after 1688*, ed. J. R. Jones (Stanford, CA, 1992), 199–230.

19. Locke, *An Essay Concerning Human Understanding*, ed. Peter Nidditch (Oxford, 1975), 353, 657; Locke, *A Letter Concerning Toleration*, ed. John Horton and Susan Mendus (London, 1991), 18; Locke, *Two Treatises on Government*, ed. Peter Laslett (Cambridge, 1960), 463; Reinhart Koselleck, *Critique and Crisis* (1959; reprint, Cambridge, MA, 1988), 53–61.

20. Locke, *Human Understanding*, 249–87; Uday Singh Mehta, *The Anxiety of Freedom* (Ithaca, NY, 1992).

21. Locke, *Human Understanding*, 101; Joseph Butler, *The Analogy of Religion, Natural and Revealed, to the Constitution and Course of Nature* (1736; reprint, Cincinnati, 1863), 326; Shaftesbury to Ainsworth, 3 June 1709, in *Life, Unpublished Letters, and Philosophical Regimen of Anthony, Earl of Shaftesbury*, ed. Benjamin Rand (London, 1900), 403–4; Jerrold Seigel, *The Idea of the Self* (Cambridge, 2005), 87–110; Neal Wood, *The Politics of Locke's Philosophy* (Berkeley, CA, 1983), 164–67.

22. Hutcheson, *An Essay on the Nature and Conduct of the Passions and Affections with Illustrations on the Moral Sense* (1728; reprint, New York, 1971), 5; Kames, *Essays on the Principles of Morality and Natural Religion* (Edinburgh, 1751), 142–43; Burke, *A Philosophical Enquiry into the Origins of Our Ideas of the Sublime and Beautiful* (Oxford, 1990), 45–46. On common sense, see John D. Schaeffer, *Sensus Communis* (Durham, NC, 1990); Hans-Georg Gadamer, *Truth and Method*, 2nd ed. (New York, 1975), 19–29; and Sophia Rosenfeld, *Common Sense* (Cambridge, MA, 2011). On the aesthetics of virtue, see Terry Eagleton, *The Ideology of the Aesthetic* (Oxford, 1990), 31–69, and John Barrell, *The Political Theory of Painting from Reynolds to Hazlitt* (New Haven, CT, 1986), 1–68.

23. J. A. W. Gunn, "Opinion in Eighteenth-Century Thought: What Did the Concept Purport to Explain?" *Utilitas* 5 (May 1993): 17–33; [James Forrester], *The Polite Philosopher* (Edinburgh, 1734), 31; Shaftesbury, *Sensus Communis*, in *Characteristiks of Men, Manners, and Opinions* (London, 1711), 64–65, 83, 96; Adam Ferguson, *An Essay on the History of Civil Society* (1767), ed. Fania Oz-Salzberger (Cambridge, 1995), 131; Richard Bushman, *The Refinement of America* (New York, 1992), 30–60; Edward A. Bloom and Lillian D. Bloom, *Joseph Addision's Sociable Animal* (Providence, RI, 1971); Peter Burke, *The Art of Conversation* (Ithaca, NY, 1993), 89–122.

24. Pocock, *Virtue, Commerce, and History* (Cambridge, 1985), 236, 47–50; Lawrence Klein, *Shaftesbury and the Culture of Politeness* (Cambridge, 1994).

25. Michael Heyd, *"Be Sober and Reasonable"* (New York, 1995); Lawrence E. Klein, "Sociability, Solitude, and Enthusiasm," in *Enthusiasm and Enlightenment in Europe, 1650–1850*, ed. Klein and Anthony J. La Volpa (San Marino, CA, 1998), 153–77; Henry More, *Enthusiasmus Triumphatus* (1662; reprint, Los Angeles, 1966); Margaret Jacob, *The Newtonians and the English Revolution, 1689–1720* (Ithaca, NY, 1976), 260–65.

26. Gunn, "Public Spirit to Public Opinion," in *Beyond Liberty and Property: The Process of Self-Recognition in Eighteenth-Century Political Thought* (Montreal, 1983), 273; Hume, "Of the First Principles of Government" (1741), in *Essays, Moral, Political, and Literary*, ed. Eugene Miller (Indianapolis, IN, 1987), 32. On Hume's use of "opinion" in this context, see Dario Castiglione, "History, Reason, and Experience: Hume's Arguments against Contract Theories," in *The Social Contract from Hobbes to Rawls*, ed. David Boucher and Paul Kelly (New York, 1994), 107–9. For a similar conception of opinion, see David Hartley, *Observations on Man, His Frame, His Duty, and His Expectations* (London, 1749), 197–209.

27. Johnson, "The False Alarm" (1770), in *The Yale Edition of the Works of Samuel*

Johnson, ed. Donald Greene (New Haven, CT, 1977), 10:317–18; Johnson, "Taxation No Tyranny" (1775), ibid., 444.

28. Donald S. Lutz, "The Relative Influence of European Writers on Late Eighteenth-Century American Political Thought," *American Political Science Review* 78 (March 1984): 188–97; Paul Merill Spurlin, *Montesquieu in America, 1760–1801* (Baton Rouge, LA, 1940).

29. Montesquieu, *The Spirit of the Laws*, trans. Thomas Nugent (New York, 1949), 19–26, 151.

30. Ibid., 232.

31. Hume, "Of Superstition and Enthusiasm," in *Hume: Political Essays*, ed. Knud Haakonssen (Cambridge, 1994), 46; John Trenchard and Thomas Gordon, *Cato's Letters; or, Essays on Liberty, Civil and Religious, and Other Important Subjects*, ed. Ronald Hamowy (Indianapolis, IN, 1995), 1:462; Mark Goldie, "Priestcraft and the Birth of Whiggism," in *Political Discourse in Early Modern Britain*, ed. Nicholas Phillipson and Quentin Skinner (Cambridge, 1993), 209–31.

32. Smith, *The Theory of Moral Sentiments* (1759), ed. D. D. Raphael and A. L. Macfie (Indianapolis, IN, 1984), 30, 36–37; Hutcheson, *Passions and Affections*, 5; Peter Silver, *Our Savage Neighbors: How Indian War Transformed Early America* (New York, 2009), 83. See also Julie Ellison, *Cato's Tears and the Making of Anglo-American Emotion* (Chicago, 1999); David Marshall, "Adam Smith and the Theatricality of Moral Sentiments," *Critical Inquiry* 10 (June 1984): 592–613.

33. Hume, "Whether the British Government Inclines More to Absolute Monarchy, or to a Republic," in *Essays, Moral, Political, and Literary*, 51; Blackstone, *Commentaries on the Laws of England* (1765–69), ed. Stanley Katz (Chicago, 1979), 1:234.

34. Brendan McConville, *The King's Three Faces* (Chapel Hill, NC, 2006); Richard Bushman, *King and People in Provincial Massachusetts* (Chapel Hill, NC, 1985). On "opinion" versus force in the governance of colonies, see Jack Greene, *Peripheries and Center* (New York, 1986), 44, 142–43.

35. Wood, "Conspiracy and the Paranoid Style: Causality and Deceit in the Eighteenth Century," *WMQ* 39 (July 1982): 409, 417.

36. "T.Q." in *Boston Gazette and Country Journal*, 18 April 1763 and 6 June 1763; "J" in *Boston Evening Post*, 23 May 1763.

37. Adams, "Letters from a Distinguished American #8" (1782), in *The Papers of John Adams*, ed. Robert J. Taylor (Cambridge, MA, 1996), 9:563.

38. On colonial communications, see Trish Loughran, *The Republic in Print* (New York, 2007), 33–104, and Richard D. Brown, *Knowledge Is Power* (New York, 1989).

39. "Candidus," *Boston Gazette*, 9 December 1771, in *The Writings of Samuel Adams*, ed. Harry Cushing (New York, 1907). 293.

40. Silver, *Our Savage Neighbors*, xix, 86–94; "Petition of the Inhabitants of Anson County, North Carolina" (9 October 1769), in *The Colonial Records of North Carolina*, ed. W. Saunders (Raleigh, NC, 1890), 3:75.

41. Gordon to Washington, 17 July 1777, in "The Letters of William Gordon," *Proceedings of the Massachusetts Historical Society* 62 (October 1929–June 1930): 347.

On the "great fear" of an American episcopacy, see Carl Bridenbaugh, *Mitre and Sceptre* (New York, 1962), 260–87.

42. Mayhew, "The Snare Broken," in *Political Sermons of the Founding Era*, 245–48.

43. Ibid., 249, 262.

44. *The Poetical Works of James Thomson* (London, 1830), 184. "Hampden" was John Hampden, an English country gentleman who famously protested the ship-money tax of 1634. American revolutionaries were notably fond of Hampden. See, for example, Stephen Hopkins, *The Rights of the Colonies Examined* (Providence, RI, 1764).

45. Dickinson, *Letters from a Farmer in Pennsylvania to the Inhabitants of the British Colonies* (Philadelphia, 1768), 38; F. Nwabueze Okoye, "Chattel Slavery as the Nightmare of American Revolutionaries," *WMQ* 37 (January 1980): 3–28; Burke, "Speech of Edmund Burke, Esq., on Moving His Resolutions for Conciliation with the Colonies, March 22nd, 1775," in *Edmund Burke: Pre-Revolutionary Writings*, ed. Ian Harris (Cambridge, 1993), 225.

46. Paine, *Common Sense* (1776), in *The Thomas Paine Reader*, ed. Michael Foot and Isaac Kramnick (New York, 1987), 99, 104, 107.

47. Daniel Leonard, "Massachusettensis, December 26, 1775," in *Tracts of the American Revolution, 1763–1776*, ed. Merrill Jensen (Indianapolis, IN, 1975), 283–85; Sewall to General Frederick Haldimand, 30 May 1775, in *Colonies to Nation, 1763–1789*, ed. Jack P. Greene (New York, 1967), 266–67; [Myles Cooper], *The Patriots of North America: A Sketch* (New York, 1775), 3.

48. *Peter Oliver's Origin and Progress of the American Rebellion*, ed. Douglass Adair and John Schutz (Stanford, CA, 1967), 6.

49. John Adams, "Dissertation on the Cannon and Feudal Law," in *The Works of John Adams*, ed. Charles Francis Adams (Boston, 1851–56), 3:452; Mercy Warren, *History of the Rise, Progress, and Termination of the American Revolution* (Boston, 1805), 3:428; Moses Coit Tyler, *The Literary History of the American Revolution* (New York, 1893), 2:279–81; Catherine Albanese, *Sons of the Father* (Philadelphia, 1976), 46–59; Chauncy quoted in David Lovejoy, *Religious Enthusiasm in the New World: Heresy to Revolution* (Cambridge, MA, 1985), 225.

50. On the revolution as a "religious war," see J. C. D. Clark, *The Language of Liberty, 1660–1832* (Cambridge, 1994), 296–381; "A Jersey Soldier," *New Jersey Journal*, 4 May 1779, is quoted on p. 302. Hume, "Of Superstition and Enthusiasm" (1777), in *Essays Moral, Political, and Literary*, 73–79; Madison, "Federalist #49," *FP*, 351.

51. James H. Hutson, "The Origins of 'The Paranoid Style in American Politics': Public Jealousy from the Age of Walpole to the Age of Jackson," in *Saints and Revolutionaries*, ed. David Hall, John Murrin, and Thad Tate (New York, 1983), 332–72; Hamilton, "Speech at New York Ratifying Convention" (24 June 1788), in *The Debates of the Several State Conventions on the Adoption of the Constitution*, ed. Jonathan Elliot (Philadelphia, 1896), 2:301.

52. Hamilton, "The Continentalist I" (1781), in *PAH*, 2:650; Ames, "Camillus III" (1787), in *Works of Fisher Ames*, ed. Seth Ames (Indianapolis, IN, 1983), 1:72; John Trumbull, *M'Fingal* (1782), in *The Connecticut Wits*, ed. Vernon Louis Parrington

(New York, 1926), 102–3; "S.C.," *Pennsylvania Gazette*, 9 July 1783, quoted in Hutson, "Public Jealousy," 355. The allusion in Trumbull's verse is to *The Tempest*, Act III, scene ii.

53. Rush "Influence of the American Revolution" (1788), in *The Selected Writings of Benjamin Rush*, ed. Dagobert Runes (New York, 1947), 333. On the prevalence of discourse about "passion," see Marshall Smelser, "The Federalist Period as an Age of Passion," *American Quarterly* 10 (Winter 1958): 391–419, and Daniel W. Howe, "The Political Psychology of *The Federalist*," *WMQ* 44 (July 1987): 485–509.

54. "Salem, Nov. 11," *Pittsburgh Gazette*, 13 January 1787; Knox to Washington, 18 October 1786, cited in Forrest and Ellen Shapiro McDonald, "The Late Disturbances in Massachusetts," in *Requiem: Variations on Eighteenth-Century Themes* (Lawrence, KS, 1988), 72–3; "Americanus," *New York Journal*, 15 March 1787.

55. "A Citizen of America" [Webster], "An Examination into the Leading Principles of the Federal Constitution" (Philadelphia, 1787), reprinted in *Friends of the Constitution*, ed. Colleen Sheehan (Indianapolis, IN, 1997), 373; Washington, "Circular to the States" (1783), in *The Writings of George Washington from the Original Manuscript Sources, 1745–1799*, ed. John C. Fitzpatrick (Washington, DC, 1931–44), 26:489.

56. Hamilton, "Federalist #29," in *FP*, 186; Hamilton, "First Speech of June 21, 1788 to the New York Ratifying Convention," in *Selected Writings and Speeches of Alexander Hamilton*, ed. Morton J. Frisch (Washington, DC, 1985), 210; Albert Furtwangler, *The Authority of Publius: A Reading of the Federalist Papers* (Ithaca, NY, 1984), 98–111.

57. Franklin, "A Comparison of the Conduct of the Ancient Jews and of the Anti-Federalists in the United States of America," in *Writings*, 9:698–703; Madison, "Federalist #49," in *FP*, 315.

58. Though the term "public opinion" appears but ten times throughout all eighty-five of *The Federalist Papers*—a relative frequency of 0.0052%—terms such as "opinion" and "sentiment" are often used in a synonymous fashion. Thomas Engeman, Edward Erler, and Thomas Hofeller, *The Federalist Concordance* (Chicago, 1988).

59. Hamilton, "Federalist #27," in *FP*, 176; Madison, "Federalist #10," ibid., 82; Madison, "Federalist #38," ibid., 234.

60. Madison, "Federalist #58," in *FP*, 360; Hamilton, "Federalist #84," ibid., 516–17; Hamilton, "Federalist #34," ibid., 204. On the absence of public communication in the *Federalist*, see Richard John, *Spreading the News* (Cambridge, MA, 1995), 29. For different readings of the constitution and the *Federalist* papers arguing that both presupposed a "public" that operated through the medium of print, see Warner, *Letters of the Republic* (Cambridge, MA, 1990), 97–117, and James Carey, *Communication as Culture* (New York, 1989), 1–9.

61. Madison, "Federalist #10," in *FP*, 46; Hamilton "Federalist #76," ibid., 455; Hamilton, "Federalist #71," ibid., 432; Madison, "Federalist #63," ibid., 385; "State Soldier II," in Sheehan, *Friends of the Constitution*, 123.

62. On elective and deliberative powers, see Gordon Wood, *The Creation of the American Republic, 1776–1787* (New York, 1972), 373–75. On compromise, see Peter

Knupfer, *The Union as It Is* (Chapel Hill, NC, 1991), 23–55. On Federalist assumptions about voting and elections, see Judith Shklar, "Alexander Hamilton and the Language of Political Science," in *The Languages of Political Theory in Early-Modern Europe*, ed. Anthony Pagden (Cambridge, 1985), 339–55.

63. Madison, "Federalist #49," in *FP*, 314; Madison, "Federalist #10," ibid., 83. One of the few interpreters to recognize the similarities between "opinion" in the *Federalist* and Montesquieu's "opinion of safety" is David F. Epstein, *The Political Theory of the Federalist* (Chicago, 1984). Madison cites the relevant passages from Montesquieu in "Federalist #47."

64. Madison, "Federalist #49," in *FP*, 314–15; Madison to John Randolph, 19 January 1787, in *PJM*, 10:355–56.

65. Hamilton, "Federalist #70," in *FP*, 429.

66. Hamilton, "Federalist #29," in *FP*, 185–86.

67. Lee to Samuel Adams, 8 August 1789, in *The Letters of Richard Henry Lee*, ed. James C. Ballagh (New York, 1970), 2:495–96. On these points, see Kenyon, "Men of Little Faith: The Anti-Federalists on the Nature of Representative Government," *WMQ* 12 (January 1955): 3–43.

68. [George Clinton], "Cato IV," and [Samuel Bryan], "Centinel #1," in *The Antifederalists*, ed. Cecilia M. Kenyon (Indianapolis, IN, 1966), 7, 308–9; "Address by Denatus," *The Complete Antifederalist*, ed. Herbert Storing (Chicago, 1991), 5:262; "Philadelphiensis #8," ibid., 3:124–27; Wood, *Creation of the American Republic*, 486–87. See also "Fallacies of the Freeman Detected by a Farmer," in Storing, *Complete Antifederalist*, 3:185.

Chapter 2 · Credit and the Political Economy of Opinion

1. See, for example, Jon Elster, "Th^pe Market and the Forum: Three Varieties of Political Theory," in *Deliberative Democracy: Essays on Reason and Politics*, ed. James Bohman and William Rehg (Cambridge, MA, 1997), 3–34, and Jean-Christophe Agnew, *Worlds Apart: The Market and the Theater in Anglo-American Thought, 1550–1750* (Cambridge, 1986), 17–56. On language as money and money as language, see Marc Shell, *Money, Language, and Thought* (Berkeley, CA, 1982).

2. The classic discussion of "confidence" and "expectations" is John Maynard Keynes, *The General Theory of Employment, Interest, and Money* (New York, 1953), 147–64.

3. Herbst, *Reading Public Opinion* (Chicago, 1998), 13; Colleen A. Sheehan, "The Politics of Public Opinion: James Madison's 'Notes on Government,'" *WMQ* 49 (October 1992): 609–27; Sheehan, "Madison and the French Enlightenment: The Authority of Public Opinion," *WMQ* 59 (October 2002): 925–56; Gordon Wood, "The Democratization of Mind in the American Revolution," in *Leadership in the American Revolution: Papers Presented at the Third Symposium on the American Revolution* (Washington, DC, 1974), 63–88; Michael Lienesch, "Thomas Jefferson and the American Democratic Experience: The Origins of the Partisan Press, Popular Political Parties, and Public Opinion," in *Jeffersonian Legacies*, ed. Peter Onuf (Charlottesville, VA,

1993), 316–39; Saul Cornell, *The Other Founders* (Chapel Hill, NC, 1999). Studies of the public sphere rarely address the more specific problem of what "public opinion" meant. For a review of this literature, see John Brooke, "Consent, Civil Society, and the Public Sphere in the Age of Revolution and the Early American Republic," in *Beyond the Founders*, ed. Jeffrey Pasley, Andrew Robertson, and David Waldstreicher (Chapel Hill, NC, 2004), 207–50. On public opinion and public finance in Europe, see Patrick Brantlinger, *Fictions of State* (Ithaca, NY, 1996), 125; John Dahlberg-Acton, "The Background of the French Revolution" (1895), in *Essays on Freedom and Power*, ed. Gertrude Himmelfarb (Boston, 1948), 267; Mackinnon, *On the Rise, Progress, and Present State of Public Opinion in Great Britain and Other Parts of the World*, 2nd ed. (London, 1828), 94–116, 160–77; Thomas Kaiser, "Money, Despotism, and Public Opinion in Early Eighteenth-Century France: John Law and the Debate on Royal Credit," *Journal of Modern History* 63 (March 1991): 1–28; Hans Speier, "The Rise of Public Opinion," in *The Truth in Hell and Other Essays on Politics and Culture, 1935–1987* (New York, 1989), 148–49; and Gerhard Oestreich, *Neostoicism and the Early Modern State*, ed. Brigitta Oestreich and H. G. Koenigsberger, trans. David McLintock (Cambridge, 1982), 190–94.

4. *The Memoirs of Stephen Burroughs* (1811; Boston, 1988), 83; Kenneth Scott, *Counterfeiting in Colonial America* (New York, 1957).

5. John Brewer, *The Sinews of Power: War, Money, and the English State, 1688–1783* (Cambridge, MA, 1988), 199–249; Peter G. M. Dickson, *The Financial Revolution in England: A Study in the Development of Public Credit, 1688–1756* (New York, 1967); Bruce Carruthers, *City of Capital: Politics and Markets in the English Financial Revolution* (Princeton, NJ, 1996); Istvan Hont, "The Rhapsody of Public Debt: David Hume and Voluntary State Bankruptcy," in *Political Discourse in Early Modern Britain*, ed. Nicholas Phillipson and Quentin Skinner (Cambridge, 1983), 321–48; J. G. A. Pocock, "The Mobility of Property and the Rise of Eighteenth-Century Sociology," in *Virtue, Commerce, and History* (Cambridge, 1985), 103–24; Pocock, *The Machiavellian Moment* (Princeton, NJ, 1975), 439–61; Emma Rothschild, *Economic Sentiments: Adam Smith, Condorcet, and the Enlightenment* (Cambridge, MA, 2001). For a larger history of the connection between public finance and popular government, see James Macdonald, *A Free Nation in Debt: The Financial Roots of Democracy* (Princeton, NJ, 2003).

6. Smith, *An Inquiry into the Nature and Causes of the Wealth of Nations*, ed. Edwin Cannan (Chicago, 1976), 2:479; Berkeley, *The Querist* (1735), in *The Works of George Berkeley*, ed. A. A. Luce and T. E. Jessop (London, 1948), 4:107, 126; Cooke, "The Planter's Looking Glass, In Verse" (1730), in *Early Maryland Poetry*, Maryland Historical Society Publications no. 36, ed. Bernard Steiner (Baltimore, 1900), 40. My generalizations about colonial finance are drawn primarily from Edwin J. Perkins, *American Public Finance and Financial Services, 1700–1815* (Columbus, OH, 1994); Bray Hammond, *Banks and Politics in America from the Revolution to the Civil War* (Princeton, NJ, 1957), 3–39; Margaret Ellen Newell, *From Dependency to Independency: Economic Revolution in Colonial New England* (Ithaca, NY, 1998), 107–236; E. James Ferguson, "Currency Finance: An Interpretation of Colonial Monetary Pol-

icies," *WMQ* 10 (1953): 153–80; Janet Riesman, "The Origins of American Political Economy, 1690–1781" (PhD diss., Brown University, 1983); John J. McCusker and Russell R. Menard, *The Economy of British America, 1607–1789* (Chapel Hill, NC, 1985); Eric P. Newman, *The Early Paper Money of America* (Racine, WI, 1967); and Curtis P. Nettels, *The Money Supply of the American Colonies* (Madison, WI, 1934).

7. Paine, "Common Sense" (1776), in *The Thomas Paine Reader*, ed. Isaac Kramnick and Michael Foote (New York, 1987), 102; "To the Creditor," *Norwich Packet*, 26 January 1778; *New England Chronicle*, 19 October 1775; *Pennsylvania Evening Post*, 21 September 1776; "Thoughts on the Paper Currency," *Connecticut Courant*, 9 March 1779; *Boston Gazette and County Journal*, 26 January 1778. On quantity theory, see Joseph Schumpeter, *History of Economic Analysis* (New York, 1954), 311–18. On revolutionary finance, see E. James Ferguson, *The Power of the Purse: A History of American Public Finance, 1776–1790* (Chapel Hill, NC, 1961), and Perkins, *American Public Finance*, 85–198.

8. Washington to James Warren, 31 March 1779, in *George Washington: A Collection*, ed. W. B. Allen (Indianapolis, IN, 1998), 127; Boston Committee of Correspondence, "Boston, June 21, 1779: Gentlemen, by the Inclosed Votes and Proceedings" (Boston, 1779), at www.masshist.org/revolution/doc-viewer.php?item_id=190; Resolves of Congress, 13 January 1779, *Journals of the Continental Congress*, ed. Worthington Ford (Washington, DC, 1909), 13:20; Jefferson to Richard Henry Lee, 17 June 1779, in *Writings of Jefferson*, ed. Andrew Lipscomb (Washington, DC, 1907), 2:298; Paine, "The Crisis #5" (1778), in *The Complete Writings of Thomas Paine*, ed. Philip S. Foner (New York, 1945), 1:109–27; Samuel Cooper, *A Sermon on the Day of the Commencement of the Constitution* (Boston, 1780), reprinted in *Political Sermons of the Founding Era*, ed. Ellis Sandoz (Indianapolis, IN, 1991), 649–50; "A Moderate Whig," *A Short Receipt for a Continental Disease* (New Malborough, NY, 1782), reprinted in ibid., 769–70.

9. Paine, "Dissertations on Government, the Affairs of the Bank, and Paper Money" (1786), in *Paine Reader*, 193–200; Benjamin Rush, "Influence of the American Revolution" (1788), in *The Selected Writings of Benjamin Rush*, ed. Dagobert Runes (New York, 1947), 331; David Ramsay, *The History of the American Revolution* (1789), excerpted in *American Political Writing during the Founding Era, 1760–1805*, ed. Charles Hyneman and Donald S. Lutz (Indianapolis, IN, 1983), 2:755.

10. Tribunus, "On Public Credit" (May 1787), *American Museum*, November 1788, 412; Alexander Hamilton to Robert Morris, December 1779, in *PAH*, 2:242; James Madison, "Money" (December 1779–March 1780), in *PJM*, 2:306; Charles Calomiris, "Institutional Failure, Monetary Scarcity, and the Depreciation of the Continental," *Journal of Economic History* 48 (March 1988): 47–68.

11. Riesman, "Origins of American Political Economy," 402, 412; Robert Morris, "Plan for Establishing a National Bank, with Observations" (1781), in *The Papers of Robert Morris*, ed. E. James Ferguson (Pittsburgh, 1973), 1:68–72; Morris, "To the Public," ibid., 1:83–86; Hamilton to Morris, 30 April 1781, in *PAH*, 2:604–35; Madison, "Money," in *PJM*, 2:304–9; Joyce Appleby, "Locke, Liberalism, and the Natural Law of Money," *Past and Present* 71 (May 1976): 43–69; Janet Riesman, "Money,

Credit, and Federalist Political Economy," in *Beyond Confederation*, ed. Richard Beeman (Chapel Hill, NC, 1987), 128–61.

12. Wilson, "Considerations on the Bank of North America" (1785), in *The Works of James Wilson*, ed. Robert G. McCloskey (Cambridge, MA, 1967), 2:827; Ferguson, *Power of the Purse*, 114–15, 149–57; Royster, *Revolutionary People at War*, 308–10; Thomas M. Doerflinger, *A Vigorous Spirit of Enterprise* (Chapel Hill, NC, 1986), 253–78.

13. Wilson, "Considerations on the Bank of North America," 824; Tribunus, "On Public Credit," 411; Sylvius, "On the Present Scarcity of Money," *American Museum*, August 1787, 109; Pelatiah Webster, "An Essay on Credit" (1786), in *Political Essays on the Nature and Operation of Money, Public Finances, and Other Subjects* (New York, 1791), 427–64; Jackson Turner Main, *Political Parties before the Constitution* (New York, 1973), 59–66, 334–40.

14. Max Edling, *A Revolution in Favor of Government* (Oxford, 2003); Calvin Johnson, *Righteous Anger at the Wicked States* (Cambridge, 2005); Roger H. Brown, *Redeeming the Republic* (Baltimore, 2000).

15. Hamilton, "Pay Book," in *PAH*, 1:391–407; Plutarch, *The Lives of the Noble Grecians and Romans*, trans. John Dryden, rev. Arthur Hugh Clough (New York, 1864), 706; Mackubin T. Owens Jr., "A Further Note on Certain of Hamilton's Pseudonyms: The 'Love of Fame' and the Use of Plutarch," *Journal of the Early Republic* 4 (Fall 1984): 275–86; Ron Chernow, *Alexander Hamilton* (New York, 2004), 110–12.

16. John Dunn, "Trust and Political Agency," in *Interpreting Political Responsibility* (Princeton, NJ, 1990), 26; Keynes, *General Theory*, 154. For a similar observation from the eighteenth century, see James Steuart, *An Inquiry into the Principles of Political Oeconomy* (Dublin, 1770) 2:444–45, 463, 625.

17. Hamilton, "Federalist #27" and "#30," in *FP*, 176, 188; Hamilton, "Report on Public Credit," in *PAH*, 6:97; "Report on the Mint," ibid., 7:505; "Report on the Bank," ibid.,7:327; Hamilton to Washington, 27 March 1791, ibid., 8:221; Hamilton to Robert Morris, December 1779, ibid., 2:242; "Report Relative to the Loans Negotiated under the Acts of the 4th and 12th of August, 1790," ibid., 14:31; Hamilton, "Speech in the New York Ratifying Convention," 21 June 1788, in *Selected Writings and Speeches of Alexander Hamilton*, ed. Morton Frisch (Washington, DC, 1985): 207; "Remarks in New York Ratifying Convention," 24 June 1788, ibid., 217–22. On the centrality of administration and state-building to Hamiltonian Federalists, see Edling, *Revolution in Favor of Government*; Lynton Caldwell, *The Administrative Theories of Hamilton and Thomas Jefferson* (New York, 1964), 10–30; and Gerald Stourzh, *Alexander Hamilton and the Idea of Republican Government* (Stanford, CA, 1970), 76–125.

18. "The Tablet #5," *GUS*, 25 April 1789; Tribunus, "Public Credit is Public Wealth," *American Museum*, February 1788, 180–81; "The Tablet #6," *GUS*, 6 May 1789; Wolcott to Theodore Sedgwick, 5 September 1793, in *Memoirs of the Administration of George Washington and John Adams Edited from the Papers of Oliver Wolcott, Jr.*, ed. George Gibbs (New York, 1846), 1:108; Wolcott to Oliver Wolcott Sr., 27 March 1790, ibid., 1:43.

19. Hamilton, "Report on the Bank," in *PAH*, 7:327.

20. Forrest McDonald, *Alexander Hamilton: A Biography* (New York, 1979), 143–210, quote on p. 189; Donald F. Swanson and Andrew P. Trout, "Alexander Hamilton, 'the Celebrated Mr. Necker,' and Public Credit," *WMQ* 47 (July 1990): 422–30; Jacques Necker, *A Treatise on the Administration of the Finances of France*, trans. Thomas Mortimer (London, 1784), 1:9, 20, 29, 65–66, 73.

21. "The Tablet #1," "#124," "#125," "#126," and "#127," *GUS*, 15 April 1789, 19 June 1790, 23 June 1790, 26 June 1790, 30 June 1790; Hamilton, "Report on a National Bank," 305–6; "The Tablet #38" and "#88," *GUS*, 22 August 1789, 13 February 1790; "To the Public," *GUS*, 15 April 1789.

22. "The Tablet #108," *GUS*, 24 April 1790. This is a reprint of an unsigned essay first published in Philadelphia. Compare to Hamilton to Washington, 27 March 1791, in *PAH*, 8:223.

23. Madison, "Discrimination between Present and Original Holders of the Public Debt," 11 February 1790, in *PJM*, 35–39; Madison, "Assumption of the State Debts," 24 February 1790, ibid., 60–63; Fisher Ames, "Speech of May 25, 1790," and "Speech of February 15, 1790," in *The Works of Fisher Ames*, ed. W. B. Allen (Indianapolis, IN, 1983), 1:756, 760–70; Madison to Rush, 7 March 1790, in *PJM*, 13:93; Rush to Madison, 27 February 1790, ibid., 67–68. Several local and poorly coordinated efforts were made to rally public opinion behind Madison's discrimination proposal. See, for example, "An Old Soldier," *(Boston) Independent Chronicle*, 25 March and 15 April 1790, and *(New Haven) Connecticut Journal*, 2 February 1791.

24. William Maclay, *The Journal of William Maclay* (New York, 1927), 189, 312, 328; Jefferson to Nicholas Lewis, 12 April 1792, in *Papers of Thomas Jefferson*, ed. Julian P. Boyd and Charles Cullen (Princeton, NJ, 1950–), 23:408; Gerry, speech before Senate, 19 February 1790, reported in *New York Daily Gazette*, 26 February 1790; William Findley, *History of the Insurrection in the Four Western Counties of Pennsylvania* (Philadelphia, 1796), 259–60; Pelatiah Webster, *Plea for the Poor Soldiers* (Philadelphia, 1790); John P. Resch, *Suffering Soldiers* (Amherst, MA, 1999).

25. Sheehan, "Madison and the French Enlightenment: The Authority of Public Opinion," *WMQ* 59 (October 2002): 925–56; Sheehan, "The Politics of Public Opinion: James Madison's 'Notes on Government,'" *WMQ* 49 (October 1992): 609–27; Madison, "Notes for the *National Gazette* Essays," [ca. 19 December 1791–3 March 1792], in *PJM*, 14:157–69. See also Richard Matthews, *If Men Were Angels* (Lawrence, KS, 1995), 158–62. On physiocrats, public opinion, and communication, see Jürgen Habermas, *The Structural Transformation of the Public Sphere*, trans. Thomas Burger (Cambridge, MA, 1989), 95–96; Armand Mattelart, *The Invention of Communication*, trans. Susan Emmanuel (Minneapolis, 1996), 26–39; and J. A. W. Gunn, *Queen of the World* (Oxford, 1995), 246–81.

26. [Madison], "Property," *NG*, 27 March 1792; "Public Opinion," *NG*, 19 December 1791.

27. [Madison], "Public Opinion," *NG*, 19 December 1791; "Charters," *NG*, 18 January 1792; "Consolidation," *NG*, 3 December 1791; "Government," *NG*, 2 January 1792.

28. [Madison], "Foreign Influence," *Philadelphia Aurora and General Advertiser*,

23 January 1799; [Madison], "Fashion," *NG*, 20 March 1792; Frank Thisthlewaite, *America and the Atlantic Community* (New York, 1959), 3–38.

29. Drew R. McCoy, *The Elusive Republic: Political Economy in Jeffersonian America* (New York, 1980), 43, 136; Major L. Wilson, "The Concept of Time and the Political Dialogue in the United States, 1828–48," *American Quarterly* 19 (1967): 619–44; Smith, *Wealth of Nations*, 128.

30. On the panic of 1792, see Cathy Matson, "Public Vices, Private Benefit: William Duer and his Circle, 1776–1792," in *New York and the Rise of American Capitalism*, ed. William Pencak and Conrad Wright (New York, 1989), 72–123; David J. Cowen, "The First Bank of the United States and the Securities Market Crash of 1792," *Journal of Economic History* 60 (December 2000): 1041–60. On opposition to Hamiltonian finance, see Cornell, *Other Founders*, 174–87; Lance Banning, *The Jeffersonian Persuasion* (Ithaca, NY, 1978), 126–60; Donald Stewart, *The Opposition Press of the Federalist Period* (Albany, NY, 1969), 33–70; Walter R. Fee, "The Effect of Hamilton's Financial Policy upon Public Opinion in New Jersey," *Proceedings of the New Jersey Historical Society* 50 (1932): 32–44; and Margaret Woodbury, *Public Opinion in Philadelphia, 1789–1801* (Northhampton, MA, 1919).

31. "Virginia Resolutions on the Assumption of State Debts," 16 December 1790, reprinted in *Documents of American History*, ed. Henry Steele Commager (New York, 1964), 155; Freneau, "Rules for Changing a Limited Republican Government into an Unlimited Hereditary One," *NG*, 4 July 1792 and 7 July 1792; "A Letter from the Democratic Society of the City of New York to the Democratic Society of Philadelphia" (1794), in *The Democratic-Republican Societies, 1790–1800*, ed. Philip S. Foner (Westport, CT, 1976), 188–89; John Taylor, *A Definition of Parties; or, The Political Effects of the Paper System Considered* (Philadelphia, 1794), 10; Manning, "Some Proposals for Making Restitution to the Original Creditors of Government" (1790), in *The Key of Liberty: The Life and Democratic Writings of William Manning, "A Laborer," 1747–1814*, ed. Michael Merrill and Sean Wilentz (Cambridge, MA, 1993), 111–16; Ruth Bogin, ed., "'Measures So Glaringly Unjust': A Response to Hamilton's Funding Plan by William Manning," *WMQ* 46 (1989): 315–31.

32. "An American Farmer" [George Logan], *Letters Addressed to the Yeomanry of the United States, Containing Some Observations on Funding and Bank Systems* (Philadelphia, 1793), 5; John Taylor, *An Inquiry into the Principles and Policy of the Government of the United States*, ed. Loren Baritz (1814; reprint, Indianapolis, IN, 1969), 216, 230–31; Taylor, *Definition of Parties*, 3; Freneau, "Modern Explanation of a Few Terms, Commonly Misunderstood," *NG*, 24 April 1794; "Sydney," "On the Injustice of the Excise Law and the Secretary's Report," *NG*, 10 May 1792; Edwin G. Burrows, *Albert Gallatin and the Political Economy of Republicanism, 1761–1800* (New York, 1986), 405, argues, "Perhaps the only distinctly American objection to Hamilton's funding and assumption schemes was that they had demoralized republicanism simply by being too complicated for ordinary citizens to understand."

33. John Taylor, *An Enquiry into the Principles and Tendency of Certain Public Measures* (Philadelphia, 1794), 9; Taylor, *Inquiry*, 425; Freneau, "Rules for Changing a Limited Republican Government"; "Valerius," *Newark Gazette*, 29 October 1794;

Joel Barlow, "Advice to the Privileged Orders" (1792), in *The Connecticut Wits*, ed. Vernon L. Parrington (New York, 1926), 372–74, 378; Logan, *Letters Addressed to the Yeomanry*, 20–21.

34. Taylor, *Definition of Parties*, 3; Taylor, *Inquiry*, 440; *Pennsylvania General Advertiser*, 5 March 1794; [Freneau], "The 'Close Relation' of Wealth and Intelligence," *NG*, 19 December 1791. On "mirrors" and "filters" as political metaphors, see Richard J. Ellis, *American Political Cultures* (New York, 1993), 63–67. On the mirror as a complementary metaphor for both public opinion and the market, see Niklas Luhmann, "Social Complexity and Public Opinion," in *Political Theory in the Welfare State*, trans. John Bednarz Jr. (Berlin, 1990), 215.

35. See, for example, Todd Estes, *The Jay Treaty Debate, Public Opinion, and the Evolution of Early American Political Culture* (Amherst, MA, 2006); James Morton Smith, *Freedom's Fetters* (Ithaca, NY, 1966); and Jeffrey Pasley, *"The Tyranny of Printers"* (Charlottesville, VA, 2001).

36. Christine Desan, "The Market as a Matter of Money: Denaturalizing Economic Currency in American Constitutional History," *Law and Social Inquiry* 30 (2005): 1–60. Farley Grubb, "Creating the U.S. Dollar Currency Union, 1748–1811: A Quest for Monetary Stability or a Usurpation of State Sovereignty for Personal Gain?" *American Economic Review* 93 (December 2003): 1778–98, concludes that it was the latter. See also Macdonald, *Free Nation Deep in Debt*, 303–6.

37. Douglas Bradburn, *The Citizenship Revolution* (Richmond, VA, 2008); Cornell, *Other Founders*, 274–302; David Waldstreicher, *In the Midst of Perpetual Fetes* (Chapel Hill, NC, 1997); John Lauritz Larson, *Internal Improvement* (Chapel Hill, NC, 2001); Paul Kahn, *The Reign of Law* (New Haven, CT, 1997), 206–29.

38. Joyce Appleby, "Locke, Liberalism, and the Natural Law of Money," *Past and Present* 71 (May 1976): 43–69; Perkins, *American Public Finance*; Bray Hammond, *Banks and Politics in America from the Revolution to the Civil War* (Princeton, NJ, 1957); Halleck, "Alnwick Castle," *The Poetical Works of Fitz-Green Halleck*, 3rd ed. (New York, 1820), 15. See also "Laureate to the Banks," "The Banks; or, Western Melodies" *Port Folio* 7 (March 1819): 248–49. Adams to Jefferson, 15 Nov. 1813 and 24 Feb. 1819, in *The Adams-Jefferson Letters*, ed. Lester Cappon (Chapel Hill, NC, 1987), 401, 535.

39. Lamoreaux, *Insider Lending* (Cambridge, 1994), 74.

40. "About the Banks," *Niles' Weekly Register* 3 (7 November 1816): 162. For similar themes and arguments, see "The Crisis," *Western Messenger*, September 1837, 47–52; "The Moral of the Crisis," *USMDR* 1 (October 1837): 108–22; Washington Irving, "A Time of Unexampled Prosperity," *Knickerbocker Magazine* 15 (April 1840): 303–24; and John Pendleton Kennedy, *Quodlibet* (Philadelphia, 1840).

41. Benton, *Thirty Years' View* (New York, 1886), 1:470; Gouge, *A Short History of Paper Money and Banking in the United States* (1833; reprint, New York, 1968), 231–32.

42. Webster, "Public Dinner at New York, March 24, 1831," in *The Papers of Daniel Webster: Speeches and Formal Writings, 1800–1833*, ed. Charles M. Wiltse (Hanover, NH, 1986), 1:452.

43. Jackson, "Fifth Annual Message, 3 Dec. 1833," *A Compilation of the Messages and Papers of the Presidents, 1789–1897*, ed. James Richardson (Washington, DC, 1897), 3:30; Bryant, "Credit System and Senator Tallmadge's Eulogy" (17 June 1836), in *Power for Sanity: Selected Editorials of William Cullen Bryant, 1829–1861*, ed. William Cullen Bryant II (New York, 1994), 46–47.

44. Emerson, "Nominalist and Realist" (1844) and "Wealth" (1860), in *Emerson: Essays and Lectures*, ed. Joel Porte (New York, 1983), 578, 997–98. For some suggestive comments on the problems of money-handling in the antebellum economy, see David Henkin, *City Reading* (New York, 1998), 137–66, and Joyce Appleby, "The Popular Sources of American Capitalism," *Studies in American Political Development* 9 (Fall 1995): 452–54.

45. Harry E. Miller, "Earlier Theories of Crises and Cycles in the United States," *Quarterly Journal of Economics* 38 (February 1924): 294; Riesman, "Republican Revisions: Political Economy in New York after the Panic of 1819," *New York and the Rise of American Capitalism*, ed. William Pencak and Conrad E. Wright (Albany, NY, 1989), 33.

46. For example, see Willard Phillips, "Seybert's Statistical Annals," *North American Review*, September 1819, 229, and Francis Wayland, *The Elements of Political Economy* (Boston, 1850), 262–88. For useful transatlantic comparisons, see Noel Thompson, *The People's Science* (Cambridge, 1984). See also Charles P. Kindleberger, *Manias, Panics, and Crashes*, rev. ed. (New York, 1989).

47. "Theories based on the uncertainty of the market, on speculation in commodities, on 'overtrading,' on the excesses of bank credit, on the psychology of traders and merchants, did indeed fit reasonably well the early 'mercantile' or commercial phase of modern capitalism. But as the nineteenth century wore on, 'captains of industry,' men who made their fortunes in great industrial enterprises, came to the fore. Investment of fixed capital in railroads, in industrial plant and equipment, in construction, became the main outlet for funds seeking a profitable return." Alvin Hansen, *Business Cycles and National Income* (New York, 1964), 226.

Chapter 3 · Partisan Manufactories of Public Sentiment

1. "Present-day polling, in its main assumptions, exemplifies the 19th-century liberal's approach to the individual as a social atom. By a convenient fiction, polling tends to treat its subject, in every social stratum, as a 'responsible citizen'—one who considers the world in terms of 'issues' and considers these issues in the terms in which they are discussed in the press and on the radio, holds a position in a political spectrum which runs in such single dimensions as left-right, or Republican-Democrat-Progressive, and feels it his duty to take sides on public issues both when polled and when called upon to vote." David Riesman and Nathan Glazer, "The Meaning of Opinion" *Public Opinion Quarterly* 12 (Winter 1948–49): 635.

2. Ronald Formisano, "State Development in the Early Republic: Substance and Structure, 1780–1840," and David Waldstreicher, "The Nationalization and Racialization of American Politics: Before, beneath, and between Parties, 1790–1840," in

Contesting Democracy, ed. Bryon E. Shafer and Anthony Badger (Lawrence, KS, 2001), 7–36, 37–64.

3. Bagehot, "The Age of Discussion," in *Physics and Politics* (1867; reprint, Boston, 1956), 114–48; David Spring, "Walter Bagehot and Deference" *AHR* 81 (June 1976): 524–31; Ronald Formisano, "Deferential-Participant Politics: The Early Republic's Political Culture, 1789–1840," *American Political Science Review* 68 (1974): 473–87.

4. On public opinion and the legitimation of party, see Niklas Luhmann, "The Theory of Political Opposition" and "Societal Complexity and Public Opinion," in *Political Theory in the Welfare State*, trans. John Bednarz Jr. (Berlin, 1990), 167–86, 203–18.

5. Some eighteenth-century British political theorists (Bolingbroke and Burke) distinguished factions (which derived from shared interests) from parties (which shared common principles). But for the most part, Americans tended to conflate the two. Terrence Ball, "Party," in *Political Innovation and Conceptual Change*, ed. Ball, James Farr, and Russell Hanson (Cambridge, 1989), 155–75.

6. Hofstadter, *The Idea of a Party System* (Berkeley, CA, 1969), ix. On anti-partyism in the early republic, see also Ralph Ketcham, *Presidents above Party* (Chapel Hill, NC, 1984); Ronald Formisano, *The Transformation of Political Culture* (New York, 1983), 85–106; and Michael Wallace, "Ideologies of Party in the Antebellum Republic" (PhD diss., Columbia University, 1973).

7. "Atticus II," *(Boston) Independent Chronicle and the Universal Advertiser*, 18 October 1787; Taylor, *A Definition of Parties; or, the Political Effects of the Paper System Considered* (Philadelphia, 1794), 2.

8. Madison, "Federalist #10," in *FP*, 122; Gordon Wood, "Interests and Disinterestedness in the Making of the Constitution," in *Beyond Confederation*, ed. Richard Beeman, Stephen Botein, and Edward Carter (Chapel Hill, NC, 1987), 69–112.

9. Hamilton, "Federalist #71," in *FP*, 432; Hamilton, "Federalist #76," ibid., 455; and Madison, "Federalist #63," ibid., 385; Cecilia Kenyon, "Men of Little Faith: The Anti-Federalists on the Nature of Representative Government," *WMQ* 12 (January 1955): 40.

10. Gerry in *Notes on Debates in the Federal Convention of 1787 Reported by James Madison* (Athens, OH, 1966), 368; Shlomo Slonin, "The Electoral College at Philadelphia: The Evolution of an Ad Hoc Congress for the Selection of a President," *JAH* 73 (June 1986): 35–58.

11. Morris in *Records of the Federal Convention of 1787*, ed. Max Farrand and David Maydole Matteson, rev. ed. (New Haven, CT, 1937), 2:500; Ackerman, *The Failure of the Founding Fathers* (Cambridge, MA, 2005), 28.

12. Lippman, *Public Opinion* (New York, 1922), 163.

13. Democratic Society of New York, "Address to the Republican Citizens of the United States, May 28, 1794," in *The Democratic-Republican Societies, 1790–1800*, ed. Phillip Foner (Westport, CT, 1976), 175, 179.

14. *Farmer's Library* (Fair Haven, VT), 17 February 1794, quoted in Sean Wilentz, *The Rise of American Democracy* (New York, 2005), 69; Democratic Society of New

York, "Address to the Republican Citizens," 175. April 19, 1775, is the date of the battles at Lexington and Concord.

15. J. G. A. Pocock, "The Classical Theory of Deference," *AHR* 81 (June 1976): 516–23.

16. The passage at issue was: "an interest in the approbation of the people, and a strong sense of accountability to them, in all official conduct, is the greatest or rather the only effectual security against abuses in those who exercise the power of government." Chipman, *Sketches on the Principles of Government*, 139. Chipman, *New York Herald*, 14 July 1794; "J. M.," *New York Journal*, 9 August 1794, reprinted in Foner, *Democratic-Republican Societies*, 290–92, 298; Chipman to Alexander Hamilton, 9 June 1794, in *PAH*, 16:465–70.

17. Washington in *A Compilation of the Messages and Papers of the Presidents*, ed. James D. Richardson (Washington, DC, 1897), 1:153; Washington to Burgess Ball, 25 September 1794, in *The Writings of George Washington*, ed. John Fitzpatrick (Washington, DC, 1940), 33:506.

18. *Annals of the Congress of the United States, 1789–1842*, 3rd Cong., 2nd sess., 906, 923 (November 1794); Edmund Randolph, *Germanicus* (Philadelphia, 1795).

19. Webster, "The Revolution in France," in *Political Sermons of the American Founding Era*, ed. Ellis Sandoz (Indianapolis, IN, 1991), 1278–79; *Annals*, 922–23.

20. *Annals*, 934–35; Madison to Monroe, 4 December 1794, in *PJM*, 15:406–7. For example, even Congressman William Findley of western Pennsylvania, who had taken part in that region's protests against the whiskey excise, believed that the Democratic societies had improperly "imitated the language, and assumed the forms of regularly constituted authority." Findley, *History of the Insurrection in the Four Western Counties of Pennsylvania* (Philadelphia, 1796), 56–57. A useful discussion of this tension between private interest and public disinterestedness in the rhetoric of the societies may be found in James Roger Sharp, *American Politics in the Early Republic* (New Haven, CT, 1995), 88–91.

21. "Constitution of the Democratic Society in the County of Addison," in Foner, *Democratic-Republican Societies*, 275; Wortman, *A Treatise Concerning Political Enquiry, and the Liberty of the Press* (New York, 1800), 265–66. Wortman's argument here leans heavily on William Godwin, *Enquiry Concerning Political Justice* (1793), ed. Isaac Kramnick (New York, 1976), 282–92.

22. Waldstreicher, *In the Midst of Perpetual Fetes* (Chapel Hill, NC, 1997), 2.

23. Steven Bullock, *Revolutionary Brotherhood* (Chapel Hill, NC, 1996); Vernon Stauffer, *New England and the Bavarian Illuminati* (New York, 1918); Amos Hoffman, "Opinion, Illusion, and the Illusion of Opinion: Barruel's Theory of Conspiracy," *Eighteenth-Century Studies* 27 (Fall 1993): 27–60; John L. Brooke, "Ancient Lodges and Self-Created Societies: Voluntary Association and the Public Sphere in the Early Republic," in *Launching the "Extended Republic": The Federalist Era*, ed. Ronald Hoffman and Peter J. Albert (Charlottesville, VA, 1996), 273–377.

24. Day, *Oration on Party Spirit* (Litchfield, CT, 1798), 8–9, 13. The long passage closely paraphrases David Hume, "On the First Principles of Government" (1758), in *Essays, Moral, Political, and Literary*, ed. Eugene Miller (Indianapolis, IN, 1985), 31.

25. Addison, *Analysis of the Report of the Committee of the Virginia Assembly* (Philadelphia, 1800), 40.

26. Jefferson to Taylor, 1 June 1798, *Works of Thomas Jefferson*, ed. Paul Ford (New York, 1904), 7:264–65; Michael Kent Curtis, *Free Speech, "the People's Darling Privilege"* (Durham, NC, 2000), 72–79.

27. Jefferson to Joseph Priestly, 21 March 1801, in *Works of Thomas Jefferson*, 7:22; Jefferson to Joel Barlow, 3 May 1802, ibid., 8:149; Jefferson to Thomas Cooper, 9 July 1807, in *Writings of Thomas Jefferson*, 11:265.

28. Jefferson to John Garland Jefferson, 25 January 1810, in *Works of Thomas Jefferson*, 12:353; Ketcham, *Presidents above Party*, 100–112; Richard McCormick, *The Presidential Game* (New York, 1982), 76.

29. Alex Keyssar, *The Right to Vote* (New York, 2000), 26–52; Tadahisa Kuroda, *The Origin of the Twelfth Amendment* (Greenwood, CT, 1994); McCormick, *Presidential Game*, 83–115.

30. Ames to John Rutledge Jr., 26 January 1801, cited in David Hackett Fischer, *The Revolution of American Conservatism* (New York, 1965), 150; Jeffrey Pasley, "The Cheese and the Words: Popular Political Culture and Participatory Democracy in the Early American Republic," in *Beyond the Founders*, ed. Jeffrey Pasley, Andrew Robertson, and David Waldstreicher (Chapel Hill, NC, 2004), 46–49.

31. Andrew Robertson, "Voting Rites and Voting Acts: Electioneering Ritual, 1790–1820," in Pasley, Robertson, and Waldstreicher, *Beyond the Founders*, 57–78; Alan Taylor, "From Fathers to Friends of the People: Political Personae in the Early Republic," in *Federalists Reconsidered*, ed. Doron Ben-Atar and Barbara Oberg (Charlottesville, VA, 1998), 225–45; Michael Wallace, "Changing Concepts of Party in the United States: New York, 1815–1828," *AHR* 74 (December 1968): 453–91.

32. Carl Richard, *The Founders and the Classics* (Cambridge, MA, 1994), 169–95; Howe, "The Political Psychology of *The Federalist*," *WMQ* 44 (July 1987): 485–509.

33. Reed, *Observations on the Growth of Mind* (Boston, 1826), 3; Everett, "Oration Delivered before the Citizens of Charlestown, on the Fourth of July, 1828," in *Orations and Speeches on Various Occasions* (Boston, 1836), 158; Francis Wayland Jr., *The Duties of an American Citizen* (Boston, 1825), 11; Story, "A Discourse Pronounced at Cambridge, before the Phi Beta Kappa Society at the Anniversary Celebration on the Thirty-First Day of August, 1826," in *American Oratory; or, Selections from the Speeches of Eminent Americans* (New York, 1880), 504–5.

34. Kammen, "The United States Constitution, Public Opinion, and the Question of American Exceptionalism," in *Sovereignty and Liberty* (Madison, WI, 1980), 111; Calhoun in *Annals*, 14th Cong., 2nd sess., 854 (4 February 1817); Virginia General Assembly, House of Delegates, *Report of the Committee on Roads and Inland Navigation, 27 Dec. 1816*, cited in John Lauritz Larson, *Internal Improvement*: (Chapel Hill, NC, 2001), 94; Richard John, *Spreading the News* (Cambridge, MA, 1995), 9–15.

35. May, *The Enlightenment in America* (New York, 1976), 307–62; Daniel Walker Howe, *The Unitarian Conscience*, rev. ed. (Middletown, CT, 1988); Wilson Smith, *Professors and Public Ethics* (Ithaca, NY, 1956); D. H. Meyer, *The Instructed Conscience* (Philadelphia, 1972).

36. Charles Jared Ingersoll, "The Influence of America on the Mind (1823)," in *American Philosophical Addresses, 1700–1900*, ed. Joseph Blau (New York, 1946), 25, estimated that there were as many as 7,500 American copies of the *Elements* in circulation. Donald Winch, "The System of the North: Dugald Stewart and His Pupils," in *That Noble Science of Politics*, ed. Stefan Collini, John Burrow, and Donald Winch (Cambridge, 1983), 23–62.

37. Stewart, *Elements of the Philosophy of the Human Mind*, 2nd ed. (London, 1802), 235, 239–40, 246, 268–69.

38. Ibid., 246–47, 259; Vincent Starzinger, *The Politics of the Center* (Alexandria, VA, 1965).

39. Winch, "System of the North," 43; Graham Burchell, "Peculiar Interests: Civil Society and Governing 'The System of Natural Liberty,'" in *The Foucault Effect*, ed. Burchell, Colin Gordon, and Peter Miller (Chicago, 1991), 119–50.

40. Carey, *The Olive Branch; or, Faults on Both Sides, Federal and Democratic*, 10th ed. (Philadelphia, 1818), 439–52. For a similar reading of Carey, see Steven Watts, *The Republic Reborn* (Baltimore, 1987), 301–5.

41. "The Patriot," *New Hampshire Patriot and State Gazette*, 21 April 1823; Taylor to Jane Taylor, 17 March 1816, cited in James S. Chase, *The Emergence of the Presidential Nominating Convention, 1789–1833* (Urbana, IL, 1973), 22; M. Ostorgorski, "The Rise and Fall of the Nominating Caucus, Legislative and Congressional," *AHR* 5 (December 1899): 253–83.

42. King in *Annals*, 18th Cong., 1st sess., 355–62 (18 March 1824); Ostorgorski, 272; *Niles' Weekly Register*, 28 June 1823, 259; "Sovereignty of the People #2," ibid., 11 September 1824, 19.

43. *Niles' Weekly Register*, 18 September 1824, 38; Joseph Walton, "Nominating Conventions in Pennsylvania" *AHR* 2 (January 1897): 262–87; McCormick, *Presidential Game*, 134.

44. Joel Silbey, *The American Political Nation, 1838–1893* (Stanford, CA, 1993), 59; Van Buren, *Inquiry into the Origin and Course of Political Parties in the United States* (New York, 1867), 226, 232; Gerald Leonard, *The Invention of Party Politics* (Chapel Hill, NC, 2002), 35–43; Larry D. Kramer, *The People Themselves* (New York, 2004).

45. Leonard, *Invention of Party Politics*, 14; Jackson, "Fifth Annual Message, 3 Dec. 1833," in Richardson, *Messages and Papers of the Presidents*, 3:30.

46. Paul Goodman, *Towards a Christian Republic: Antimasonry and the Great Transition in New England, 1826–1836* (New York, 1988); Steven C. Bullock, *Revolutionary Brotherhood: Freemasonry and the Transformation of the American Social Order, 1730–1840* (Chapel Hill, NC, 1996), 277–307.

47. *Proceedings of the Antimasonic Republican Convention of Massachusetts, Held at Boston, September 11, 12, & 13, 1833* (Boston, 1833), 6; *Anti-Masonic Review and Magazine* 1, no. 3 (1828): 76; "Address to the Electors of New York, June 21, 1832, by the New York Antimasonic Convention of 1832," in *History of United States Political Parties*, ed. Arthur Schlesinger Jr. (New York, 1973), 1:669; Formisano, *Transformation of Political Culture*, 222.

48. Ratcliffe, "Antimasonry and Partisanship in Greater New England, 1826–1836," *JER* 15 (Summer 1995): 199–239, quote on p. 215; Adams, *Letters and Addresses on Freemasonry* (1833; reprint, Dayton, OH, 1875), 274; "Address to the People of New York, 1829, by the New York Antimasonic Convention," in Schlesinger, *History of Political Parties*, 1:639; *Anti-Masonic Review and Magazine* 1, no. 1 (1828): 36; "Proceedings of a Convention of Young Men of the Country of Washington, New York Opposed to the Masonic Institution, Hartford, April 16th, 1830," reprinted in ibid. 2, no. 7 (1830): 222.

49. Throop, "Special Messages," in *Messages from the Governors of New York*, ed. Charles Z. Lincoln (Albany, NY, 1909), 3:274–76; *Albany Evening Journal*, 1 October 1831; Robert O. Rupp, "Parties and the Public Good: Political Anti-Masonry in New York Reconsidered," *JER* 8 (Autumn 1988): 253–79.

50. Bullock, *Revolutionary Brotherhood*, 302–7, 313; Power, *Secrecy: A Poem* (Boston, 1832), 25.

51. On pluralism and the second party system, see, for example, Silbey, *American Political Nation*, 43, and William G. Shade, "Political Pluralism and Party Development: The Creation of a Modern Party System: 1815–1852," in *The Evolution of American Electoral Systems*, ed. Paul Kleppner (Westport, CT, 1981), 77–111. On republicanism, see Major Wilson, "Republicanism and the Idea of Party in the Jacksonian Period," *JER* 8 (Winter 1988): 419–42, and Marc Kruman, "The Second American Party System and the Transformation of Revolutionary Republicanism," *JER* 12 (Winter 1992): 509–37.

52. Tocqueville, *Democracy in America*, ed. and trans. Harvey Mansfield and Debra Winthrop (Chicago, 2000), 246; "A Citizen of the United States," *Vindiciae Americanae* (London, 1837); "European Views of American Democracy," *USMDR* 1 (October 1837): 102–4.

53. Camp, *Democracy* (New York, 1841), 199–205.

54. For example, "On the Intelligence of the People," *USMDR* 8 (November 1840): 361, argued that "faith in the instinctive intelligence of the people, separated entirely from those forms of the understanding which are necessary for the expression of that intelligence through the medium of language—and without any reference to what is termed Education—has always been the fundamental doctrine of democracy." Bancroft, "The Office of the People in Art, Government, and Religion: An Oration Delivered before the Adelphi Society of Williamstown College in August of 1835," in *Social Theories of Jacksonian Democracy*, ed. Joseph Blau (New York, 1954), 267, 269.

55. Baker, *Affairs of Party* (Ithaca, NY, 1983), 124.

56. William Leggett, "The Division of Parties" (1834), in *Democratick Editorials*, ed. Lawrence White (Indianapolis, IN, 1984), 242–46; "Political Tolerance," *USMDR* 3 (September 1838): 64; O'Sullivan, "Introduction," *USMDR* 1 (October 1837): 1.

57. O'Sullivan, "Introduction," 2, 9, 13.

58. "H," "Political Parties," *New England Magazine* 7 (October 1834): 269; Calhoun, "Second Speech on the Bill for the Admission of Michigan" (1837), in *The Papers of John C. Calhoun*, ed. Clyde Wilson (Columbia, SC, 1980), 13:346–49. On

conventions and popular sovereignty, see Gordon Wood, *Creation of the American Republic* (New York, 1972), 306–43.

59. "The Progress of the Ultra-Democratic Principle," *American Monthly Magazine* 6 (August 1838): 110; Daniel Walker Howe, *The Political Culture of the American Whigs* (Chicago, 1979), 29–30; Michael Holt, *The Rise and Fall of the American Whig Party* (New York, 1999), 30–32; William Brock, *Parties and Political Conscience* (Milwood, NY, 1971).

60. Calvin Colton, *Thoughts on the Religious State of the Country* (New York, 1836), 176–77; Colton, *The Crisis of the Country* (New York, 1840), 16; Channing, "Self Culture" (1838), in *The Works of William Ellery Channing* (New York, 1970), 27.

61. Lieber, *Manual of Political Ethics*, 2nd ed. (Philadelphia, 1838), 2:273; Marshall, "The Strange Stillbirth of the Whig Party," *AHR* 72 (January 1967): 461.

62. Choate, "The Position and Function of the American Bar, as an Element of Conservativism in the State" (1845), in *Addresses and Orations of Rufus Choate* (Boston, 1891), 137–38, 143–44; Jean V. Matthews, *Rufus Choate* (Philadelphia, 1980).

63. Choate, "Position and Function of the American Bar," 149–56.

64. "Address by Chairman James Barbour of Virginia to the Whig National Convention of 1839," in Schlesinger, *History of Political Parties*, 1:402–3; *Speech of Mr. Ogle, of Pennsylvania, on the Regal Splendor of the President's Palace* (Washington, DC, 1840); M. Bradley to Thurlow Weed, 29 August 1839, cited in Robert Gunderson, *The Log-Cabin Campaign* (Lexington, KY, 1957), 52.

65. Harrison, "Inaugural Address," in Richardson, *Messages and Papers of the Presidents*, 4:19; Ullmann, *An Address Delivered in the Tabernacle, before the Tippecanoe and Other Harrison Associations of the City of New York* (New York, 1841), 26–27, 36–38. See also John Duer, *An Introductory Lecture on the Evils, Social, Moral, and Political, That Flow from Our Party Divisions, and the Prevalence of Party Spirit* (New York, 1841).

66. Ullmann, *Address*, 39–40. Ullmann practiced what he preached. In the New York gubernatorial election of 1854, he ran (unsuccessfully) as the Know-Nothing Party nominee, moved on to the Republican Party, and served as a Brigadier General in the Corps d'Afrique during the Civil War.

67. William B. Sprague, *A Voice of the Rod* (Albany, NY, 1841), 14; Bethune, *A Discourse on the Death of William Henry Harrison* (Philadelphia, 1841), 12; Smith, *Sermon Occasioned by the Death of William Henry Harrison* (Hallowell, ME, 1841), 14–15.

68. Colton, *The Junius Tracts* (New York, 1844), 10.

69. Cobb, speech on 1 July 1848, *Appendix to Congressional Globe*, 30th Cong., 1st sess., 775–76.

Chapter 4 · The Importance of Having Opinions

1. Mill, *Diary*, 13 January 1854, cited in Walter Houghton, *The Victorian Frame of Mind, 1830–1870* (New Haven, CT, 1957), 13. I have poached the title for this chap-

ter from Albert Hirschman, "Having Opinions—One of the Elements of Well-Being?" *American Economic Review* 79 (May 1989): 75–79.

2. Benjamin Franklin, *Poor Richards's Almanack* (Waterloo, IA, 1914), 44; Habermas, *The Structural Transformation of the Public Sphere*, trans. Thomas Burger (Cambridge, MA, 1991), 129–40. See also Alan Kahan, *Aristocratic Liberalism: The Social and Political Thought of Jacob Burckhardt, John Stuart Mill, and Alexis de Tocqueville* (Oxford, 1992), 65–68; Biancamaria Fontana, *Benjamin Constant and the Post-Revolutionary Mind* (New Haven, CT, 1991), 81–97; and Vincent Starzinger, *Middlingness: Juste Milieu Political Theory in France and England, 1815–1848* (Charlottesville, VA, 1965).

3. Emerson, "Historic Notes of Life and Letters in New England," in *Complete Works of Ralph Waldo Emerson*, ed. Edward Waldo Emerson (Boston, 1903–4), 10:326. On "self-talk," see Jan Goldstein, *The Post-Revolutionary Self: Politics and Psyche in France, 1750–1850* (Cambridge, MA, 2005), 1–21. Daniel Walker Howe, *Making the American Self* (Oxford, 1997), 107–35.

4. James, "The Will to Believe," in *The Writings of William James*, ed. John McDermott (Chicago, 1977), 719. In contemporary philosophy, this problem is known as "doxological voluntarism." See, for example, Bernard Williams on "Deciding to Believe" in *Problems of the Self* (Cambridge, 1976), 136–51.

5. Bailey, *Essays on the Formation and Publication of Opinions and Other Subjects*, 2nd ed. (London, 1826), 42, 103, 132. While largely neglected by historians, Bailey (the "Hallamshire Bentham") was an important figure in British utilitarianism. His *Essays* was reprinted six times in Britain between 1821 and 1861, and twice in America. James Mill praised the book as second only to Adam Smith's *Wealth of Nations* in the canon of modern philosophy. Keith Quincy, "Samuel Bailey and Mill's Defence of Freedom of Discussion," *Mill Newsletter* 21 (Winter 1986), 4–18.

6. Brougham, "Inaugural Discourse on Being Installed Lord Rector of the University of Glasgow, April 6, 1825," in *Works of Henry Lord Brougham* (Edinburgh, 1879), 3:139–40; Walwyn, "The Compassionate Samaritan," in *Tracts on Liberty in the Puritan Revolution, 1638–1647*, ed. William Haller (New York, 1933), 3:67–68. See also the appendix on the "Psychology of Freedom" (a term introduced by the legal scholar Mark DeWolfe Howe) in Levy's *Legacy of Suppression: Freedom of Speech and Press in Early American History* (Cambridge, 1964), 313–20.

7. Jefferson, "The Virginia Statute on Religious Freedom," in *The Papers of Thomas Jefferson*, ed. Julian P. Boyd (Princeton, NJ, 1950) 2:545; *Journal of the House of Delegates of the Commonwealth of Virginia* (Richmond, VA, 1828), 95, 143–44; Madison, "Property" (1792), in *PJM*, 14:266.

8. Thomson, *An Enquiry Concerning the Liberty, and Licentiousness of the Press, and the Uncontrollable Nature of Mind* (New York, 1801), 15, 24, 61, 75.

9. Wortman, *A Treatise Concerning Political Enquiry, and the Liberty of the Press* (New York, 1800), iv. Leonard Levy argued that this was "the book that Jefferson did not write but should have." *Emergence of a Free Press* (Oxford, 1985), 328. Saul Cornell has contended that it represents the "most important effort at a theory of the

public sphere to counter the Federalist political and constitutional vision." *The Other Founders* (Chapel Hill, NC, 1999), 254.

10. Wortman, *Treatise*, 32, 53, 64, 67.

11. Ruth Bloch, *Visionary Republic* (Cambridge, 1980), 197–98; Wortman, *An Oration upon the Influence of Social Institutions upon Human Morals and Happiness* (New York, 1796).

12. Wortman, *Treatise*, 23–24. On the "irreversibility thesis" in democratic thought, see Don Herzog, *Poisoning the Minds of the Lower Orders* (Princeton, NJ, 2000), 86–88.

13. Wortman, *Treatise*, 45–46, 122. On the relation between opinion and voluntary action, see William Godwin, *Enquiry Concerning Political Justice* (1793; reprint, New York, 2009), 116–46.

14. Thomas Green Fessenden, *Democracy Unveiled* (New York, 1806), 1:xxiii; Edmund Burke, *Reflections on the Revolution in France* (1790; reprint, New York, 2009), 95; Seth Cotlar, "The Federalists' Transatlantic Cultural Offensive of 1798 and the Moderation of American Political Discourse," in *Beyond the Founders*, ed. Jeffrey Pasley, Andrew Robertson, and David Waldstreicher (Chapel Hill, NC, 1996), 274–99; Douglas Bradburn, "A Clamor in the Public Mind: Opposition to the Alien and Sedition Acts," *WMQ* 65 (July 2008): 565–600.

15. Rachel Hope Cleves, *The Reign of Terror in America* (Cambridge, 2011); Peter S. Field, *Crisis of the Standing Order* (Amherst, MA, 1998); David Hackett Fischer, *The Revolution of American Conservatism* (Chicago, 1965); Linda Kerber, *Federalists in Dissent* (Ithaca, NY, 1970).

16. Webster, "Oration on Opinion, Dartmouth, 1801," *The Papers of Daniel Webster: Speeches and Formal Writings, 1800–1833*, ed. Charles M. Wiltse (Hanover, NH, 1986), 1:492–93, 499–502; [Webster], "Review of Wortman's Political Inquiry," *Monthly Anthology and Boston Review* 3 (October 1806): 544–46.

17. Rush, "The Influence of Physical Causes on the Moral Faculty" (1786), in *American Philosophic Addresses*, ed. Joseph Blau (New York, 1946), 317–25; Rush "Influence of the American Revolution" (1788), in *The Selected Writings of Benjamin Rush*, ed. Dagobert Runes (New York, 1947), 333; Michael Meranze, *Laboratories of Virtue* (Chapel Hill, NC, 1996), 87–127; Jefferson to Nathaniel Burwell, 14 March 1818, in *Writings of Thomas Jefferson*, 15:166; Murray, "On the Equality of the Sexes" (1790), in *American Political Thought*, ed. Isaac Kramnick and Theodore Lowi (New York, 2008), 507. For similar pathologies of imagination, see Grant Powers, *Essay upon the Influence of the Imagination on the Nervous System Contributing to a False Hope in Religion* (Andover, NH, 1828), and John Haygarth, *Of the Imagination, as a Cause and a Cure of Disorders of the Body* (London, 1800).

18. Rosenfeld, *Common Sense: A Political History* (Cambridge, MA, 2011), 182.

19. Irving, *History, Tales, and Sketches* (New York, 1983), 144, 545. On Irving, Jefferson, and "logocracy," see Christopher Looby, *Voicing America* (Chicago, 1996), 13–96.

20. Everett, *Common Sense in Dishabille: or, The Farmer's Monitor* (Worcester, MA, 1799), 9–10.

21. *Biblical Repertory and Theological Review* 4 (1832): 397, 402, 408. The editor of the *Review* (and possibly Bailey's reviewer), Professor Charles Hodge of Princeton University, once boasted that he had, in fifty years of teaching, never broached a new or original idea. Perry Miller, *The Life of the Mind in America* (New York, 1965), 17.

22. Hall, "Responsibility for Opinion," *Christian Examiner* 47 (September 1849): 209–16.

23. Newman, "The Tamworth Reading Room" (1841), in *Newman: Prose and Poetry*, ed. Geoffrey Tillotson (Cambridge, MA, 1957), 83.

24. Herttell, *The Demurrer; or, Proofs of Error in the Decision of the Supreme Court of the State of New York* (New York, 1828); Cooper, *A Treatise on the Law of Libel and the Liberty of the Press* (New York, 1830), 42; James S. Kabala, "'Theocrats' vs. 'Infidels': Marginalized Worldviews and Legislative Prayer in 1830s New York," *Journal of Church and State* 51 (Winter 2009): 78–101; Ronald Formisano and Stephen Pickering, "The Christian Nation Debate and Witness Competency," *JER* 29 (Summer 2009): 219–48.

25. David Sehat, *The Myth of American Religious Freedom* (Oxford, 2011), 51–69.

26. Robert Abzug, *Cosmos Crumbling* (Oxford, 1994); Richard Carwardine, *Evangelicals and Politics in Antebellum America* (New Haven, CT, 1993); John Brooke, "Cultures of Nationalism, Movements of Reform, and the Composite-Federal Polity: From Revolutionary Settlement to Antebellum Crisis," *JER* 29 (Spring, 2009): 11.

27. Beecher, *The Practicality of Suppressing Vice* (New Haven, CT, 1804), 8–9; Beecher, "A Reformation of Morals Practicable and Indispensable" (1812), in *Sermons Delivered on Various Occasions* (Boston, 1828), 69–96.

28. *A Brief Account of the Origin and Progress of the Divisions in the First Presbyterian Church in the City of Troy* (Troy, NY, 1827), 34–36; "Philalethes," *The Importance of Revivals as Exhibited in the Late Convention at New Lebanon* (New York, 1827); James Walker, "The Oneida and Troy Revivals," *Christian Examiner* 4 (May–June 1827): 242–65; Beecher, *The Autobiography of Lyman Beecher* (Cambridge, MA, 1961), 2:72–73. See also Charles Hambrick-Stowe, *Charles G. Finney and the Spirit of American Evangelism* (Grand Rapids, MI, 1996), 36–73.

29. Finney, "The Religion of Public Opinion," in *Lectures to Professing Christians* (New York, 1837), 86–87; Finney, *Lectures on Revivals of Religion* (1835), ed. William G. McGloughlin (Cambridge, MA, 1960), 7–23.

30. Miller, *The Life of the Mind in America* (New York, 1970), 7; Nathan Hatch, *The Democratization of American Christianity* (New Haven, CT, 1989); James Bratt, "Religious Anti-Revivalism in Antebellum America," *JER* 24 (Spring 2004): 65–106; Colton, *Thoughts on the Religious State of the Country* (New York, 1836), 176–78.

31. Channing, "Discourse at the Dedication of the Second Congregational Unitarian Church, New York, 1826," in *Discourses, Reviews, and Miscellanies* (Boston, 1830), 400. Channing's language here provoked some controversy. Lyman Beecher thought it would destroy his reputation among "sober Unitarians." Lyman Beecher to Catharine Beecher, 3 February 1827, in Beecher, *Autobiography*, 2:64; Miller, *The Life of the Mind in America*, 3–35. On Unitarianism, see Daniel Walker Howe, *The Uni-*

tarian Conscience: Harvard Moral Philosophy, 1805–1861, rev. ed. (Middletown, CT, 1988), and Conrad Wright, *The Beginnings of Unitarianism in America* (Boston, 1955).

32. [Dewey], *Letters of an English Traveler to His Friend in England on the "Revivals of Religion" in America* (Boston, 1828), 117–18, 120–21, 122–25; Colton, *Thoughts on the Religious State of the Country; with Reasons for Preferring the Episcopacy* (New York, 1836), 176–78. For the same argument stated less succinctly, see Ephraim Perkins, *A "Bunker Hill" Contest, A.D. 1826* (Utica, NY, 1826).

33. Walker, *Smooth Preaching* (New York, 1823), 4–9; Walker, "Dissensions among the Revivalists," *Christian Examiner* 6 (March 1829): 101–7. On Walker, see Howe, *Unitarian Conscience*, 313–14.

34. Channing, "Letter on Catholicism," *The Works of William Ellery Channing* (New York, 1970), 321–33; Jenny Franchot, *Roads to Rome: The Antebellum Protestant Encounter with Catholicism* (Berkeley, CA, 1994), 221–33; Andrew Delblanco, *William Ellery Channing: An Essay on the Liberal Spirit in America* (Cambridge, MA, 1981), 36–37.

35. Beecher, *The Evils Suffered by American Women and American Children: The Causes and the Remedy* (New York, 1846), 21–23.

36. Stanley Elkins, *Slavery: A Problem in American Institutional and Intellectual Life* (1959; reprint, Chicago, 1976); Lewis Perry, *Radical Abolitionism: Anarchy and the Government of God in Antislavery Thought* (Ithaca, NY, 1973).

37. Channing, "Spiritual Freedom: Discourse Preached at the Annual Election, May 26, 1830," in *William Ellery Channing: Selected Writings*, ed. David Robinson (New York, 1985), 196, 200–201, 205–9.

38. Ware, "Sober Thoughts on the State of the Times Addressed to the Unitarian Community" (1835), in *The Works of Henry Ware, Jr.* (Boston, 1847), 2:115–18; Dewey, *Moral Views of Commerce, Society, and Politics in Twelve Discourses* (New York, 1838), 146–47, 170–73, 182; Parker, *Lessons from the World of Matter and the World of Man*, in *The Collected Works of Theodore Parker*, ed. Francis Power Cobbe (London, 1872), 101–2. While it is tempting to suggest Channing as a source for Tocqueville's "tyranny of the majority"—Reino Virtanen, "Tocqueville and William Ellery Channing," *American Literature* 22 (March 1950): 21–28, suggested as much—Tocqueville does not appear to have read this sermon. He met with Channing but spoke mostly on religious matters not pertinent to the theme. Tocqueville did have a copy of Channing's *Discourses, Reviews, and Miscellanies* (1830) in his library and might have picked up some sense of how public opinion punished the theologically unorthodox from such pieces as "The System of Exclusion and Denunciation in Religion Considered," 557–70. George Wilson Pierson, *Tocqueville and Beaumont in America* (Baltimore, 1996), 421–23, 730.

39. Bourdieu, *Distinction*, trans. Richard Nice (Cambridge, MA, 1984), 415–16.

40. Channing, *Self-Culture* (Boston, 1843), 20; Ware, "Formation of a Christian Character" (1831), in *Works*, 4:311–13. On "character," see Burton Bledstein, *The Culture of Professionalism* (New York, 1978), 129–58; Karen Halttunen, *Confidence Men and Painted Ladies* (New Haven, CT, 1982); and Stefan Collini, *Public Moralists* (Oxford, 1991), 91–120.

41. Robert Riegel, "The Introduction of Phrenology to the United States," *AHR* 39 (October 1933): 73–78. For the scientific background, consult Robert M. Young, *Mind, Brain, and Adaptation in the Nineteenth Century* (Oxford, 1970). On popular interest in the body, see Michael Sappol, *A Traffic of Dead Bodies* (Princeton, NJ, 2002).

42. Charles Follen, *Funeral Oration Delivered before the Citizens of Boston Assembled at the Old South Church* (Boston, 1832).

43. Beecher's testimonial is cited in Nelson Sizer, *Forty Years in Phrenology* (New York, 1882), 14.

44. Donald Scott, "The Popular Lecture and the Creation of a Public in Mid-Nineteenth Century America," *JAH* 66 (March 1980): 791–809; Paul Starr, *The Creation of the Media* (New York, 2004), 113–50; Isabelle Lehuu, *Carnival on the Page* (Chapel Hill, NC, 2000); David Henkin, *The Postal Age* (Chicago, 2007).

45. Madeline Stern, *Heads and Headlines* (Norman, OK, 1971), 80; Stephen Pearl Andrews, *The Phonographic Reader* (Boston, 1846); Isaac Pitman, *Exercises in Phonography* (Philadelphia, 1849); Pliny Miles, *American Phreno-Mnemotechny, Theoretical and Practical* (New York, 1846). For similar efforts, see Jill Lepore, *A Is for American* (New York, 2002).

46. [Hedge], "Pretensions of Phrenology Examined," *Christian Examiner* 17 (November 1834): 267; Anthony Albert Walsh, "Johann Gaspar Spurzheim and the Rise and Fall of Scientific Phrenology in Boston, 1832–1842" (PhD diss., University of New Hampshire, 1974).

47. Parker, "Theodore Parker's Experience as a Minister" (1859), in *The Transcendentalists*, ed. Perry Miller (Cambridge, MA, 1950), 487; Emerson, "The Spirit of the Times" (1848–1856), in *The Selected Lectures of Ralph Waldo Emerson*, ed. Ronald Bosco and Joel Myerson (Athens, GA, 2005), 132; Emerson, "Experience," in *Ralph Waldo Emerson, Essays and Lectures*, ed. Joel Porte (New York, 1983), 475; Stephen Conroy, "Emerson and Phrenology," *American Quarterly* 16 (Summer 1964): 215–17; John B. Wilson, "Phrenology and the Transcendentalists," *American Literature* 28 (May 1956): 220–25; George Willis Cooke, *An Historical and Biographical Introduction to Accompany "The Dial"* (Cleveland, 1902), 2:72.

48. Charles Colbert, *A Measure of Perfection* (Chapel Hill, NC, 1997); David Reynolds, *Walt Whitman's America* (New York, 1995); David Reynolds, *Beneath the American Renaissance* (New York, 1988); Edward Hungerford, "Poe and Phrenology," *American Literature* 2 (November 1930): 209–31; Stern, *Heads and Headlines*; John D. Davies, *Phrenology* (New Haven, CT, 1955).

49. Secord, *Victorian Sensation* (Chicago, 2000), 437–70. On morphology and romanticism, see Robert J. Richards, *The Romantic Conception of Life* (Chicago, 2002). See also Trevor Levere, "Samuel Taylor Coleridge and the Human Sciences: Anthropology, Phrenology, and Mesmerism," in *Science, Pseudo-Science, and Society*, ed. Marsha Hanen, Margaret Osler, and Robert Weyant (Waterloo, ON, 1980), 171–92.

50. Channing to Lucy Aikin, 8 January 1833, in *The Correspondence of William Ellery Channing and Lucy Aikin from 1826 to 1842* (Boston, 1874), 158–59. The Unitarian *Christian Examiner* shared Channing's confusion, publishing a positive review

of phrenology before publishing Hedge's denunciation in November of that year. Isaac Ray, "Moral Aspects of Phrenology," *Christian Examiner* 16 (May 1834): 221–48.

51. "Phrenology," *North American Review*, July 1833, 75, 83; Brownson, "The Pretensions of Phrenology," in *The Works of Orestes Brownson*, ed. Henry Brownson (New York, 1966), 9:242. These arguments had already been well rehearsed in Scotland. G. N. Cantor, "Phrenology in Early Nineteenth-Century Edinburgh: A Historiographical Discussion," *Annals of Science* 32 (1975): 195–218; Stephen Shapin, "Phrenological Knowledge and the Social Structure of Early Nineteenth-Century Edinburgh," *Annals of Science* 32 (1975): 219–43; and A. Cameron Grant, "Combe on Phrenology and Free Will: A Note on 19th-Century Secularism," *Journal of the History of Ideas* 26 (January–March 1965): 141–47. See also Roger Cooter, *The Cultural Meaning of Popular Science: Phrenology and the Organization of Consent in Nineteenth-Century Britain* (Cambridge, 1984), 25.

52. John Byrne, *Anti-Phrenology; or, A Chapter on Humbug* (Washington, DC, 1843), 4; Frank H. Hamilton, *Lecture on Phrenology* (Rochester, NY, 1841); Thomas Sewall, *An Examination of Phrenology in Two Lectures*, 2nd ed. (Boston, 1839); Emerson, *Journals and Miscellaneous Notebooks*, ed. Ralph Orth (Cambridge, MA, 1966), 6:222.

53. "Professions," *American Phrenological Journal and Miscellany* 2 (February 1845): 61.

54. R. W. Haskins, *History and Progress of Phrenology* (Buffalo, NY, 1839); J. V. C. Smith, "Statistics of Phrenology in the United States," *American Medical Almanac* (1840), excerpted in *American Phrenological Journal and Miscellany* 3 (January 1841): 185–90; Watson, *Public Opinion; or, Safe Revolution through Self-Representation* (London, 1848); "Hewett C. Watson," *The Dictionary of National Biography*, ed. Leslie Stephen and Sidney Lee (Oxford, 1917), 20:918–20; Frank Egerton, "In Quest of a Science: Hewett Watson and Victorian Phrenology," *Essays in the Arts and Sciences* 24 (October 1995): 1–20; Watson, *Statistics of Phrenology* (London, 1836).

55. Elisha Bartlett, *An Address Delivered at the Anniversary Celebration of the Birth of Spurzheim, and the Organization of the Boston Phrenological Society* (Boston, 1838), 20–22; Stowe quoted in Stern, *Heads and Headlines*, 82.

56. [Warren Burton], *Uncle Sam's Recommendation of Phrenology to the Millions of Friends in the United States in a Series of Not Very Dull Letters* (New York, 1842), 109–10. This meant that a pronounced organ of "approbativeness" had overshadowed the frontal organ of "firmness." See also "The Heads of Our Great Men," *American Phrenological Journal* 1 (May 1839): 286–94, and Madeleine Stern, comp., *A Phrenological Dictionary of Nineteenth-Century Americans* (Westport, CT, 1982).

57. Sizer, *Forty Years in Phrenology* (New York, 1882), 31–34.

58. Henkin, *City Reading* (New York, 1998); Sizer, *Forty Years in Phrenology*, 395; Beecher, *Eyes and Ears* (Boston, 1863), 21–25. On science as a genteel "hunt," see William Eamon, *Science and the Secrets of Nature* (Princeton, NJ, 1994). Graphology—the science of reading handwriting for character traits and forgeries—drew much of its inspiration and authority from phrenology. Tamara Plakins Thornton, *Handwriting in America* (New Haven, CT, 1996).

59. "Horace Mann's Opinion of Phrenology from Thoughts for a Young Man," *American Phrenological Journal and Repository of Science* 13 (January–July 1851): 31; Christopher Lasch, "The Common Schools: Horace Mann and the Assault on Imagination," in *Revolt of the Elites* (New York, 1995), 141–60; Howe, *A Discourse on the Social Relations of Man; Delivered before the Boston Phrenological Society* (Boston, 1837), 28–32; Amariah Brigham, *Observations on the Influence of Religion upon the Health and Physical Welfare of Mankind* (Boston, 1835); David Meredith Reese, *Phrenology Known by Its Fruits, Being a Brief Review of Doctor Brigham's Late Work, Entitled "Observations on the Influence of Religion upon the Health and Physical Welfare of Mankind"* (New York, 1836); William Sims Bainbridge, "Religious Insanity in America: The Official Nineteenth Century Theory," *Sociological Analysis* 45 (1984): 229–31.

60. Luna M. Hammond, *Trials and Triumphs of an Orphan Girl: The Biography of Mrs. Deiadamia Chase, Physician and Phrenologist* (Cortland, NY, 1859), 110–11, 116–17, 167–93.

61. Fowler, "Republicanism IX," *American Phrenological Journal* 9 (November 1847): 370; Sizer, "Debate in Cranium," *American Phrenological Journal* 12 (March 1850): 119–23; "Debate in Crania," in *The Phrenological Miscellany; or, The Annuals of Phrenology and Physiognomy from 1865 to 1873 Revised and Combined in One Volume* (New York, 1887), 11–28; S. T. Spears, "A Convention of the Faculties," ibid., 240–42.

62. *Phreno-Magnetic Vindicator* 1 (October 1842): 5–6; Fowler, "Republicanism the True Form of Government," *American Phrenological Journal* 7 (February 1845): 61; Fowler, "Republicanism VII," *American Phrenological Journal* 9 (October 1847): 276. For an extended phrenological analysis of popular "sanction," see Amos Dean, *The Philosophy of Human Life* (Boston, 1839), 163–89. Arthur Wrobel, "Phrenology as Political Science," in *Pseudo-Science and Society in Nineteenth-Century America*, ed. Wrobel (Lexington, KY, 1987), 122–43, identifies phrenology as "Jacksonian."

63. One of the few explicit references to the "middle class" in the 1830s appears in an article discussing their interest in physical culture: "The Middle Classes," *Journal of Health* 1 (1830): 357–58.

64. Emerson, "The Rule of Life" (1867–71), in *Selected Lectures*, 351–52. On the "middling style," see Kenneth Cmiel, *Democratic Eloquence: The Fight over Popular Speech in Nineteenth-Century America* (Berkeley, CA, 1990), 55–93.

65. *Buchanan's Journal of Man* 1 (January 1849): 32; Robert H. Collyer, *Psychography; or, The Embodiment of Thought with an Analysis of Phreno-Magnetism, "Neurology," and Mental Hallucination* (Philadelphia, 1843), 9; John Bovee Dodds, *The Philosophy of Electrical Psychology: In a Course of Twelve Lectures* (New York, 1851), 30–31.

66. "Impressibility," *Buchanan's Journal of Man* 1 (August 1849): 322, 329; "Sympathetic Impressibility," ibid., 1 (October 1849): 356–57; R. T. Trall, "A New Theory of Population," *American Phrenological Journal* 16 (1852): 88.

67. "Animal Magnetism," *USMDR* 9 (December 1841): 515–27; [O'Sullivan], "Neurology," *USMDR* 9 (January 1843): 79–93. Mr. R. later asked Buchanan to show him how to excite his wife's organ of "excitability."

68. Dodds reprints an invitation from senators George W. Jones, John P. Hale, Henry Clay, Thomas Rusk, Sam Houston, H. S. Foote, and Daniel Webster, dated 12 February 1850, in his *Philosophy of Electrical Psychology*, 13. He began his lectures three days later. J. H. Bennett, *The Mesmeric Mania of 1851, with a Physiological Explanation of the Phenomena Produced* (Edinburgh, 1851).

69. See, for example, John Newman, *Fascination, or the Philosophy of Charming* (New York, 1847).

70. Neil Harris, *Humbug: The Art of P. T. Barnum* (Boston, 1973); Henri Ellenberger, *Discovery of the Unconscious* (New York, 1970); Winter, *Mesmerized: Powers of Mind in Victorian Britain* (Chicago, 1998), 343.

71. John Durham Peters, *Speaking into the Air* (Chicago, 1999), 93–94; Emerson, "New England: Genius, Manners, and Customs," in *Selected Letters of Ralph Waldo Emerson*, ed. Robert Busco and Joel Myerson (Athens, GA, 2005), 111.

Chapter 5 · *The Fatal Force of Public Opinion*

1. James Q. Whitman, "Enforcing Civility and Respect: Three Societies," *Yale Law Journal* 109 (2000): 1279–1398.

2. William Crafts Jr., *An Oration on the Influence of Moral Causes on National Character* (Cambridge, MA, 1817), 5–6.

3. Hazel Dicken-Garcia, *Journalistic Standards in Nineteenth-Century America* (Madison, WI, 1989), 162.

4. *Stow v. Converse*, 4 Conn. 8, 33 (1822); *Root v. King*, 7 Cow. 613, 628 (NY 1827).

5. James Kent, *Commentaries on American Law*, 2nd ed. (New York, 1832), 2:23.

6. Jeffrey L. Pasley, *"The Tyrrany of Printers"* (Charlottesville, VA, 2001); Culver Smith, *The Press, Politics, and Patronage* (Athens, GA, 1977); Robert W. T. Martin, "From the 'Free and Open' Press to the 'Press of Freedom': Liberalism, Republicanism, and Early American Press Liberty," *History of Political Thought* 15 (Winter 1994): 505–34; Stephen Botein, "'Meer Mechanics' and an Open Press: The Business and Political Strategies of Colonial American Printers," *Perspectives in American History* 9 (1975): 130–211; Botein, "Printers and the American Revolution," in *The Press and the American Revolution*, ed. Bernard Bailyn and John Hench (Boston, 1981), 11–58.

7. On the decline of printers, see Milton Hamilton, *The Country Printer* (New York, 1936); Osman C. Hooper, *History of Ohio Journalism, 1793–1933* (Columbus, 1933), 77–78; and Ava Baron, "Acquiring Manly Competence: The Demise of Apprenticeship and the Remasculinization of Printer's Work," in *Meanings for Manhood*, ed. Mark Carnes and Clyde Griffen (Chicago, 1990), 152–63.

8. Marcus Daniel, *Scandal and Civility* (Oxford, 2009); Michael Durey, *Transatlantic Radicals and the Early American Republic* (Lawrence, KS, 1997); Mathew Carey, *The Plagi-Scuriliad* (Philadelphia, 1786); Carey, *A Plumb Pudding for the Humane, Chaste, Valiant, Enlightened Peter Porcupine* (Philadelphia, 1799); William F. Steirer Jr., "Riding 'Everyman's Hobby Horse'; Journalism in Philadelphia, 1764–1794," in *Newsletters to Newspaper*, ed. Donavan Bond and W. Reynolds McLeod (Morgantown, WV, 1977), 263–76; Allan Nevins, *The Evening Post* (New York, 1922), 9–62.

9. Brackenridge, *Modern Chivalry*, ed. Claude M. Newlin (New York, 1937), 395–97; Brackenridge, "Sermon on the Duel" (1789), in *A Hugh Henry Brackenridge Reader*, ed. Daniel Marder (Pittsburgh, 1970), 144–47; George T. Fleming, ed., *History of Pittsburgh and Environs* (New York, 1922), 2:323–43; John Binns, *Recollections of the Life of John Binns* (Philadelphia, 1854), 183–91.

10. Franklin, "An Account of the Supremest Court of Judicature in Pennsylvania, viz., The Court of the Press," *Federal Gazette*, 12 February 1789. James Morton Smith, *Freedom's Fetters* (Ithaca, NY, 1956), 137, reads Franklin's essay as mere "horseplay," whereas Leonard W. Levy, *Emergence of a Free Press* (Oxford, 1985), 192, is less amused. On violence against (and by) printers in Philadelphia, see Richard Rosenfeld, *American Aurora* (New York, 1997), and "The Trial of William Duane, James Reynolds, Robert Moore, and Samuel Cuming for Riot, Philadelphia, Pennsylvania, 1799," in *AST*, 7:676.

11. On civility, see Richard Bushman, *The Refinement of America* (New York, 1992), 30–99.

12. Franklin to Thomas Percival, 17 July 1784, in *The Writings of Benjamin Franklin*, ed. Albert H. Smyth (New York, 1907), 9:236–37; "U," "On Private Revenge," *Boston Gazette*, 1 August 1763, reprinted in *The Works of John Adams*, ed. Charles Francis Adams (Boston, 1851), 3:429; Paine, "Duelling" (1775), in *The Complete Writings of Thomas Paine*, ed. Philip Foner (New York, 1945), 2:28–32.

13. Royster, *A Revolutionary People at War* (Chapel Hill, 1979), 210; "General Harrison on Duelling," *Niles' National Register*, 7 Nov. 1840, 153–54; Evarts B. Greene, "The Code of Honor in Colonial and Revolutionary Times, with Special Reference to New England," *Proceedings of the Colonial Society of Massachusetts: Transactions, 1924–1926* (March, 1926), 367–89; Marcus Cunliffe, *Soldiers and Civilians* (Boston, 1968); "Anti-Duellist," "On the Increasing Prevalence of Duelling # 1," *(New York) Balance, and Columbian Repository*, 4 January 1803.

14. Montesquieu, *The Spirit of the Laws*, trans. Thomas Nugent (New York, 1949), 19–28; Bertram Wyatt-Brown, "Honour and American Republicanism: A Neglected Corollary," in *Ideology and the Historians*, ed. Ciaran Brady (Dublin, 1991), 52. On honor in the early republic, see Joanne B. Freeman, *Affairs of Honor* (New Haven, CT, 2001).

15. Adams, "Discourses on Davilla" (1790), in *Works*, 6:274–76.

16. Beecher, *The Remedy for Duelling*, in *Lyman Beecher's Works* (Boston, 1852), 2:47–49. On the "polity of courts and parties," see Stephen Skowronek, *Building and New American State* (Cambridge, 1982), 19–46.

17. *Lansingsburg Gazette*, 28 July 1829. On editors and "deadbeat readers," see Thomas Leonard, *News For All* (New York, 1995), 33–47. On the meaning of "hireling" in antebellum culture, see David Roediger, *The Wages of Whiteness*, rev ed. (New York, 1999), 44–50.

18. Twain, "Journalism in Tennessee" (1869), in *Mark Twain: Collected Tales, Sketches, Speeches, and Essays, 1852–1890*, ed. Louis J. Budd (New York, 1992), 312; "A Virginian" [Bagby], "The Virginia Editor," *Harper's New Monthly Magazine* 64 (December 1856): 66–69; *New York Times*, 9 December 1856, 1.

19. Robert M. Hughes, "The Fighting Editor: Address of Robert M. Hughes be-

fore the Virginia Press Association, Farmville, Va., January 15, 1926," *WMQ* 7 (January 1927): 1–16.

20. Frederick Hudson, *Journalism in the United States, 1690–1872* (New York, 1872); Lambert Wilmer, *Our Press Gang* (Baltimore, 1859), 294–311; Ben C. Truman, *The Field of Honor* (New York, 1884), 300–333; Lorenzo Sabine, *Notes on Duels and Dueling* (Boston, 1855).

21. In another admittedly unscientific survey, John Nerone, *Violence against the Press* (New York, 1989), 252 n78, found around fifty.

22. Steven Hughes, "Men of Steel: Dueling, Honor, and Politics in Liberal Italy," in *Men and Violence*, ed. Pieter Spierenburg (Columbus, 1996), 64–81; David S. Parker, "Law, Honor, and Impunity in Spanish America: The Debate over Dueling, 1870–1920," *Law and History Review* 19 (Summer 2001): 311–41; Pablo Piccato, "Politics and the Technology of Honor: Dueling in Turn-of-the-Century Mexico," *Journal of Social History* 33 (Winter 1999): 331–54; William Reddy, "Condottieri of the Pen: Journalists and the Public Sphere in Postrevolutionary France (1815–1850)," *AHR* 99 (December 1994): 1546–70; Robert A. Nye, *Masculinity and Male Codes of Honor in Modern France* (New York, 1993), 187–90; Ute Frevert, *Men of Honour*, trans. Anthony Williams (Cambridge, 1995).

23. "The Trial of William P. Darnes for the Killing of Andrew Jackson Davis, St. Louis, Missouri, 1840," in *AST*, 16:78–322. The Darnes case is briefly mentioned in Rosenberg, *Protecting the Best Men* (Chapel Hill, NC, 1986), 134. See also Perry McCandless, "Punishment under the Law or by the Cudgel: The Case of William P. Darnes, 1840," *Missouri Historical Review* 93 (January 1999): 121–32, and Cynthia DeHaven Pitcock, "The Involvement of William Beaumont, M.D., in a Medical-Legal Controversy: The Darnes-Davis Case, 1840," *Missouri Historical Review* 59 (October 1964): 31–45.

24. "Anti-Sardanapalus," *Saint Louis Commercial Bulletin*, 28 May 1840. The allusion here is to a 1785 William Cowper poem ("The Diverting History of John Gilpin") about an inept horseman.

25. My best guess is that he had a good explanation but that it was not one which he could reveal with propriety. Gannt may have been courting—or wished to court—Carroll's niece. He married Mary Carroll Tabbs in 1845. William Hyde and Howard Conard, eds., *Encyclopedia of the History of St. Louis* (St. Louis, 1899), 2:865. The Carroll family was not of dunghill breed: they were related to the Charles Carroll of Maryland, signer of the Declaration of Independence

26. Beaumont was vulnerable to this charge. The treatise that had made him famous—*Experiments and Observations on the Gastric Juice* (1833)—resulted from experiments performed on an unfortunate French Canadian whose upper abdomen had been rendered visible by a freak gunshot wound.

27. Secrets I can only speculate on. But it seems likely that numerous board members of Benton's Bank of St. Louis (perhaps Benton himself) were *Argus* creditors. Proprietorship of the *Argus* immediately returned to the previous owner—Abel R. Corbin—(a board member of the Bank of St. Louis) upon Davis's death. Walter B. Stevens, *St. Louis* (St. Louis, 1909), 206–7.

28. For example, Thomas S. Nelson's *A Full and Accurate Account of the Trial of William P. Darnes* (Boston, 1841) went through two editions. On national interest in the trial during the campaign of 1840, see Robert Gunderson, *The Log Cabin Campaign* (Lexington, 1957), 146. On Geyer, see *Encyclopedia of the History of St. Louis*, 2:893–94; W. V. N. Bay, *Reminiscences of the Bench and Bar of Missouri* (St. Louis, 1878), 143–52; and Frances Lea McCurdy, *Stump, Bar, and Pulpit* (Columbia, MO, 1969), 132–42.

29. *AST*, 16:163–64.

30. Ibid., 308, 235, 165. Geyer made frequent allusions to Richard Sheridan's *The Rivals*, a comedy in which the hot-blooded Luscious O'Trigger (Colonel Gilpin) and the cowardly dandy Bob Acres (Captain Grimsley) incompetently arrange a double duel with the hero and his alter ego.

31. Ibid., 304, 171, 183–84, 132 ("Mr. [Joseph] Crockett's Speech for the Prisoner").

32. Ibid., 310. In his speech, defense co-counsel Beverly Allen likewise asserted that "Mr. Darnes was compelled by the force of public opinion, to punish Davis; he was under moral duress to chastise him." Ibid., 103.

33. Ibid., 287–88.

34. Ibid., 305, 308.

35. Ibid., 143–47, 322. The fine was a steep one for an unemployed carpenter, but it was probably subsidized by political friends.

36. Ibid., 133, 178.

37. Speech of Samuel Dexter, "Report of the Trial of T. O. Selfridge, Esq.," reprinted in Francis Wharton, *A Treatise on the Law of Homicide in the United States* (Philadelphia, 1855), 452–54. For details surrounding this incident, see Charles Warren, *Jacobin and Junto* (Cambridge, MA, 1931), 187–214, and Thomas Selfridge, comp., *The Trial of Thomas O. Selfridge, Attorney at Law[,] before the Hon. Isaac Parker for Killing Charles Austin* (Boston, 1807).

38. "The Trial of Judge Wilkinson, Dr. Wilkinson, and John Murdaugh for the Murder of John Rothwell and Alexander H. Meeks, Kentucky, 1839," *AST*, 1:294–96.

39. Calvin Colton, *The Life of Henry Clay, the Great American Statesman* (New York, 1855), 1:90–93.

40. Richard Maxwell Brown, *No Duty to Retreat* (Norman, OK, 1994), 3–37; Joseph H. Beale Jr., "Retreat from a Murderous Assault," *Harvard Law Review* 16 (1902–3): 567–82; Rollin M. Perkins, "Self-Defense Re-Examined," *UCLA Law Review* 1 (1953–54): 133–62.

41. *Erwin v. State*, 29 Ohio St. 186 (1876); *Runyan v. State*, 57 Ind. 80 (1877); *Brown v. United States*, 256 U.S. 335 (1921). Holmes quoted in Brown, *No Duty to Retreat*, 3. On changing conceptions of manhood in the late nineteenth century, see Gail Bederman, *Manliness and Civilization* (Chicago, 1995).

42. "Private" businessmen, it would seem, had less latitude. Several years later, Geyer made a similar argument in a civil case brought by a cudgeled editor. Defending an insurance agent who had severely beaten the editor over an article concerning his wife's indiscretions, Geyer sought to introduce the article into evidence as a miti-

gating factor. The trial court rejected this evidence, and the state Supreme Court agreed. *Coxe et al. v. Whitney,* 9 Mo. 531 (1845).

43. *AST,* 16:171–76.

44. Reddy, *The Invisible Code* (Berkeley, CA, 1997), 10.

45. Hartog, "Lawyering, Husband's Rights, and 'the Unwritten Law' in Nineteenth-Century America," *JAH* 84 (June 1997): 67–96; Ireland, "The Libertine Must Die," *Journal of Social History* 23 (Fall 1989): 27–44.

46. Glenn Altschuler and Stuart Blumin, *Rude Republic* (Princeton, NJ, 2000), 33–34; Ronald Formisano, "The New Political History and the Election of 1840," *Journal of Interdisciplinary History* 23 (Spring 1993): 661–82.

47. Missouri law defined third-degree manslaughter as the use of a "deadly weapon" in "the heat of passion." Fourth-degree manslaughter was defined as the "involuntary killing of another by a weapon, or by means neither cruel nor unusual, in the heat of passion." *AST,* 16:320.

48. Robert Ireland, "Insanity and the Unwritten Law," *American Journal of Legal History* 32 (April 1988): 157–72; "Recognition of the Honor Defense under the Insanity Plea," *Yale Law Journal* 43 (1934): 809–14.

49. *The Charge of Sir Francis Bacon Touching Duels* (New York, 1968), 11–13. On the origins of dueling, see Edward Muir, *Mad Blood Stirring: Vendetta in Renaissance Italy* (Baltimore, 1998).

50. *Bentham's Theory of Legislation: Principles of the Penal Code,* trans. and ed. Charles Milner Atkinson (New York, 1914), 2:87–94, 99–100. See also, Donna T. Andrew, "The Code of Honour and Its Critics: The Opposition to Dueling in England, 1700–1850," *Social History* 5 (October 1980): 409–34, and Rousseau, *Letter to M. d'Alembert on the Theatre,* trans. Allan Bloom (Ithaca, NY, 1960), 67–75.

51. Wayne Minnick, "A Case Study in Persuasive Effect: Lyman Beecher on Dueling," *Speech Monographs* 38 (November 1971): 262–76; Livingston, "Code of Crimes and Punishments," in *The Complete Works of Edward Livingston on Criminal Jurisprudence,* ed. Salmon P. Chase (Montclair, NJ, 1968), 2:149–50.

52. *The Diary of Philip Hone,* ed. Bayard Tuckerman (New York, 1889), 1:309–10. For similar commentary on Graves's speech, see J. H. Young, "Trials by Ordeal and Single Combat," *Methodist Magazine and Quarterly Review* 21 (1839): 159–60.

53. William Leggett, *New York Evening Post,* 2 March 1838; "Statement of Thomas Hart Benton," *Niles' National Register,* 10 March 1838; Jackson to Martin Van Buren, 26 March 1838, reel #19, Martin Van Buren Papers, Library of Congress, Washington, DC; "The Martyrdom of Cilley," *USMDR* 1 (March 1838): 493; *Congressional Globe,* 25th Cong., 2nd sess., 329–33 (25 April 1838). For a concise summary of legal arguments against the committee report, see Asher C. Hinds, *Hinds' Precedents of the House of Representatives of the United States* (Washington, DC, 1907), 2: 1116–19.

54. *Congressional Globe,* 25th Cong., 2nd sess., 282–84 (5 April 1838).

55. David Grimstead, *American Mobbing, 1828–1861* (New York, 1998); Paul Gilje, *Rioting in America* (Bloomington, 1996); Leonard Richards, *"Gentlemen of Property*

and Standing" (Oxford, 1970); Nerone, *Violence against the Press*, 84–110; Smith, *The Dominion of Voice* (Lawrence, KS, 1999), 51–85.

56. Philip J. Ethington, *The Public City* (Berkeley, CA, 2001), 43–169; Sarah J. Hale, "The Poor Scholar," in *Sketches of American Character* (Philadelphia, 1843), 147–78; Ralph Lockwood, "Arthur Lennox; or, The Challenge," *Southern Literary Messenger* 17 (December 1851): 730–41; David Brion Davis, *Homicide in American Fiction, 1798–1860* (Ithaca, NY, 1957), 277–83.

57. For a concise summary of these developments, see Gerald J. Baldasty, *The Commercialization of News in the Nineteenth Century* (Madison, WI, 1992). See also Andi Tucher, *Froth and Scum* (Chapel Hill, NC, 1994); James Crouthamel, *Bennett's New York Herald and the Rise of the Popular Press* (Syracuse, NY, 1989); and Michael Schudson, *Discovering the News* (New York, 1978), 52–60.

58. *New York Herald*, 9 May 1836; *New York Sun*, 10 May 1836.

59. Rosenberg, *Protecting the Best Men*, 153–89; Timothy Gleason, *The Watchdog Concept* (Ames, IA, 1990).

60. "Louisiana," *DeBow's Review* 1 (1846): 428; speech of William C. Bullitt in *Report of the Debates and Proceedings of the Convention for the Revision of the Constitution of the State of Kentucky*, rep. R. Sutton (Frankfort, 1849), 816–17; Benton, *Thirty Years' View* (New York, 1854–56), 2:148–49.

61. Wilson, *The Code of Honor* (Charleston, SC, 1838), 13.

62. Simms, *Beauchampe* (New York, 1854–56), 337–38, 342–43. See also Simms's defense of dueling in "Lorris," *Charleston Mercury*, 9 and 17 May 1855, and Sabine, *Notes on Duels and Dueling*, 317–18.

63. Frederick Law Olmsted, *The Cotton Kingdom*, ed. Arthur Schlesinger (New York, 1996), 330, 558–59; John D. Allen, "Journalism in the South," in *Culture in the South*, ed. W. T. Couch (Chapel Hill, NC, 1935), 135–38.

64. Clyde N. Wilson, *Carolina Cavalier* (Athens, GA, 1990), 85; Kenneth S. Greenberg, *Honor and Slavery* (Princeton, NJ, 1996), 3–12; Sabine, *Notes on Duels and Dueling*, 138.

65. *The Diary of Edmund Ruffin*, ed. William K. Scarborough (Baton Rouge, LA, 1972), 1:329–30; Barbara J. Griffin, ed., "Thomas Ritchie and the Code Duello," *Virginia Magazine of History and Biography* 92 (1984): 71–95; John S. Wise, *The End of an Era* (Boston, 1900), 94–96; Craig M. Simpson, *A Good Southerner* (Chapel Hill, NC, 1985), 178–89; Lillian A. Kibler, *Benjamin F. Perry* (Durham, NC, 1946), 124–35.

66. Drew Gilpin Faust, *James Henry Hammond and the Old South* (Baton Rouge, LA, 1982), 44–57.

67. Henry S. Foote, *Casket of Reminiscences* (Washington, DC, 1874), 377–87; Edwin Miles, "The Mississippi Press in the Jackson Era, 1824–1841," *Journal of Mississippi History* 19 (1957): 1–20; Wilmuth Rutledge, "Dueling in Antebellum Mississippi," ibid., 24 (1964): 181–91. "Notice of the Organization of Mississippi Anti-Dueling Society" (1844), in *The Papers of Jefferson Davis*, ed. James T. McIntosh (Baton Rogue, LA, 1974), 2:142–65.

Chapter 6 · Irrepressible Conflicts, Impending Crises

1. Forbes, *The Missouri Compromise and its Aftermath* (Chapel Hill, NC, 2007), 9; Robin Einhorn, *American Taxation, American Slavery* (Chicago, 2006); David Roediger, *Wages of Whiteness*, rev. ed. (New York, 1999).

2. James Brewer Stewart, *Wendell Phillips, Liberty's Hero* (Baton Rouge, LA, 1998); Richard Hofstadter, *The American Political Tradition* (New York, 1954), 137–63.

3. Phillips, "Public Opinion," in *Speeches, Letters, and Writings* (Boston, 1894), 38–39, 47.

4. Ibid., 41, 43; Phillips, *Review of Webster's Speech on Slavery* (Boston, 1850).

5. Robert D. Marcus, "Wendell Phillips and American Institutions," *JAH* 55 (June 1969): 45–47; Phillips, "Public Opinion," 42, 52–53, Phillips, "Idols," in *Speeches, Letters, and Writings*, 249; Phillips, "Daniel O'Connell" (1875), in *Speeches, Lectures, and Letters* (Boston, 1891), 399–400.

6. On the significance of public opinion and publicity to the rhetoric and tactics of the abolitionists, see Robert Fanuzzi, *Abolition's Public Sphere* (Minneapolis, 2003), and Trish Loughran, *The Republic in Print* (New York, 2007), 303–440.

7. Douglass, "An Appeal to the British People" (1846), in *Frederick Douglass: Selected Speeches and Writings*, ed. Philip Foner (Chicago, 2000), 39; Bernard Boxill, "Fear and Shame as Forms of Moral Suasion in the Thought of Frederick Douglass," *Transactions of the Charles S. Peirce Society* 31 (Fall 1995): 713–44.

8. Edward D. Barber, *Oration Delivered before the Addison County Anti-Slavery Society* (Middlebury, VT, 1836), 16, excerpted in "Eloquent Extracts," *Liberator*, 15 October 1836.

9. "History of Slavery in Massachusetts," *Liberator*, 26 February 1831; Timothy Breen, "Making History: The Force of Public Opinion and the Last Years of Slavery in Revolutionary Massachusetts," in *Through a Glass Darkly: Reflections on Personal Identity in Early America*, ed. Ronald Hoffman, Mechal Sobel, and Fredrike Teute (Chapel Hill, NC, 1997), 67–95. On British and American abolitionism, see Sam Haynes, *Unfinished Revolution: The Early American Republic in a British World* (Charlottesville, VA, 2010), 177–203, and Frank Thistlethwaite, *America and the Atlantic Community* (New York, 1959), 103–20.

10. Robert Abzug, *Cosmos Crumbling: American Reform and the Religious Imagination* (Oxford, 1994), 129–62; Lewis Perry, *Radical Abolitionism: Anarchy and the Government of God in Antislavery Thought* (Ithaca, NY, 1973); Ronald Walters, *The Antislavery Appeal: American Abolitionism after 1830* (New York, 1984), 37–53; James Brewer Stewart, *Holy Warriors: The Abolitionists and American Slavery* (New York, 1976).

11. Chapman, *Right and Wrong*, quoted in Fanuzzi, *Abolition's Public Sphere*, xii; Daniel Walker Howe, *What Hath God Wrought* (New York, 2007), 426–27.

12. "A Northern Man" [Calvin Colton], *Abolition a Sedition* (Philadelphia, 1839), 29. On anti-abolitionism, see Lorman Ratner, *Powder Keg: Northern Opposition to the Anti-Slavery Movement, 1831–1840* (New York, 1968), and Leonard Richards,

Gentlemen of Property and Standing: Anti-Abolition Mobs in Jacksonian America (Oxford, 1970).

13. Susan Wyly-Jones, "The 1835 Anti-Abolition Meetings in the South: A New Look at the Controversy over the Abolition Postal Campaign," *Civil War History* 47 (December 2001): 289–309; Bertram Wyatt-Brown, *Lewis Tappan and the Evangelical War against Slavery* (Cleveland, 1969), 143–45; Richard John, *Spreading the News: The American Postal System from Franklin to Morse* (Cambridge, MA, 1995), 257–63.

14. David Grimstead, *American Mobbing, 1828–1861* (New York, 1998), 3–32; John Nerone, *Violence against the Press* (New York, 1994), 88–89.

15. Channing, *Slavery*, 4th ed. (Boston, 1836), 54–55.

16. Reese, *Humbugs of New York: Being a Remonstrance against Popular Delusion* (New York, 1838), 164–65; Dewey, *Discourse on Slavery and the Annexation of Texas* (New York, 1844), 5–6, 12; Beecher, *An Essay on Slavery and Abolitionism, with Reference to the Duty of American Females*, 2nd ed. (Philadelphia, 1837), 35–36, 46–47.

17. On slavery and antebellum political persuasions, see Robert Forbes, *The Missouri Compromise and Its Aftermath: Jonathan Earle, Jacksonian Antislavery and the Politics of Free Soil, 1824–1854* (Chapel Hill, NC, 2003); Leonard Richards, *The Slave Power: The Free North and Southern Domination, 1780–1860* (Baton Rouge, LA, 2000); John Ashworth, *Slavery, Capitalism, and Politics in the Antebellum Republic*, vol. 1: *Commerce and Compromise, 1820–1850* (Cambridge, 1995); William Freehling, *The Road to Disunion: Secessionists at Bay, 1776–1854* (New York, 1990).

18. Douglass, "What to the Slave Is the Fourth of July?" (1852), in *The Frederick Douglass Papers*, ed. John Blassingame (New Haven, CT, 1982), 2:370–71.

19. On these points, see Kim Smith, *The Dominion of Voice: Riot, Reason, and Romance in Antebellum Politics* (Lawrence, KS, 1999); Don Herzog, *Poisoning the Minds of the Lower Orders* (Princeton, NJ, 1998), 140–90; and Lynn Sanders, "Against Deliberation," *Political Theory* 25 (June 1997): 347–76.

20. Elisabeth Noelle-Neumann, "Public Opinion and Rationality," in *Public Opinion and the Communication of Consent*, ed. Theodore Glaser and Charles Salmon (New York, 1995), 33–54; Noelle-Neumann, *The Spiral of Silence: Public Opinion— Our Social Skin* (Chicago, 1993).

21. Alfred Cave, *An American Conservative in the Age of Jackson: The Political and Social Thought of Calvin Colton* (Fort Worth, TX, 1969); "A Protestant" [Colton], *Protestant Jesuitism* (New York, 1836), 204.

22. [Colton], *Abolition a Sedition*, 12.

23. "An American in London" [Colton], *The Americans* (London, 1833); Colton, *History and Character of American Revivals of Religion* (London, 1832); Colton, *A Manual for Emigrants to America* (London, 1832); Colton, *Church and State in America* (London, 1834).

24. Stephen Nissenbaum, *Sex, Diet, and Debility in Jacksonian America* (Westport, CT, 1980). [Colton], *Protestant Jesuitism*, 52, 148–9; [Colton], *Abolition a Sedition*, 59, 61.

25. [Colton], *Abolition a Sedition*, 61, 112; [Colton], *Protestant Jesuitism*, 52,

111; Colton, *Colonization and Abolitionism Contrasted* (Philadelphia, 1839); Douglas Egerton, " 'Its Origin Is Not a Little Curious': A New Look at the American Colonization Society," *JER* 5 (Winter 1985): 463–80.

26. Schlesinger, *The Age of Jackson* (Boston, 1945), 281; Barnard, *A Plea for Social and Popular Repose* (New York, 1845), 7–8.

27. "An American Gentleman" [Colton], *A Voice from America to England* (London, 1839), 38–39, 54, 76.

28. Lincoln, "Address to the Young Men's Lyceum of Springfield, Illinois," *Lincoln: Speeches, Letters, Miscellaneous Writings*, ed. Don Fehrenbacher (New York, 1989), 29, 32, 35–36; George Forgie, *Patricide in the House Divided* (New York, 1979), 55–87.

29. *St. Louis Observer*, 21 July 1836, reprinted in Owen and Joseph Lovejoy, *Memoir of the Rev. Elijah P. Lovejoy* (New York, 1838), 174–75.

30. Lovejoy and Lovejoy, *Memoir*, 175–79.

31. *Philadelphia Commercial Herald* quoted in Michael Kent Curtis, *Free Speech, "the People's Darling Privilege"* (Durham, NC, 2000), 233. See also Russel B. Nye, *Fettered Freedom* (East Lansing, MI, 1963), and William Lee Miller, *Arguing about Slavery* (New York, 1995).

32. Lacy K. Ford, *Deliver Us from Evil: The Slavery Question in the Old South* (New York, 2011); Grimstead, *American Mobbing*, 85–178; Clement Eaton, *The Freedom-of-Thought Struggle in the Old South* (New York, 1964).

33. Green, in *United States Telegraph*, 4 September 1835, cited in Freehling, *Road to Disunion*, 291.

34. McCord, "Slavery and the Abolitionists," *Southern Quarterly Review* 15 (April 1849): 182–83. Elizabeth Fox-Genovese and Eugene Genovese, *The Mind of the Master Class: History and Faith in the Southern Slaveholder's Worldview* (Cambridge, 2005), 365–82.

35. *Speech of Mr. Preston, of South Carolina, in the Senate of the United States, March 1, 1836, on the Abolition Question*, cited in Haynes, *Unfinished Revolution*, 197; *Southern Literary Messenger* 33 (1861): 237; *Compendium of the Seventh United States Census*, ed. J. D. B. DeBow (Washington, DC, 1854), 15. On Southern readership of Northern journals, see Jonathan Wells, *The Origins of the Southern Middle Class, 1800–1861* (Chapel Hill, NC, 2004), 41–65, and Eaton, *Freedom-of-Thought Struggle*, 335–52.

36. Pringle, "The People," *Southern Quarterly Review* 9 (January 1854): 53; Wigfall quoted in William Howard Russell, *My Diary North and South* (Boston, 1863), 179; Carruthers, *The Kentuckian in New York* (New York, 1834), cited in David Henkin, *City Reading* (New York, 1998), 19. On the "myth of the Southern orator," see *Oratory in the Old South, 1828–1860*, ed. Waldo Braden (Baton Rouge, LA, 1970), 3–18, and Kenneth Greenberg, *Masters and Statesmen: The Political Culture of American Slavery* (Baltimore, 1985), 12–15.

37. Daniel R. Hundley, *Social Relations in Our Southern States* (1860), ed. William Cooper Jr. (Baton Rouge, LA, 1979), 62–63. For other examples of this perspective, see "Instability of Public Opinion," *Southern Literary Messenger* 14 (June 1848): 377–

82, and, more generally, Dickson Bruce Jr., *Violence and Culture in the Antebellum South* (Austin, TX, 1979), 188–93.

38. Fitzhugh, *Cannibals All!; or, Slaves without Masters* (1856), ed. C. Vann Woodward (Cambridge, MA, 1988), 131, 249; Laura Edwards, *The People and their Peace* (Chapel Hill, NC, 2009).

39. Strangely, the meaning of "fire-eater" is rarely recognized in Southern historiography. Eric Walther, *The Fire-Eaters* (Baton Rouge, LA, 1992), 2, asserts that "the term *fire-eater* is shrouded in mystery." On the "fire-eaters" of Ireland, see Sir Jonah Barrington, *Personal Sketches of His Own Life and Times* (London, 1827), 2:5–28. For a similar comparison between southern debate and dueling, see Christine Leigh Heyrman, *Southern Cross* (Chapel Hill, NC, 1997), 246–47.

40. Thornton, *An Inquiry into the History of Slavery* (Washington, DC, 1841), 85; Holcombe, "Is Slavery Consistent with Natural Law?" *Southern Literary Messenger* 27 (1858): 47–48; Tucker, "An Essay on the Moral and Political Effect of the Relation between the Caucasian Master and the African Slave, Part One," *Southern Literary Messenger* 10 (June 1844): 333; "A Planter," "Treatment of Slaves in the South-West," *Southern Literary Messenger* 7 (November 1841): 774.

41. Harper, "Memorial on Slavery" (1837), in *The Pro-Slavery Argument, as Maintained by the Most Distinguished Writers of the Southern States* (Charleston, SC, 1852), 64–65; Fox-Genovese and Genovese, *Mind of the Master Class*, 375.

42. Weld, *American Slavery as It Is* (New York, 1839), 151–52, 185–88. On Weld's use of newspapers as evidence, see Thomas Leonard, *News for All* (New York, 1995), 75–79. Loughran, *Republic in Print*, 354–59.

43. See, for example, Susan-Mary Grant, *North over South* (Lawrence, KS, 2000); Melinda Lawson, *Patriot Fires* (Lawrence, KS, 2005); and Drew Gilpin Faust, *The Creation of Confederate Nationalism* (Baton Rouge, LA, 1990).

44. *Albany Evening Journal*, 23 May 1856; *Richmond Enquirer*, 3 June 1856.

45. *Appendix to the Congressional Globe*, 33rd Cong., 1st sess., 374; Manisha Sinha, "The Caning of Charles Sumner: Slavery, Race, and Ideology in the Age of Civil War," *JER* 23 (Summer 2003): 233–62; William Gienapp, "The Crime against Sumner: The Caning of Charles Sumner and the Rise of the Republican Party," *Civil War History* 25 (September 1979): 218–45.

46. Loughran, *Republic in Print*, xx, 345.

47. Lewis, *An Essay on the Influence of Authority in Matters of Opinion* (London, 1849), 401; Alan S. Kahan, *Aristocratic Liberalism* (Oxford, 2001), 65–8; Dror Wahrman, *Imagining the Middle Class* (Cambridge, 1995), 190–200; Jürgen Habermas, *The Structural Transformation of the Public Sphere*, trans. Thomas Burger (Cambridge, MA, 1989), 129–40.

48. Grimke, *The Nature and Tendency of Free Institutions* (Cambridge, MA, 1968), 397–99, 401, 419, 519–20. On Grimke, see Maxwell Bloomfield, *American Lawyers in a Changing Society* (Cambridge, MA, 1976), 235–70.

49. Grimke, *Nature and Tendency of Free Institutions*, 147, 417–37, 594; *Historical Magazine* 7 (April 1863): 136.

50. Winthrop, "The Obligations and Responsibilities of Educated Men in the Use

of the Tongue and the Pen" (1852), in *Addresses and Speeches on Various Occasions* (Boston, 1867), 19–20.

51. Ibid., 31, 44–45. On a similar theme, see Mark A. DeWolfe Howe, *Public Opinion, Directed and Impelled by Conflicting Tendencies* (Hartford, CT, 1852).

52. Walker, "Public Opinion," in *Reason, Faith, and Duty* (Boston, 1877), 228–29, 234. For a similar argument, see Francis Wayland, "Slavery to Public Opinion," in *Sermons to the Churches* (New York, 1858), 178–205.

53. Parker, *A Discourse Occasioned by the Death of Daniel Webster* (Boston, 1853), 12; Lori Ginzberg, "'Moral Suasion Is Moral Balderdash': Women, Politics, and Social Activism in the 1850s," *JAH* 73 (December 1986): 601–22; George Fredrickson, *The Inner Civil War* (New York, 1965), 7–52.

54. Heinzen, "Public Opinion: A Lecture Delivered in the City of New York," *Liberator*, 18 May 1860.

55. Heinzen, *Der Mord* (Zurich, 1849), quoted in Mischa Honeck, "'Freemen of All Nations, Bestir Yourselves': Felice Orsini's Transnational Afterlife and the Radicalization of America," *JER* 30 (Winter 2010): 598; Carl Wittke, *Against the Current* (Chicago, 1945).

56. Calhoun, *A Disquisition on Government*, in *Union and Liberty*, ed. Ross M. Lence (Indianapolis, IN, 1992), 7, 66–67; Lacy K. Ford, "Inventing the Concurrent Majority: Madison, Calhoun, and the Problem of Majoritarianism in American Political Thought," *Journal of Southern History* 40 (February 1994): 19–58.

57. Calhoun, *Disquisition*, 55–57.

58. Ibid., 31, 49–50; Hofstadter, *The American Political Tradition* (New York, 1954), 69.

Conclusion · Corn-Pone Opinions

1. Lincoln, "Speech on the Dred Scott Decision at Springfield, Illinois" (1857), in *Abraham Lincoln: Speeches and Writings, 1832–1858*, ed. Don Fehrenbacher (New York, 1989), 396–97; *Dred Scott v. Sanford* 60 U.S. 393 (1856); Lincoln, "Speech at Hartford, Connecticut" (1860), in *Collected Works of Abraham Lincoln*, ed. Roy Basler (New Brunswick, NJ, 1953), 4:3–6.

2. John Burt, *Lincoln's Tragic Pragmatism* (Cambridge, MA, 2013), 174; David Zarefsky, "'Public Sentiment Is Everything': Lincoln's View of Political Persuasion," *Journal of the Abraham Lincoln Association* 15 (1994): 23–40; Lincoln, "Speech at Ottawa," in *The Complete Lincoln-Douglas Debates*, ed. Paul M. Angle (Chicago, 1991), 2:120.

3. Twain, "Corn-Pone Opinions," in *Europe and Elsewhere*, ed. Albert B. Paine (New York, 1923), 399–406.

4. On the rejection of idealism and the turn to realism in the postwar period, see George Fredrickson, *The Inner Civil War* (New York, 1965), 183–238; Thomas Haskell, *The Emergence of Professional Social Science* (1977; reprint, Baltimore, 2000); and David Shi, *Facing Facts* (Oxford, 1996).

5. John G. Sproat, *"The Best Men": Liberal Reformers in the Gilded Age* (Chicago,

1968); Leslie Butler, *Critical Americans* (Chapel Hill, NC, 2007), 175–220; Michael McGerr, *The Decline of Popular Politics* (New York, 1986); Nancy Cohen, *The Reconstruction of American Liberalism, 1865–1914* (Chapel Hill, NC, 2002).

6. E. L. Godkin, "The Growth and Expression of Public Opinion," in *Unforeseen Tendencies of Democracy* (Boston, 1898), 222; Godkin, "Opinion-Moulding," *Nation*, 12 August 1869, 126.

7. James to Henry L. Higginson, 8 February 1903, in *Letters of William James*, ed. Henry James (Boston, 1920), 2:182.

8. Bryce, *Studies in Contemporary Biography* (New York, 1903), 368.

9. Godkin, "Aristocratic Opinions of Democracy," *North American Review* 100 (April 1865): 194–232, reprinted in Godkin, *Problems of Modern Democracy*, ed. Morton Keller (1896; reprint, Cambridge, 1966), 54–55; Mill to Godkin, 24 May 1865, in *The Letters of John Stuart Mill*, ed. Hugh S. R. Elliot (London, 1910), 2:35.

10. Walter Bagehot, *Physics and Politics* (London, 1872), 101–29.

11. *Nation* 1 (1865): 5, 39. On liberal reformers and journalism, see Butler, *Critical Americans*, 175–220; and McGerr, *Decline of Popular Politics*, 107–37.

12. Godkin, "The Democratic View of Democracy," *North American Review* 101 (July 1865): 114, 116.

13. Bowles in *Views and Interviews on Journalism*, ed. Charles Frederick Wingate (New York, 1875), 46–47. Such themes are quite prominent in the first history of American "journalism," Frederic Hudson, *Journalism in the United States from 1690 to 1872* (New York, 1873).

14. Godkin, "Democratic View of Democracy," 117–19; Godkin in Wingate, *Views and Interviews on Journalism*, 212; Godkin to Charles Elliot Norton, [Fall 1866], in *The Gilded Age Letters of E. L. Godkin*, ed. William M. Armstrong (Albany, NY, 1974), 93.

15. Haskell, *Emergence of Professional Social Science*; Sven Beckert, "Democracy in the Age of Capital: Contesting Suffrage Rights in Gilded Age New York," in *The Democratic Experiment*, ed. Meg Jacobs, William Novak, and Julian Zelizer (Princeton, NJ, 2003), 146–74.

16. Lippmann, *Public Opinion* (New York, 1922), 228; Jürgen Habermas, *The Structural Transformation of the Public Sphere*, trans. Thomas Burger (Cambridge, MA, 1989), 236; Godkin, "Democratic View of Democracy," 129–30.

17. Godkin, "Popular Government and High Tariffs," *Nation*, 14 April 1870, 234–35; Godkin, "Some Political Aspects of the Tariff," *New Princeton Review* 1 (1887): 164–76, reprinted in Godkin, *Problems of Modern Democracy*, 106–7, 117.

18. Godkin, "Public Opinion and the Currency," *Nation*, 27 April 1873, 144; Godkin, "The Political Situation in 1896," *Forum* 21 (1896): 257–70, reprinted in Godkin, *Problems of Modern Democracy*, 249, 260.

19. See Bernard Porter, *Critics of Empire* (London, 1968), 140–6, and Butler, *Critical Americans*, 221–61.

20. Godkin, *Unforeseen Tendencies of Democracy* (Boston, 1898), 194.

21. Ibid., 213, 225; Godkin, "The Economic Man" (1891), in *Problems of Modern Democracy*, 169–79.

22. Godkin to Bryce, 9 January 1896, in *Gilded Age Letters*, 478.

23. Bryce, *The American Commonwealth* (1889; reprint, Indianapolis, IN, 1995), 2:912.

24. Benjamin Franklin, *Poor Richard's Almanack* (Waterloo, IA, 1914), 44; Bryce, *American Commonwealth*, 2:942, 994, 999, 1001–2.

Essay on Sources

Although there are no book-length studies and no more than a handful of scholarly articles on the history of the concept of public opinion in the United States, it would be misleading to say that American historians have ignored public opinion. After all, the historical study of public opinion leads us into no undiscovered archives and taps no distinctive cache of evidence. It draws on the same public documents—newspapers, books, periodicals, government reports, pamphlets, prints, and broadsides—that generally inform research in political, intellectual, and cultural history. Indeed, it would be nearly impossible to write American history without something akin to "public opinion" lurking in the background.

Historians of the United States have occasionally urged their colleagues to pay more attention to public opinion, to deploy the concept with more care and precision, and perhaps even to learn from the methods and ideas of public opinion researchers and theorists. Michael Kammen, to cite one notable example, once complained of the "somewhat random, episodic, and hortatory, rather than systematic and substantive" notice given to the subject: "The United States Constitution, Public Opinion, and the Question of American Exceptionalism," in *Sovereignty and Liberty: Constitutional Discourse in American Culture* (Madison, WI, 1988). The most influential call for more critical studies of past public opinion came from Lee Benson, who repeatedly urged historians to replace casual generalizations about popular opinion with the rigorous empirical analysis of election results, newspaper content, and demographic data. See his "Research Problems in American Political Historiography," in *Common Frontiers of the Social Sciences*, ed. Mirra Komarovsky (Glencoe, IL, 1957), and "An Approach to the Scientific Study of Past Public Opinion," in *Towards the Scientific Study of History: Selected Essays* (New York, 1972). Many practitioners of the "new" political history attempted to do just this. But the pollster's conception of public opinion as an aggregate of individual opinions did not travel back in time well, at times resulting in "ethno-cultural" interpretations of politics that took the public out of public opinion by attributing differences (and similarities) of opinion to a multitude of ethnic and religious allegiances largely unmoved by public debate and deliberation.

By the mid-1980s, the "public opinion" presented by American historians seemed less the product of a shared political history and more a passive reflection of a fragmentary and privately lived social history. Several critics of this trend—Thomas Bender,

"Wholes and Parts: The Need for Synthesis in American History," *Journal of American History* 73 (June 1986), being one of the most notable—looked to the concept of "the public" as a way to counter these tendencies and find new grounds for "synthesis." An English translation of German philosopher Jürgen Habermas's 1962 *The Structural Transformation of the Public Sphere: An Inquiry into a Category of Bourgeois Society* (Cambridge, MA, 1989) appeared at a convenient moment. Habermas's concept of the "public sphere"—a network of institutions, associations, and communicative practices that mediated between the "private" domain of a commercial society and the official jurisdiction of the modern state—offered a promising framework for organizing American historians' revitalized interest in the public realm. As a sociological and descriptive model of public communication, the "public sphere" was not a particularly innovative conceit. Rather, the significance of Habermas's work lay in its theoretically sophisticated yet historically grounded explanation of the emergence and transformation of modern norms of publicity and public reason.

Although Habermas's historical narrative was limited to Western Europe, American historians found many uses for his conceptual vocabulary. Over the next few decades, the "public sphere" worked its way into histories of women, African American politics, public festivities, religion, the postal service, Masonic lodges, law, printing, reform, belles-lettres, music, civic architecture, and countless other subjects. Public sphere theory proved especially alluring to historians aiming to connect the traditional "high" political history of parties, elections, and public officials to the everyday politics of the street, the tavern, the civic association, and the newspaper. For an extensive review of this scholarship, see John Brooke, "Reason and Passion in the Public Sphere: Habermas and the Cultural Historians," *Journal of Interdisciplinary History* 29 (Summer 1998).

To be sure, the concept of the public sphere has its limitations. Scholars of race, class, and gender have rightly called attention to the myriad ways that universalistic claims about public reason can mask, if not perpetuate, realities of exclusion and subordination. Others have proposed alternative models for proletarian or African American public spheres that differ considerably from Habermas's "bourgeois" sphere: Johanna Meehan, ed., *Feminists Read Habermas: Gendering the Subject of Discourse* (New York, 1995); Alexander Kluge and Oskar Negt, *Public Sphere and Experience: Toward an Analysis of the Bourgeois and Proletarian Public Sphere* (Minneapolis, 1993); The Black Public Sphere Collective, eds., *The Black Public Sphere* (Chicago, 1995). Habermas himself has taken some of these criticisms into account, most fully in *Between Facts and Norms: Contributions to a Discourse Theory of Law and Democracy* (Cambridge, MA, 1996). The extensive literature concerning civil society should also be consulted. Jeffrey Alexander, *The Civil Sphere* (Oxford, 2008), and Charles Taylor, *Modern Social Imaginaries* (Durham, NC, 2004), offer two illuminating points of entry into this scholarship. John Brooke's "Consent, Civil Society, and the Public Sphere in the Age of Revolution and the Early American Republic," in *Beyond the Founders: New Approaches to the Political History of the Early American Republic*, ed. Jeffrey Pasley, Andrew Robertson, and David Waldstreicher (Chapel Hill, NC, 2004), is the best application of public sphere and civil society theories to the context American history.

For all that the aforementioned works can teach us about public culture and the formation of public opinion, most do not directly address the question of what "public opinion" meant. That is a task for historians of ideas and historically minded literary scholars and political scientists. Like most other public opinion theorists, Habermas regarded the concept of public opinion as a distinctive product of liberalism. By erecting abstract yet impermeable boundaries between public and private, state and society, market life and home life, masculine and feminine, and reason and emotion, liberalism did much to make the concept of public opinion conceivable. But there are good reasons to believe that the concept has a more complicated genealogy. After all, classical republicans and civic humanists had much to say about the public and worried over the fickle instability of opinion. Michael Warner, *Letters of the Republic: Publication and the Pubic Sphere in Eighteenth-Century America* (Cambridge, MA, 1992), contends that "the public" of revolutionary Americans rested on a particular and short-lived "republican" understanding of print. Protestant insistence on the sacred rights of conscience, when applied to society writ large, also informed developing conceptions of public opinion. Timothy H. Breen, "Retrieving Common Sense: Rights, Liberties, and the Religious Public Sphere in Late Eighteenth Century America," in *To Secure the Blessings of Liberty: Rights in American History*, ed. Josephine Pacheco (Fairfax, VA, 1993), makes this case convincingly. Sentimentalism, in many respects a hybrid of liberalism and Protestantism, also exerted a considerable influence on concepts of public opinion. Sarah Knott's *Sensibility and the American Revolution* (Chapel Hill, NC, 2009) and Glenn Hendler's *Public Sentiments: Structures of Feeling in Nineteenth-Century American Literature* (Chapel Hill, NC, 2001) are two notable entries in a larger pool of works that show how distinctions between public and private, and reason and feeling, were not as clear as often assumed. Finally, the concept of public opinion has often intersected with the sort of democratic and populist traditions discussed by Nancy Ruttenburg, *Democratic Personality: Popular Voice and the Trial of American Authorship* (Stanford, CA, 1998); Kimberly Smith, *The Dominion of Voice: Riot, Reason, and Romance in Antebellum Politics* (Lawrence, KS, 1997); Jason Frank, *Constituent Moments: Enacting the People in Postrevolutionary America* (Durham, NC, 2010); and Sophia Rosenfeld, *Common Sense: A Political History* (Cambridge, MA, 2011)

Public opinion is one entry in a lexicon of political "keywords" or concepts that have received extensive scholarly attention. Daniel Rodgers, *Contested Truths: Keywords in American Politics since Independence* (New York, 1987), and Terrence Ball, James Farr, and Russell Hanson, eds., *Political Innovation and Conceptual Change* (Cambridge, 1989), provide excellent introductions to the history of concepts. William Connolly, *The Terms of Political Discourse*, 3rd ed. (Princeton, NJ, 1993), and Reinhart Koselleck, *The Practice of Conceptual History: Timing History, Spacing Concepts* (Stanford, CA, 2002), are helpful guides to the analysis of "essentially contested concepts" such as public opinion.

The essential contestability of "public opinion" should not be taken to mean that no definition of public opinion is better than any other, or that theorizing public opinion is a futile enterprise. My interest in public opinion was first stirred by the "debate" between Walter Lippmann and John Dewey over mass communications and democracy in the 1920s. Dewey's *The Public and Its Problems* (New York, 1927) and Lippmann's *Public Opinion* (New York, 1922) and *The Phantom Public* (New York, 1925) are still worth reading, as are V. O. Key, *Public Opinion and American Democracy* (New York, 1961), and Francis Graham Wilson, *A Theory of Public Opinion* (Chicago, 1962). A more recent summation of public opinion research and theory may be found in Carroll Glynn, Susan Herbst, Garrett O'Keefe, and Robert Shapiro, *Public Opinion*, 2nd ed. (Boulder, CO, 2004). Herbst, *Numbered Voices: How Opinion Polling has Shaped American Politics* (Chicago, 1993), and Benjamin Ginsberg, *The Captive Public: How Mass Opinion Promotes State Power* (New York, 1988), should be of particular interest to historians.

Chapter 1

"Opinion" has a much longer and varied history than "public opinion," which did not make its way into the English language until the eighteenth century. Before then, "opinion" might refer to an uncertain or subjective judgment, the reputation or honor of a person, popular wisdom or delusion, or even a force that compelled individuals to conform. On the latter, see Elizabeth Noelle-Neumann, *The Spiral of Silence: Public Opinion—Our Social Skin*, 2nd ed. (Chicago, 1993). Kirk Wetters, *The Opinion System: Impasses of the Public Sphere from Hobbes to Habermas* (New York, 2008); John Durham Peters, "Historical Tensions in the Concept of Public Opinion," in *Public Opinion and the Communication of Consent*, ed. Theodore L. Glasser and Charles T. Salmon (New York, 1995); and Paul Lazarsfeld, "Public Opinion and the Classical Tradition," *Public Opinion Quarterly* 21 (Spring 1957), highlight some key differences between "opinion" and "public opinion."

Given that the concept of public opinion originated in France, and that French *philosophes* influenced British and American thinking on the subject during the age of democratic revolutions, the early history of the concept has a heavy French accent. My discussion of that history in chapter 1 draws on Keith Michael Baker's "Public Opinion as Political Invention" in *Inventing the French Revolution* (Cambridge, 1990), and works by J. A. W. Gunn on both the English and French histories of the concept: "Public Spirit to Public Opinion," in *Beyond Liberty and Property: The Process of Self-Recognition in Eighteenth-Century Political Thought* (Kingston, ON, 1983), and *Queen of the World: Opinion in the Public Life of France from the Renaissance to the Revolution* (Oxford, 1995). Additionally, Mona Ozouf, "Public Opinion at the End of the Old Regime," *Journal of Modern History* 60 (September 1988), and Jon Cowans, *To Speak for the People: Public Opinion and the Problem of Legitimacy in the French Revolution* (London, 2001), offer some critical analyses of the limits of *opinion publique* in French revolutionary politics.

Chapter 1 also benefits from many excellent studies of communications and the public sphere in the colonial and revolutionary periods. Two books by Richard D. Brown, *Knowledge Is Power: The Diffusion of Information in Early America, 1700–1865* (Oxford, 1989) and *The Strength of a People: The Idea of an Informed Citizenry in America, 1650–1870* (Chapel Hill, NC, 1996), wisely take a long view to better illustrate the limits of eighteenth-century communication and the significance of the "communications revolution" of the nineteenth. Comparably broad and illuminating approaches appear in Richard M. John, *Spreading the News: The American Postal System from Franklin to Morse* (Cambridge, MA, 1998); Paul Starr, *The Creation of the Media: Political Origins of Modern Communications* (New York, 2005); and Trish Loughran, *The Republic in Print: Print Culture in the Age of U.S. Nation Building, 1770–1870* (New York, 2007). More fine-grained studies of the colonial and revolutionary public spheres offer more clues as to how "opinion" or "public opinion" was thought to operate. See, for example, Christopher Grasso, *A Speaking Aristocracy: Transforming Public Discourse in Eighteenth-Century Connecticut* (Chapel Hill, NC, 1999); T. H. Breen, "Making History: The Force of Public Opinion and the Last Years of Slavery in Revolutionary Massachusetts," in *Through a Glass Darkly: Reflections on Personal Identity in Early America*, ed. Ronald Hoffman, Mechal Sobel, and Fredrika J. Teute (Chapel Hill, NC, 1997); and the forum "Alternative Histories of the Public Sphere" in *William and Mary Quarterly* 62 (January 2005).

If the concept of public opinion began its career as a fiction of constitutional law, it derived much of its force from the idea of popular sovereignty. Edmund Morgan, *Inventing the People: The Rise of Popular Sovereignty in England and America* (New York, 1989), is indispensible on this subject. Larry Kramer, *The People Themselves: Popular Constitutionalism and Judicial Review* (Oxford, 2005), and Christian Fritz, *American Sovereigns: The People and America's Constitutional Tradition before the Civil War* (Cambridge, 2009), carry the history of popular sovereignty and constitutionalism forward into the early national and antebellum periods. Saul Cornell, *The Other Founders: Anti-Federalism and the Dissenting Tradition in America, 1788–1828* (Chapel Hill, NC, 1999), makes an interesting case that the "public sphere" was a central and distinguishing feature of anti-Federalist, Jeffersonian, and Jacksonian constitutionalism and political thought.

Chapter 2

Historians of Europe have long recognized the connections between public finance and public opinion. On France, see Thomas Kaiser, "Money, Despotism, and Public Opinion in Early Eighteenth-Century France: John Law and the Debate on Royal Credit," *Journal of Modern History* 63 (March 1991). On Britain, John Brewer, *The Sinews of Power: War, Money, and the English State, 1688–1783* (Cambridge, MA, 1988), and Bruce Carruthers, *City of Capital: Politics and Markets in the English Financial Revolution* (Princeton, NJ, 1996), should be consulted. Patrick Brantlinger, *Fictions of State: Culture and Credit in Britain, 1694–1994* (Ithaca, NY, 1996), and James Macdonald, *A Free Nation Deep in Debt: The Financial Roots of Democracy* (Princeton, NJ, 2006), offer overviews of the cultural and political implications of public credit.

While the relationship between public opinion and public credit has not received comparable attention from historians of the United States, this does not at all mean that scholars have minimized the political significance of public finance. Indeed, Charles A. Beard's *An Economic Interpretation of the Constitution of the United States* (New York, 1913) famously contended that a desire to protect creditors, especially large holders of war debt, played a decisive role in the constitutional convention of 1787. Subsequent critiques of Beard's evidence, most notably Forrest McDonald, *We the People: The Economic Origins of the Constitution* (Chicago, 1958), while valid in many respects, did little to diminish the significance of financial controversies to early national politics. Interest in the "republican" ideas and ideologies of the founders shed new light on their differing political-economic visions and their anxieties regarding public and private debt. On the former, see Drew McCoy, *The Elusive Republic: Political Economy in Jeffersonian America* (Chapel Hill, NC, 1980). On the latter, Herbert Sloan, *Principle and Interest: Thomas Jefferson and the Problem of Debt* (Oxford, 1995), is especially illuminating. Moreover, the Beard thesis has experienced something of a revival since 2000, as seen in Robert McGuire, *To Form a More Perfect Union: A New Economic Interpretation of the United States Constitution* (Oxford, 2003); Woody Holton, *Unruly Americans and the Origins of the Constitution* (New York, 2008); and Terry Bouton, *Taming Democracy: "The People," the Founders, and the Troubled Ending of the American Revolution* (Oxford, 2007).

A concurrent interest in state building and administration has produced studies of public finance more sympathetic to Alexander Hamilton and his system. Two books by Max Edling, *A Revolution in Favor of Government: Origins of the U.S. Constitution and the Making of the American State* (Oxford, 2003) and *A Hercules in the Cradle: War, Money, and the American State, 1783–1867* (Chicago, 2014), best represent this line of thought. Edwin J. Perkins, *American Public Finance and Financial Services, 1700–1815* (Columbus, OH, 1994), and E. James Ferguson, *The Power of the Purse: A History of American Public Finance, 1776–1790* (Chapel Hill, NC, 1961), are helpful guides to the complexities of eighteenth-century finance. Readers interested in the larger political history of public finance, money, and banking can still profit from Bray Hammond, *Banks and Politics in America from the Revolution to the Civil War* (Princeton, NJ, 1957).

Chapter 3

The history of political parties is another subject that has been examined extensively, if not exhaustively, but scholarship on the relationship between parties and public opinion remains surprisingly sparse and underdeveloped. The main reason for this, I suspect, is that the relationship between parties and public opinion generally seems so obvious as to require little explanation, and the simultaneous "rise" of both in nineteenth-century America often reinforces this view. By bringing social history and public opinion research to bear on the study of parties and elections, the "new" political history of the 1960s aimed to complicate the then common tendency to identify public opinion exclusively with the contest of parties and the results of elections. Subsequent interest in "political culture" and the "public sphere" helped historians to expand their understandings of "the political" and to produce a more rich and refined view of the relationship between parties and public opinion. Studies of taverns, clubs, parades, holidays, and other forms of popular recreation and festivity frequently discovered the fingerprints of party organizers and, more surprisingly, a good deal of ambivalence about partisanship. Len Travers, *Celebrating the Fourth: Independence Day and the Rites of Nationalism in the Early Republic* (Amherst, MA, 1997), and David Waldstreicher, *In the Midst of Perpetual Fetes: The Making of American Nationalism, 1776–1820* (Chapel Hill, NC, 1997), offer particularly illuminating analyses of this conundrum. John Brooke, *Columbia Rising: Civil Life on the Upper Hudson from the Revolution to the Age of Jackson* (Chapel Hill, NC, 2010), employs an admirably concrete yet nuanced understanding of the public sphere to explain partisanship as a response to the failure of civil society to secure consensus through public opinion.

Given this, it is not surprising that the concept of public opinion played a pivotal role in anti-party thought. Richard Hofstadter, *The Idea of a Party System: The Rise of Legitimate Opposition in the United States, 1780–1840* (Berkeley, CA, 1969), and Ralph Ketcham, *Presidents above Party: The First American Presidency, 1789–1829* (Chapel Hill, NC, 1984), are two valuable guides to this tradition, along with Mark Voss-Hubbard's *Beyond Party: Cultures of Anti-Partisanship in the Northern Politics before the Civil War* (Baltimore, 2002). Gerald Leonard, *The Invention of Party Politics: Federalism, Popular Sovereignty, and Constitutional Development in Jacksonian Illinois* (Chapel Hill, NC, 2002), offers the best discussion of arguments for party organization, especially those of Martin Van Buren. Glenn C. Altschuler and Stuart M. Blumin's *Rude Republic: Americans and Their Politics in the Nineteenth Century* (Princeton, NJ, 2000) is less a study of anti-party thought than a provocative mapping of the cultural and social "space" occupied by politics that asks what it meant to be "political."

Chapter 4

"Having" opinions became increasingly important to being political and, as I argue in chapter 4, having a self. My understanding of the history of the self has been shaped by Jerrold Seigel, *The Idea of the Self: Thought and Experience in Western Europe since the Seventeenth Century* (Cambridge, 2005); Charles Taylor, *Sources of the Self: The Making of Modern Identity* (Cambridge, MA, 1992); and Jan Goldstein, *The Post-Revolutionary Self: Psyche and Politics in France, 1750–1850* (Cambridge, MA, 2008). The American context is explored by Daniel Walker Howe, *Making the American Self: Jonathan Edwards to Abraham Lincoln* (Oxford, 1997), and Wilfred McClay, *The Masterless: Self and Society in Modern America* (Chapel Hill, NC, 1994).

Perry Miller's posthumous *The Life of the Mind in America: From the Revolution to the Civil War* (New York, 1970) laid great emphasis on the significance of debates over revivalism to American intellectual history. Most subsequent histories of revivalism, however, have been more concerned with the social, cultural, and political significance of revivalism and evangelicalism. Nathan Hatch, *The Democratization of*

American Christianity (New Haven, CT, 1989); Richard Carwardine, *Evangelicals and Politics and Antebellum America* (New Haven, CT, 1993); and Christine Heyrman, *Southern Cross: The Beginnings of the Bible Belt* (Chapel Hill, NC, 1998), provide three notable examples of this perspective. The psychology of revivalism received due consideration in Ann Taves's *Fits, Trances, and Visions: Experiencing Religion and Explaining Experience from Wesley to James* (Princeton, NJ, 1999) and Charles Hambrick-Stowe's *Charles G. Finney and the Spirit of American Evangelicalism* (Grand Rapids, MI, 1996). The introductory essay in James D. Bratt, ed., *Antirevivalism in Antebellum America: A Collection of Religious Voices* (New Brunswick, NJ, 2005), is essential to understanding this diverse yet influential group of critics. On Unitarians and moral philosophy, see Daniel Walker Howe, *The Unitarian Conscience: Harvard Moral Philosophy, 1805–1861* (Cambridge, MA, 1970), and D. H. Meyer, *The Instructed Conscience: The Shaping of the American National Ethic* (Philadelphia, 1972).

The history of phrenology in America still awaits a comprehensive, book-length treatment. Charles Colbert's excellent *A Measure of Perfection: Phrenology and the Fine Arts in America* (Chapel Hill, NC, 1997) comes close, but it is necessarily focused on art at the expense of phrenology as a science, business, and philosophy. John Davies's *Phrenology: Fad and Science; a Nineteenth Century Crusade* (New Haven, CT, 1955) and Madeleine Stern's *Heads and Headlines: The Phrenological Fowlers* (Norman, OK, 1972) are informative yet outdated. Michael Sappol's study of popular anatomy, *A Traffic of Dead Bodies: Anatomy and Embodied Social Identity in Nineteenth-Century America* (Princeton, NJ, 2004), hints at what could be done with phrenology. Alison Winter, *Mesmerized: Powers of Mind in Victorian Britain* (Chicago, 1998), provides a model study of a closely related "pseudo-science."

Chapter 5

The newspaper press and its history are obviously integral to understanding public opinion. But as was the case with political parties, the relationship between newspapers and public opinion has often been more assumed than explained; a present-minded tendency to view early American newspapers as "the media"—as a distinct institution or "fourth estate"—obscured the many connections between the press, the state, and other social, religious, civil, and political institutions. Jeffrey Pasley, *"The Tyranny of Printers": Newspaper Politics in the Early Republic* (Charlottesville, VA, 2002), rightfully recognizes newspaper editors as the organizers and day-to-day leaders of political parties. Culver Smith, *The Press, Politics, and Patronage: The American Government's Use of Newspapers, 1789–1875* (Athens, GA, 1977); Hazel Dicken-Garcia, *Journalistic Standards in Nineteenth-Century America* (Madison, WI, 1989); and David Paul Nord, *Faith in Reading: Religious Publishing and the Birth of Mass Media in America* (Oxford, 2004), provide other helpful correctives. There are many fine books on the emergence of the "penny press." Andie Tucher's *Froth and Scum: Truth, Beauty, Goodness, and the Ax Murder in America's First Mass Medium* (Charlotte, NC, 1994) is an especially lively read, and James Crouthamel's *Bennett's New York Herald and the Rise of the Popular Press* (Syracuse, NY, 1989) is a critical biography of the most significant penny press editor. Isabelle Lehuu, *Carnival on the Page: Popular Print Media in Antebellum America* (Chapel Hill, NC, 2000), and David Henkin, *City Reading: Written Words and Public Spaces in Antebellum New York* (New York, 1998), situate newspapers within a larger environment of texts.

Newspaper politics did not, however, sit comfortably with received notions of masculine honor, especially (and increasingly) in the South. The works of Bertram Wyatt-Brown loom large here, especially *Southern Honor: Ethics and Behavior in the Old South* (Oxford, 1983) and *The Shaping of Southern Culture: Honor, Grace, and War* (Chapel Hill, NC, 2001). Kenneth S. Greenberg, *Honor and Slavery* (Princeton, NJ, 1996), is particularly insightful on the subject of Southern dueling, while Joanne B. Freeman, *Affairs of Honor: National Politics in the Early Republic* (New Haven, CT, 2002), concentrates on the founders and their sense of honor. Violence against the press, and the evolving political and legal responses to it, are addressed by John C. Nerone, *Violence against the Press: Policing the Public Sphere in U.S. History* (Oxford, 1994), and Michael Kent Curtis, *Free Speech, "the People's Darling Privilege": Struggles for Freedom of Expression in American History* (Durham, NC, 2000).

Chapter 6

Abolitionist meetings and publications were frequently answered with violence and soon followed with calls for the legal suppression of abolitionist ideas. Leonard Richards, *"Gentlemen of Property and Standing": Anti-Abolition Mobs in Jacksonian America* (Oxford, 1970); David Grimstead, *American Mobbing, 1828–1861: Toward Civil War* (Oxford, 1998); Russel B. Nye, *Fettered Freedom: Civil Liberties and the Slavery Controversy* (East Lansing, MI, 1949); and William Lee Miller, *Arguing about Slavery: John Quincy Adams and the Great Battle in the United States Congress* (New York, 1998), are well worth consulting on this topic. The abolitionist faith in the power of moral suasion was sustained by some distinctive beliefs about public opinion and the power of print. Robert Fanuzzi, *Abolition's Public Sphere* (Minneapolis, 2003), and Jeannine Marie DeLombard, *Slavery on Trial: Law, Abolitionism, and Print Culture* (Chapel Hill, NC, 2007), offer sympathetic portraits of these ideas.

In the vast sea of Abraham Lincoln biography, two books are especially illuminating regarding his understanding of, and experience with, public opinion: Richard Carwardine, *Lincoln: A Life of Purpose and Power* (New York, 2007), and Harold Holzer, *Lincoln and the Power of the Press: The War for Public Opinion* (New York, 2014). David Zarefsky, "'Public Sentiment Is Everything': Lincoln's View of Political Persuasion," *Journal of the Abraham Lincoln Association* 15 (1994), demonstrates the complexity and nuance of Lincoln's understanding of public opinion, as do J. David Greenstone, "The Transient and Permanent in American Politics: Standards, Interests, and the Concept of the Public," in *Public Values and Private Power in American Politics*, ed. Greenstone (Chicago, 1982); Greenstone, *The Lincoln Persuasion: Remaking American Liberalism* (Princeton, NJ, 1993); and John Burt, *Lincoln's Tragic Pragmatism: Lincoln, Douglas, and Moral Conflict* (Cambridge, MA, 2013).

Index